The Junior Executive

By Justin Saye

Fourth Edition

Published by SG Publishing: Ventura, California.

Library of Congress Cataloging-in-Publication Data is available.
ISBN 978-0-9882102-4-0
Printed in the United States of America.

"A HUMAN BEING SHOULD BE ABLE TO CHANGE A DIAPER, PLAN AN INVASION, BUTCHER A HOG, CONN A SHIP, DESIGN A BUILDING, WRITE A SONNET, BALANCE ACCOUNTS, BUILD A WALL, SET A BONE, COMFORT THE DYING, TAKE ORDERS, GIVE ORDERS, COOPERATE, ACT ALONE, SOLVE EQUATIONS, ANALYZE A NEW PROBLEM, PITCH MANURE, PROGRAM A COMPUTER, COOK A TASTY MEAL, FIGHT EFFICIENTLY, DIE GALLANTLY. SPECIALIZATION IS FOR INSECTS."

- Robert Anson Heinlein

Preface

Generally speaking, the term "executive" is rarely elaborated. It is referenced, described and used mostly as a cultural and organizational marker. It is the subject of ten-step plans and frameworks for learning along with different theoretical approaches. For the most part and for most people, these are useless. At its core, being an executive is a mindset and way of behaving. Education, experience, intelligence, confidence, and people-skills are all necessary, but they don't combine of themselves. For those who seek an executive role and to be successful in the role, a more holistic and integrated approach is needed. That is the purpose of this book—to provide insight into the mindset and behaviors that will bring it all together for you.

The Junior Executive is organized into three sections with ten total chapters. The first section will help any person who aspires to an executive role in any organization understand what is required to reach their goal. That is, by evaluating themselves in relation to the presented concepts, the reader will gain insight into their suitability for the executive role. The list of presented topics is not exhaustive, but covers deeply important aspects of our working persona. This section can serve as a guide for reflection and a roadmap for study and improvement for those who choose to take on the challenge.

The second section will assist any person who has attained the executive role to be successful from the outset. Going beyond prescriptive toolsets, this section addresses the chasm between theory and practice. This section is the heart of the book, exploring both traditional leadership concepts and adjacent ideas that are less often addressed. In management, as in athletics, exercising the big muscles is only effective if the smaller, more finely controlled muscles stay in shape as well.

The third section provides the foundation of achievement as a junior executive and introduces what is necessary to advance to senior leadership. Executive leadership requires many different skillsets and outlooks which cannot truly be understood without proximity as a junior executive. The concepts presented in this section are a foundation for the junior executive to advance in their organization.

Finally, as we believe that executives are made over a lifetime of broad learning and not born, each section includes a suggested reading list that represents some of the best thinking as well as counterintuitive exposition on the themes presented. This book and the suggested readings sketch a framework for charting our individual path through a life of leadership.

To reflect the unique nature of one's identity as a leader, each topic or concept is presented in a short vignette for individual consideration, and this book can thus be read in piecemeal fashion. The Junior Executive is not organized as a narrative, but it is meant to be read in order of presentation.

The executive role is a central role in all organizations, regardless of function, scope, or title. Many of the examples and scenarios in this book are related to business, but I have attempted to use situations drawn from many different types of organizations to demonstrate the core of the executive role. Every organization needs leadership, and leadership is the work of the executive.

Contents

Place in Time

Chapter 1 Self Selection

"Woe betide[s] those who live by way of examples! Life is not with them. If you live according to an example, you thus live the life of that example, but who should live your own life if not yourself? So live yourselves."

-Carl Jung (The Red Book)

GENERALIST VS. EXPERT

There are many arguments for and against being a generalist in pursuit of career advancement. Many advocate for expertise in a particular area of business in order to focus and establish a domain of excellence as proof of value. The argument goes that, if we can establish excellence in a given domain, then our pursuit of advancement will be evaluated within that context. For example, an ambitious software engineer named Samantha focuses on database software design and development as her domain of excellence. Over time, she becomes the best database software developer at her company. This is a solid achievement, but to her managers, there is no reason to advance Samantha beyond "head", "lead" or "senior" database software developer. Her options for advancement are structurally limited to the maximum utility that a database engineer can deliver to the company. From a compensation standpoint, the upper limit of what Samantha can extract from her employer stops at the cost ceiling of database engineering services in the company. Practically, both Samantha's career advancement and compensation are limited to the maximum value associated with the constrained domain of her expertise. In the vast majority of cases, she is stuck.

By its very definition, being a generalist yields too low of a value to one's employer to justify elevating such a person to the ranks of executive leadership. Generalists often end up at the opposite end of the capability spectrum from experts. They have no particular skillset that differentiates them. At best, they find a position that provides a platform for their broad-but-shallow knowledge base. At worst, particularly if they are ambitious, generalists turn into manipulators: individuals attempting to gain authority or power through means other than value delivery for their company or organization. These individuals tend to rely on personal relationships (and smoke and mirrors) to create the appearance of competence. While the expert is valuable to the company even if not promotable, the ambitious generalist, under the traditional analysis, can be a detriment.

Yet all executive leaders are generalists.

So how do we explain this disconnect? Most career advice over simplifies: Do more. That is to say, Samantha will have to not only demonstrate expertise in database software, but also make additional effort to gain generalist knowledge and experience in related domains. Frustratingly vague, but this challenge seems less imposing when we acknowledge that, for the most part, all knowledge is derivative and interconnected. While expertise in a particular discipline fosters advancement in that particular discipline from a task-based perspective, we must also do the work to draw connections between derivative and complementary domains. These connections allow us to keep our footing in a particular domain while also establishing a foundation for understanding the ecosystem of organizational components and integrating higher-level goals into our work. Thus, it is growth from domain expertise into a generalist mindset.

We must have varied interests and pursuits that will allow us to connect with others, empathize with their needs and communicate clear expectations for interaction. This higher level of communication and collaborative functioning is only possible through a generalist's capacity for learning and compartmentalization.

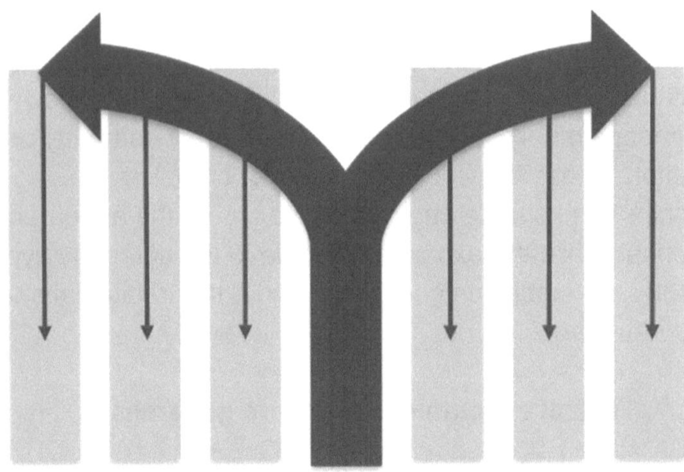

Figure 1 - Domain expertise provides a basis for generalist cross-disciplinary insight and learning.

The Junior Executive should be an expert in their domain and a generalist in the organization.

ACTION

"A good plan violently executed right now is far better than a perfect plan executed next week."

- George S. Patton

An executive's attitude and cultivated instinct toward action define their professional character. No concept in business offers a higher risk to reward ratio. Our age and perceived experience with regard to action will affect all external perceptions of our ability. These perceptions will factor into the machinations of our rivals, the trust of our subordinates, and the faith of our senior leaders and customers. Despite mountains of business books and advice chiding organizations to change their attitudes toward action to allow for a greater acceptance of failure, we should not oversimplify. We need to interrogate the idea of action for executives: What is at the core of a strong action bias and what does it mean to make a mistake in our organization? The first is arguably universal, but the second will require us to examine nuances of our organizational culture.

Action bias presents a spectrum that we all fall on: from inaction to mindless action. In our working lives, all of us start somewhere on that spectrum due to the variability of our upbringing. As we ascend the corporate ladder, the impetus for when, how, and where we act falls more and more under our individual control. Further, causal and derivative actions of other individuals and organizations become increasingly influenced by our actions. The impact of this can either yield to friction or leverage for the organization—our success will depend on it being the latter.

There is sage and wildly divergent advice on this topic, but no simple maxim can guide one's attitude toward action. Successful action bias elegantly marries preparedness and courage. Miscalculate on either side and our action bias will create friction. But when properly paired, these aspects can create tremendous leverage for our organization and thus demonstrate our suitability for leadership. We must examine what it means to be prepared and what it means to have courage—definitions that are often different for everyone.

Because action is high risk and high reward, others will judge our attitude toward it as a test for advancement. Unfortunately, the way forward is to not only get it right, but to be perceived as getting it right through our consideration and not through luck or circumstance. This is where pundits and thought-leaders get it partly right when they say that failure is virtuous. Mistakes and successes will happen—that much is true. The key to identifying the appropriate bias for action lies in how these events are perceived and handled within our organization.

So, what qualifies as a mistake with regard to action? The simplest definition for a mistake is as an outcome that was not expected that negatively affects an organization. There are myriad ways to deal with the expectation gap, which will be discussed at greater length later in the book. But, central to understanding these methods is the idea that how an organization judges mistakes has to do with how that organization perceives the level of control an individual has over the future. This idea of prescience is generally the underlying basis for how mistakes are judged. Intriguing research (Gabriel, 1996) on the anthropologic basis for gambling reveals that we all subconsciously attribute a great deal of worth to the perceived ability of an individual to divine the future.

We should ask ourselves the following question: To what degree does my organization value prescience? How is this expressed in everyday behaviors? The answer will not necessarily determine a value judgment of the organization, but it should yield an understanding about how the organization judges a mistake and will help determine where our bias for action should fall on the spectrum. If our organization highly values prescience, then our bias for action should be tempered. Organizations that highly value prescience are likely to judge mistakes harshly. As such, a strong bias for action will likely yield mistakes that characterize us as "rash," "untested," or "inexperienced." Whether these characterizations are true is irrelevant. Conversely, organizations that understand the variability of conditions in their market will put a lower value on prescience (we must acknowledge that it will always be valued to some degree). In these settings, a stronger bias for action may still yield mistakes, but managers are more likely to characterize these as "learnings" and the sign of a "hard-driver." Even in more cautious organizations, there can be room for a stronger bias for action, if they have a low value for prescience.

In addition to revealing our bias for action, weighing the value of prescience can also reveal our capacity to change that bias. In the end, we need to know how we handle the complexity around action. Can we handle nuance and tailor our attitude accordingly, or do we require explicit rules of engagement? Depending upon our organization, the latter could be a severe career limiter. The former must be cultivated.

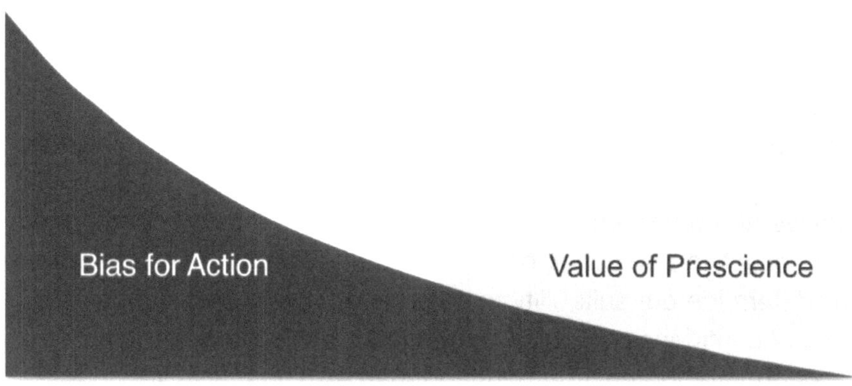

Figure 2 - Bias for Action decreases as the organization's Value of Prescience increases.

The Junior Executive will tailor their bias for action to fit with the culture of their organization.

CONFIDENCE

Like many leadership traits, confidence is something we do not have if we have to talk about it or explain that we have it. Most of us understand confidence as an innate belief that we can accomplish any task that we face. There is a flip side to that statement, one that nods at the argument made by pessimists of one type or another: confidence is simply a degree of delusion. There is a middle ground.

We will define confidence as the innate belief that we can accomplish any task that we may face, tempered by the understanding that there are limits to what can be done, in terms of resources, time, or physics. The idea of confidence has both objective and relative aspects. The objective view of confidence is a belief in ability against objective targets—e.g., I can climb that mountain. The relative view of confidence is a belief in ability in relation to other people—e.g., I can climb that mountain better than Tom. It is important not to confuse these aspects of confidence. Relative confidence is generally boundless while objective confidence is bounded by environmental constraints. Our manifest expression of either will greatly affect how we are perceived and treated. As noted previously, our age and experience will color the opinions others have about us. This is especially true as relates to confidence. In a business setting, relative confidence is a firm belief that we and our team can be better than competitors in the market. The collective perception of circumstances that surround this belief will determine our suitability to be an executive. Anyone judging our level of confidence will form an opinion against his or her own knowledge of the environment and market. Thus, relative confidence must be supported by evidence and this can only be obtained by doing our homework. That is, studying our environment and market. In terms of success, extreme examples are not necessary, as even subtle mistakes can delay or fully scuttle our advancement—often attributed to overconfidence. If, for example, we state that our team will beat company X to market with the next product release, we had better be: 1) right; 2) fully disclosed; 3) prepared to push our team very hard; and, 4) fully prepared to explain the intricacies of the situation if circumstances diverge from plan. Hubris is a very tough attribute to overcome and despite any examples from movies or literature to the contrary, no one in senior leadership likes surprises: good or bad. In this framework, relative confidence is the most difficult to get right and carries the greatest damage if expressed incorrectly. Thus, the successful junior executive has boundless relative confidence, but does the homework to back it up.

Objective confidence requires subtle handling as well, if not as much as relative confidence. The basis for objective confidence is grounded less in preparation than in developed talent and ambition. It is a trait that we cultivate. Bounded by environmental constraints, objective confidence should be manifest in method and energy. That is, we must have a method for approaching and overcoming any obstacle and the energy to do more than we imagine will be required to be successful. We don't prescribe any particular method, but it can often be cultivated through extreme experiences or led exercises (directed leadership training, military service, etc.) that allow for trial/error and stretch goals. Conscious attention to our capacity for objective confidence will allow for opportunistic advancement: succeeding where others fear to tread.

Many individuals are promoted because of the gamesmanship around relative confidence as more experienced executives create layers of hedging and obfuscation within internal operations. This can lead to opportunities for us to break out of the pack. But breakouts are only possible with a high degree of objective confidence. Objective confidence supports a higher risk-to-reward ratio. The opportunity to breakout is the unstated flipside of the old maxim "give them enough rope to hang themselves."

We must understand ourselves well to truly know our level of confidence: both relative and objective. Insufficient confidence will preclude us from advancing, while unjustified or unwarranted confidence will stall or end our advancement. Only through the measured application of confidence to operations can we take advantage of opportunities and advance.

The Junior Executive will ground their confidence in objective achievement and educated relative comparison.

TOE VS. HEEL

It is impossible to know exactly what motivates other people. This is particularly true in organizations, where one's persona is often extremely disjoined and more nuanced ethical boundaries inform choices. Let us follow the advice of Saul Bellow and treat people on the value of their external actions—internally, they are likely a mess.

Many interactions are a conflict of some sort and the posture of the conflicting parties will typically be either toe or heel, in the parlance of fighting. If we are on our toes, then we are able to maneuver, adjust, block, strike—but, most importantly, we are able to move at our own initiative and not only in reaction. From an organizational standpoint, a toe position lets us maintain position or pull the organization forward in our direction.

If we are on our heels, we can maneuver, adjust, block—but our ability to strike is much weaker and we are not able to move forward. This is a position from which we cannot execute effectively. At all times we must assess whether we are in toe or heel position. The most obvious indication of a heel position is constantly fighting fires or running from one crisis to another. A preference for crisis work is not necessarily a bad trait for an individual, if they find some level of happiness in that position. But it is not a position of strength from which to grow into an executive role.

To know our suitability for an executive position, we must understand our natural inclination—some people are genuinely more comfortable in a heel position. In general, responding is easier and requires less creativity and initiative. This is not to say that if we are comfortable in a heel position that we cannot move up, but we will need to develop a higher capability in the toe position.

Figure 3 - A toe position allows us to press forward, whereas a heel position simply reacts.

The Junior Executive will maintain a posture of active readiness.

INTUITION

Intuition is a mysterious and mostly unquantifiable attribute. In general, it is understood as the ability to subconsciously sense the true nature of a situation without the benefit of overt indicators. Intuitive knowledge is a part of human nature, and required for survival. We perceive of our intuition at a very early age as our brain begins to make sense of sight stimuli. As we differentiate the windowpane from the rest of the wall, we realize that there are things behind the windowpane and by extension, behind the wall. As we get older the skill is honed—when reading a cartoon in the Sunday paper, we intuit what action is taking place between panels to maintain the logical plotline of the story. There has been a great deal written on the nature of intuition as well as how we might enhance this form of understanding. We are primarily concerned with the application of intuition in the organization. The expert use of intuition is an absolute requirement for success in any organization. As a junior executive we must intuitively interact with those in our spheres of influence, and also understand and act upon various stimuli from the market, competitors, media, etc. In the stock market, we pay close attention to the hype around initial public offerings to project how well a stock might perform in the initial days. Do we sense that the hype associated with an initial offering means that the stock will run up a 10% gain in the first day and then drop, or perhaps make a steady run up to a 100% gain in the first month? Developing a strong sense of intuition through experience provides critical balance to technical analysis.

That the richness of our interactions with others is analyzed in an educated, disciplined manner is paramount. Like any other innate attribute, a predisposition toward intuition provides advantages. But, if lacking, intuition can be nurtured through conscious effort—by learning about the main heuristics of human nature (anthropology, sociology, psychology) and doing a great deal of introspection and experimentation. A healthy appreciation for duplicity and sociopathic behavior is very helpful as well. As Machiavelli tells us, individuals often attempt to gain power without having earned it through merit. One of the greatest benefits of intuition is to detect such characters early.

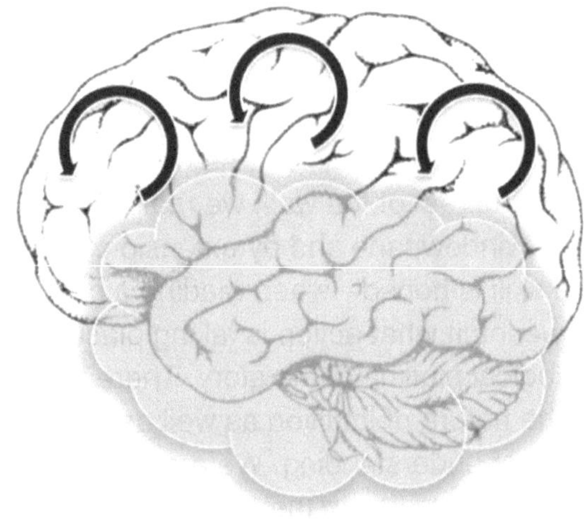

Figure 4 - Intuition is based in the sub-cortex area of the brain but can be consciously exercised.

The Junior Executive will hone a strong sense of intuition.

OVER DELIVER

As an executive candidate, over-delivering must be our normal course of business. But, our future success as an executive will depend on how we over-deliver. We must train ourselves to think of over-delivery as the base level of performance. In individual and group performance we often see a predilection to deliver to minimum standards. There is nothing generally wrong with this, but it does not signal a capacity for improvement. Clearly, achieving greater than minimum standards sends a positive signal, but there is more. The nuance of over-delivery is not so easy. For example:

> If the requirement is for production of 10 widgets in 10 minutes and we deliver to that requirement, then the minimum standard has been achieved. Expectations were met and so any evaluative thinking around this outcome is not triggered. It may happen, but will not be compelled to happen by circumstances.

This circumstance provides an opportunity for the simplest form of over-delivery: Deliver more units in the same time or the same units in less time or some combination of both. Over-delivery is beating the expectation associated with this particular process. This sort of incremental over-delivery is commendable, but not inspiring. To continue the example:

> Production of 10 widgets is achieved in 9 minutes, thus increasing throughput capacity with the same resources through process efficiency. This is the sort of improvement expected of a line supervisor or a motivated worker. However, this increase is not enough to demonstrate executive-level talent.

For future executives, over-delivery not only beats expectations, but also provides a basis for leverage. That is, the improvement made must yield benefits beyond the linear arithmetic of whatever is being delivered. The basis for leverage means that whatever is being delivered not only beats the expectations, but also provides a benefit to some other part of the organization or some other function outside of the scope of the delivery. This is what defines an executive: achieving leveraged results that could not be achieved through individual effort. To continue the example:

> The executive candidate in charge of the production line makes several line changes while over-delivering on the task of increasing production throughput (the 10% efficiency noted before). She identifies that by reconfiguring the line she can decrease the wait duration between two processes,

> while also enabling faster transactions between her line and an upstream line. Additionally, she introduces a signaling system visible to downstream lines, which allows them to more quickly anticipate transitions. These changes over-deliver on the task by not only increasing throughput on her line, but by also increasing throughput on upstream and downstream lines.

Over-delivery to this degree not only demonstrates tactical competence that is valuable to the company, but also operational and even strategic competence that is valuable in leaders. It is operational and strategic competence that provide the basis for confidence in promotion to the executive ranks. Executing to expectations on a day-to-day, tactical level will rarely, if ever, result in promotion to the executive ranks.

The Junior Executive will over-deliver not only their tactical goals but also expand the capacity of a broader group to over-deliver on theirs.

EXECUTION

As myriad business books have told us, one of the most important attributes of an aspiring executive is the ability to execute. There are countless methods aimed at improving our ability to execute effectively. But there is no checklist or protocol that will provide a shortcut. Effective execution requires a mindset, an approach to problem solving, and the culmination of many other traits—matured through experience, but not solely dependent upon it. The ability to execute effectively requires imagination, humility, timing, flexibility and the capacity to conduct a large amount of analysis given ever-changing variables. Effective execution seems terribly complex, and as such is often unnecessarily assigned to the domain of intuition.

What does it mean for a leader to execute effectively? A leader who vacillates upon every decision, fails to follow up on decisions made and denies responsibility or accountability for decisions is not able to execute effectively—that much we know. Yet neither is the classically strong leader in most instances. Is the stolid decision maker who makes a bold directive and then doggedly follows it to the bitter end good at execution? More often than not, this leads to folly and sunk cost. To execute effectively, we must first understand what is meant by the term: to execute is to implement a decision through an action. The success of that decision is evaluated by the consequences. Was the goal of the decision achieved? How did the decision affect peripheral entities? Was the cost of the decision in line with expectations? How have the consequences of the decision affected subsequent choices? Each of these lines of inquiry can be further decomposed and evaluated as extensively as resources allow.

Execution has an extended meaning beyond the ability of a leader to follow the plan that has been laid out. While "executing to plan" is an admirable linear task, it is not what we mean by the term execution. Rather, our meaning of execution is to "execute to vision." If we understand that the vision is the goal, then our path toward it can be flexible, affording us opportunity for humility, course correction and sensitivity to timing. Throughout this book, we will touch upon many foundational aspects of execution to gain a deeper understanding of what it means for the successful executive. The key insight at this point is that the ability to execute is not rooted in dogmatic discipline or toughness. Rather, execution is a higher-order skill based on courage built from intelligence, creativity and will.

The Junior Executive will develop the ability to execute to vision rather than plan.

ACCOUNTABILITY

Accountability is a topic that gets a lot of attention—and for good reason. It represents the trust that we have in a backstop. That is, if we have a good system of accountability and ensure that all essential functions are represented and monitored within that system, then our processes are backstopped, and any problems will be noted and contained. As a theory, this tends to hold true. If accountability is properly assigned and we have a rational belief in the ability and intent of individuals to honor that assignment, then backstopping will work. But in reality this rarely happens. In our discussion, we will discount instances of malfeasance or impropriety, as the repercussions of accountability in those cases are clear. Rather we will focus on the measure of tolerance within organizations for chance.

Accountability is the mature acknowledgement of responsibility for a task, an asset, a function, or a dependent. It is the sober reality that someone must make decisions and accept the consequences. Successfully executing all assignments of accountability is a prerequisite to advancement. In assessing our ability to rise to the executive level, it is crucial to understand not only what it means to be accountable, but also how our accountability will be tested. The problem is that accountability can feel like a trap. If an individual is accountable for some function and that function fails, a moral dilemma is presented. It could be argued that this particular moral dilemma is the root of a great number of bad decisions as the consequences of the failure are brought to bear—the cover up and blame avoidance being worse than the crime. It is only a trap under circumstances where the assignee is in over their head, has taken on more than can be controlled or lacks the necessary integrity.

As will be noted often, having what it takes to be an executive does not mean demonstrating one or two traits. Rather, it is the sum total of disciplined work to excel in many traits. Accountability is a bellwether of the degree of demonstrated excellence. This is not to say that demonstrating excellence means merely accepting and following through with the accountability assigned to particular functions. Rather it is a constraint which helps guide the decisions we make every day. By accepting accountability for something, we are empowered to use our talents to allocate work and resources to secure that accountability. If we are accountable for cleaning the table every evening, then we are free to purchase a washcloth. The greater the accountability, the greater our need for resources. This is the very reason that in the corporate environment, those with budgetary accountability must approve every purchase and allocate resources to ensure that the budget is spent according to the approved plan. Again, this is the theoretical line of reasoning for accountability. But for the prospective executive, this is also where a potential trap lies—being set up for failure.

When considering assignments of accountability, it is critical to understand the scope of accountability, the stakeholders and resources involved, any constraints on resources, the goals of the assigners of accountability and how much influence and power we have to ensure that we are successful in our assignment. Finally, we must clearly understand the consequences of failure. When we are offered a position of accountability, we have three choices:

> Decline outright. This action will very likely result in the delay or complete scuttling of our advancement, regardless of the circumstances.
>
> Accept with conditions. This may result in those conditions being denied. If so, we can decline in good conscience and consider another organization. This particular point is an excellent way to know if those in our current company make a habit of setting people up to fail. If our conditions are met, then we should accept the assignment and execute fully. In general, "accept with conditions" denotes two potential problems: it demonstrates either that senior leadership in our current company does not have a clear understanding of what is required to fulfill an assignment of accountability or that we may be too difficult or timid to be successful. Fortunately, the latter can be overcome through diligent, aggressive execution of our duties.
>
> Accept the assignment outright and willfully allocate

> necessary resources. This is our best choice for advancement.

Once we have accepted an assignment of accountability, we must fully execute it with integrity. If we are successful, we will gain the rewards of that success with a clear conscience and full legitimacy. If we are unsuccessful and we accept the consequences with dignity, we will most likely be given another chance. This is particularly likely if the senior executive who gave the assignment is experienced enough to understand the circumstances of the failure and our honorability in accepting the consequences. Leaders who maturely accept and execute positions of accountability are not easily replaced. It is far less expensive to accept a single failure by a reliably accountable executive than to risk an executive who shirks accountability or tries to weasel their way out of failures.

However, it is critical that the circumstances of a failure are transparent and acknowledged by both the participants and senior leadership. Of course, no one is perfect and good senior leaders understand that. But in the harried environment of most executive suites, perspective can be easily lost amid noise of other issues or positioning by adversaries. Be consistent and persistent in demonstrating reliable and mature accountability. Like all skills, accountability requires practice.

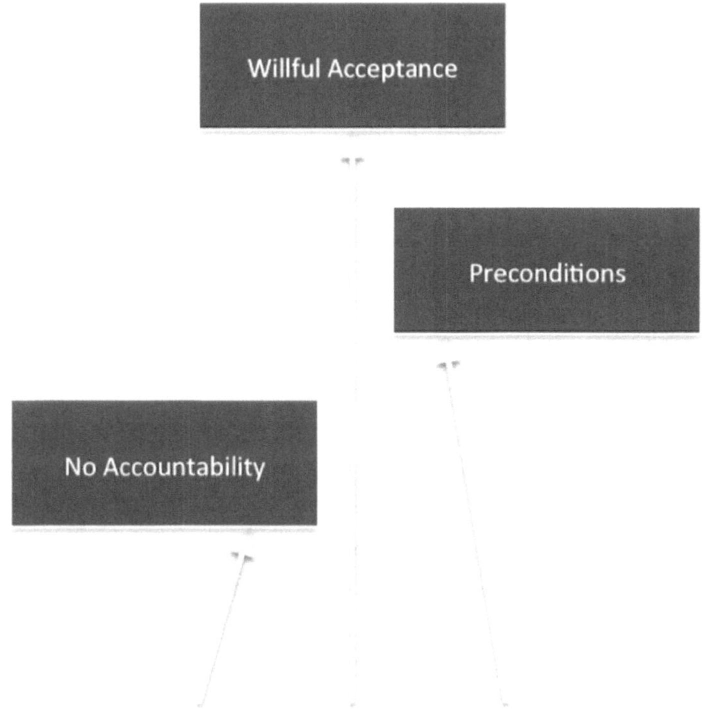

Figure 5 - Of the three choices available to us for accountability, willful acceptance presents a path forward.

The Junior Executive will accept assignments of accountability—with a clear understanding of the consequences—and execute with integrity.

EDUCATION

Education is the most important activity that an individual can undertake to position themselves for advancement. But education is broad and complex, and we must decompose the concept and identify the core aspects. Viewed from a holistic perspective, education is really the act of learning. To be more specific, it is the act of learning in a disciplined manner: subject, curriculum and verification of understanding, etc.

For aspiring executives, education has a multiplier effect on experience, and in the majority of situations, it is a prerequisite for advancement. There are inevitably exceptions: so-and-so never graduated college and is CEO, etc. Such cases are very rare and relying on them as precedent amounts to gambling. We will not dwell on the merits of higher education other than to say that it is a prerequisite. A junior executive must have a Bachelor's degree and should have a Master's degree. The particular education discipline of a degree is less important than the following two key aspects:

<u>What was the scope of learning?</u> Do not believe the false promise of specialization. An executive is not a specialist but a polymath, and has the ability to synthesize information and concepts across disciplines for productive application. This is not often a natural talent and must be learned over time. Structured educational environments provide the best place and time to learn to work across and between disciplines. The stronger the foundation built in formal education, the smarter the executive will be in the future. A structured education curriculum must cover a broad array of subjects and we must work hard to draw meta-conclusions from these subjects. This is how greater understanding of the world is obtained and how confidence is supported—the confidence that one can understand, operate and actually change the world. Individual subjects are like the cogs of a watch mechanism. We are only able to understand how they interrelate through individuation and deductive comparison. As we are exposed to more and more pieces, our point of view is elevated and we begin to see the pieces

for what they are—an operating mechanism that receives inputs, does work and yields something valuable. This vantage is only achievable through thoughtful education.

How did we do? There are few things more wasteful than coasting through classes. Money and time are expended and the resulting degree can fool employers into allocating trust to graduates who did not learn well, which will very likely end in failure. Structured education is not hard, but it requires work to be useful. A successful executive candidate will have not only taken the right courses, but excelled in them. The goal of structured education is not a piece of paper; it is learning. A degree is a trophy that helps to motivate work with results that cannot easily be shown in a finite manner. The particular school is not that important. The quality of content is what matters. The successful executive will attend an accredited university with an excellent selection of content appropriate to their field, and will excel in their coursework. The chasm between those who learn and those who do not is not necessarily reflected in a comparison of grades, but it will tell in the long term.

In the executive context, education must never end. Structured education provides the foundation for more learning. Once a Master's has been earned, there is no reason for more structured education in a seated context. The individual can develop and execute their own structured lessons outside of the classroom.

Building on the above, we add two points regarding education: target and application. The subject, curriculum, and verification of learning are necessary; but there must also be motivation and a return earned.

> **Target**: Junior executives should heed an organizational motivation for education. Within our existing or target domain, what needs to change? Should we pursue more structured project management or more efficient service delivery? Better customer service? Product innovation? Better morale? The target should be substantial, difficult and

subject to high-level and incremental goal management. Individually-directed education is challenging and requires a strong motivator.

Application: The biggest complaint that we hear in the workplace with regard to continuing education is that it is often not applied and therefore wasted. But this criticism frequently masks complacency with the status quo. If a target motivator has been identified and validated, this indicates strongly that the status quo is not sufficient and will not improve without positive action. Thus any educational endeavor in the organizational environment must have a clear plan for application. Preferably that planning takes place within the context of a disciplined measurement system to track the impacts.

Once the target has been identified, a subject is outlined, a curriculum is developed, and measures for learning proof are put in place a plan for application of the learning is ready to be implemented. Education is a substantial differentiator among executive candidates—not only the education earned to date, but also the demonstrated skill of disciplined and self-directed education.

The Junior Executive will demonstrate academic success in higher education and maintain a dedicated plan of learning throughout their career.

Chapter 2 Worldview

SYSTEMS THINKING

Systems Thinking is an important skill for any position of authority or role requiring integration of functions. But for the junior executive, Systems Thinking is mandatory. Executives promoted within organizations that have a strong functional alignment bias will feel this necessity acutely. Functionally-aligned organizations (i.e. featuring dedicated Engineering, Marketing, Sales, etc. departments) must work hard to integrate operations and ensure smooth team operation across functions. Most companies start as functionally-aligned and thus this type of organization features in the majority of scenarios. Functionally-aligned organizations are characterized by strong territorial domains that receive an input from one function, execute a process or processes and then send an output to another function or an external party. Many organizations operate efficiently in this configuration, but generally as the result of great effort by individuals within the functions under strong leadership. Functionally-aligned organizations are not efficient from a structural standpoint and are easily susceptible to breakdowns within the individual links. A strong understanding of Systems Thinking is more important for executives in functionally-aligned organizations than in matrix-aligned organizations, because matrix-aligned organizations are structured (if done correctly) as systems. Thus, Systems Thinking is baked into how such organizations operate.

Essentially, Systems Thinking is a clear understanding of the "system" required to deliver the end-goals of the organization. If the end goal of the organization is to manufacture and sell bicycles, then there must be a system in place for delivery of finished bicycles. Within a functionally-aligned organization, this would entail departments executing their individual functions under direction of central leadership. If the company sets a goal of 1,000 bicycles sold per month, then the Sales department needs to allocate resources to appropriate markets to secure orders. The Marketing department needs to allocate resources to advertising, business development activities, trade shows, etc. to generate interest. The timing of their activities needs to be brokered across the interface between the departments, perhaps through dedicated liaison personnel or automation via enterprise resource planning applications. Based on the forecast and projections from Sales, Manufacturing needs to create a production schedule that will ensure timely delivery. These forecasts and production schedules need to be continually updated, negotiated and communicated. Our success as an executive candidate in such an organization will hinge to a large degree on our ability to understand the system that is in place to sell 1,000 bicycles per month. Understanding how all the functions fit together is simple enough. The key is in understanding the constraints on each function and its individual employees, both structurally and circumstantially. For example, imagine we have been promoted to Vice President of Research and Development at the bicycle manufacturer. How does the Research and Development function fit within the underlying system? It requires substantial inputs:

Sales: What are customers requesting?
Marketing: What are our competitors doing?
Procurement: What are the material constraints from our suppliers?
Manufacturing: What is the level of sophistication of our production line, personnel and processes?
Human Resources: How difficult is it to acquire and keep researchers and developers?
Finace: How is budget allocated to the R&D function?
Administrative: What are the internal resource, process and funding constraints?

Additionally, it requires substantial outputs:

Sales: What is our product roadmap?
Marketing: When can they announce new developments?
Procurement: What will our Bills of Material require for product updates, new products, etc.?
Manufacturing: What are the new specifications, training requirements, tooling requirements, Quality Assurance requirements, etc.?
Human Resources: What new personnel do we need?
Finance: What budget do we need?
Administrative: How are we performing?

This is only a small sample of the typical inputs and outputs, but they demonstrate the concept. All functions within an organization are interrelated and interdependent. A change in one function will yield consequences in another, all of which will aggregate to affect the company's ability to sell 1,000 bicycles per month. This is what many military theorists often refer to as "friction." Although the individual functions and duties are relatively simple, minor points of variability inevitably add up to a quantity of friction within the system, leading to substantial cost and delay. As an executive, it will be our responsibility to reduce friction as much as possible, and this can only be accomplished by Systems Thinking. If we understand the idiosyncrasies of the other functions and our interface with them, we have the framework of information required to anticipate points of friction and allocate resources to address those points. For example, if we know that Procurement is chronically understaffed, we can modify the interface with Procurement to automate some manual functions and reduce administrative overhead. Or we could identify the resource SME (Subject Matter Expert) within R&D with the most intimate knowledge of the materials needed for a new product and cross-train that person in Procurement, which can reduce or remove a point of friction.

For those candidates promoted within a matrix-aligned organization, the tasks and goals are much the same, but the points of friction are often reduced. In a matrix-aligned organization, groups of resources are typically arranged in a system-like structure, whereby individual functional resources are allocated to a system with a discrete goal. Often, the discrete goal is encapsulated in a project or program. Thus, the points of friction resulting from functional leadership disagreements are mitigated and the interfaces between functions are torn down to the bare minimum. Given that much of the structural friction is reduced in a matrix-aligned organization, the major tasks are to ensure continuity between matrix units, optimize administrative performance, and avoid redundancy and destructive competition among matrix units.

Continuity among matrix units is often handled most efficiently at the senior leadership level, where the inputs and outputs of matrix units are more clearly understood. As an executive, our task is to support senior leadership so that decisions regarding unit harmony and planning synchronicity are executed efficiently. Fundamentally, this means strategic planning, which we'll discuss later in the book.

Finally, politics and internal issues are not fully mitigated by a matrix-aligned organization. Where a functionally-aligned business sees its silos fighting over resources and control, the matrix-aligned organization sees its units fighting for lines of business and clients. For example, if one matrix unit is responsible for government business while another is responsible for private business, which is responsible for public-private partnerships? Which is responsible for serving a private customer who is in turn serving a government customer? These types of issues can have a devastating effect on systems optimization. In our work as junior executives, this issue needs only to be highlighted and brought to light with suggested courses of action. It is up to senior leadership to resolve these types of conflicts decisively.

From a Systems Thinking vantage, units fighting for business is a high-level constraint that should be understood and neutralized as a source of friction.

Once the underlying system is understood and the idiosyncrasies of the various functions and interfaces are integrated into planning, the executive can begin to monitor, control and optimize their role in the system. Overall, Systems Thinking means understanding how our particular domain affects and is affected by other domains within the organization, and pushing our organization toward system optimization.

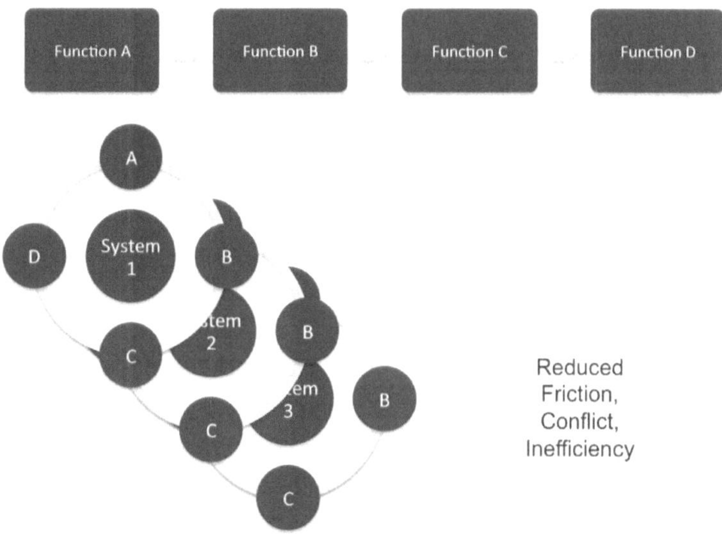

Figure 6 - Systems Thinking allows us to structurally transition our organizations to reduce functional friction, conflict and inefficiency.

The Junior Executive will develop a capacity for Systems Thinking and work toward greater functional integration and reduced friction.

MORALITY AND ETHICS

Executive candidates, like all intelligent people, will have spent a significant amount of time trying to make sense of the world and, in particular, considering the nature of justice. As executive candidates, we are concerned principally with the basis for decision-making, and thus with internally controllable outcomes associated with everyday actions to make firm our basis for determining right and wrong. When this determination—the question of what is just—is considered, the trap of fatalism (a submissive belief that all events are predetermined) often presents itself. We will not survey this topic to any great extent, except to highlight the importance of morality and ethics in light of it. For fatalism is the source of a great deal of negativity: nihilism, apathy, and damaging thinking in general. We are concerned with the damage that can be wrought by this on the psyche of the executive candidate. Is our basis for right and wrong influenced by a sense of fatalism or by something better?

There are two concepts that can serve as a bulwark against this melancholy: beauty and honor. We will leave detailed discussion of beauty aside and simply state that it must be found by the individual, for it is intrinsically important as a component of individuation ("...beauty in things exists in the mind which contemplates them."—David Hume) (Hume, 2003). In a world of injustice and uncertainty, beauty is a safe harbor of comfort and a fount of support for morality and ethical behavior. Honor, for us, is the constraint that ensures we act in a manner consistent with our code of morality and ethics. It is the state of being whereby we determine the right action given the circumstances. But what defines right action? We argue that an instantiated definition is intuited based upon the framework established by our conscious application of an internalized code of behavior. This sense of honor guides our code of behavior—it is a gatekeeping mechanism of our decision-making process that adjudicates right from wrong.

But how is a code of moral and ethical behavior developed? That is out of scope for our discussion as we are merely concerned that it is created and provides the recurring impetus for honorable action (and thus a defense against fatalism). Many major systems of belief have a high-degree of commonality on what is right and wrong: do not lie, cheat or steal and associated derivatives. It is neither complex nor difficult to understand—the challenge is maintaining fidelity to right and wrong. We must place a high priority on acting honorably in relation to our ethical and moral code.

Why is this important in the organizational context? The simple answer is that both our subconscious and the world at large will perpetually conspire to capture, judge and punish us according to this set of ethics and morals. There are no exceptions. Our subconscious will keep score and adjust both the basis for scoring and the criteria for success or failure. But if we are honorable, the basis for scoring and the criteria for success or failure are static. With a static sense of justice, the subconscious will permit peace within the individual and several consequences will result:

- We will be able to get a decent night's sleep.
- We will demonstrate consistently that we can be trusted.
- We will be able to allocate more of our conscious thought to value-yielding endeavors.
- We will strengthen our chances for long-term success.

If we consider the alternative, whereby there is no solid basis for honor or there exists no will to adhere to a code of ethics and morals, we see the underlying reasons for the resulting calamity. As the subconscious keeps score and the failures add up, the basis for scoring or criteria for success and failure must be adjusted. That is, our standards are lowered in relation to perceived or real inconsistencies in our external environment: hypocrisy, unfairness, etc.

This is a dangerous cycle, for the door to fatalism has been opened. How will the subconscious be adjusted? What are the consequences of such dissonance?

- We do not get a good night's rest.
- We are at risk of not being trusted.
- We will lose conscious capacity to address the deficiency, as thoughts manifest from the subconscious.
- We are at risk of losing our hold on honor.

If we can return our subconscious to a state of equilibrium by working through our code of morals and ethics by making amends, evaluating and adjusting the criteria in line with accepted societal norms, etc., then the situation can be recovered and action can be reliably based on honor. However, if fatalistic sources are allowed to influence the adjustment, failure will result. Typically, the subconscious will continually struggle with the dissonance in such a way that there is no intuitive definition of right behavior. The conscious mind will be forced to rationalize actions in situational contexts to make up for the deficiency. We see this happening on many occasions, from the petty to the grandiose. What would cause a co-worker to take a soda that they knew did not belong to them from the communal refrigerator if not for a lack of empathy? What would cause a leader to embezzle funds? These are not honorable actions and are not based on moral and ethical standards. Rather, they are the actions of a dissonant subconscious and nihilistic thinking. A lack of honor will inexorably result in failure. It is only a matter of time and circumstance.

This topic deserves a great deal of study and internal contemplation. The successful executive candidate will base their actions on honor and work to ensure that the basis for honor is a strong code of morals and ethics.

The Junior Executive will develop a strong code of morality and ethics to guide honorable decisions and actions.

PASTORAL THINKING

There are few better lessons to learn than to witness a leader who does not care for nor look after their subordinates. It is the surest path to failure in any organization.

An organization and its teams are distinctive entities and must be treated as such. In many respects, they are like an accumulation of thoughts and actions that aggregate for a very short time for a particular purpose, much like a Heideggerian thought (Heidegger, 1962). In the case of companies and teams, the thought is the intent of the team or organization. The individuals each bring a particular component to the thought and then execute in concert to achieve the intent of that thought. In basic terms the whole purpose of an organization or team is the aggregation of entities for the execution of thought(s). As such, it is the responsibility of the executive to ensure that the accumulation of individuals and resources is effective. This is the pastoral role of the executive leader, and it is often overlooked. The term "pastoral" has connotations that may seem parochial or outdated, but this function is vital to the effective performance of a team or organization—particularly as it relates to the purposeful accumulation of resources.

How does an executive ensure that an accumulation of resources works in concert and at potential long enough to fulfill the intent? Motivation and incentive should be employed, but the overarching concern should reside with how resources are treated. Pastoral thinking is an acknowledgement of the power differential in a team or organization and acceptance of responsibility by those with the power. At a minimum, the executive is responsible for providing a physically and psychologically safe work environment. Pastoral thinking moves beyond these basic points of care. It takes an interest in the betterment of the employees to ensure that they fulfill their potential. A good example of the benefits of this is the Hawthorne effect, as demonstrated in a classic study. Workers greatly improved performance not because of changes to physical condition, hours or task, but due simply to being considered and involved (Mayo, 1945). The circumstances of executing the study—interviews, feedback, involvement and show of concern—were the actual influencers on performance, not the mechanics of the work. As an executive candidate, we must develop a capacity for pastoral thinking and demonstrate it consistently to our subordinates. A few simple questions will help guide us:

Are we looking after the careers of our subordinates? They certainly are. If we do not provide opportunities to advance their careers in line with their aspirations, they will leave. In order to maintain team and organizational cohesion in pursuit of goals, we must ensure that all resources view their involvement in the organization as a means to further their career goals. Typically, this means ample delegation and challenging them to learn new skills with the tools we provide.

Do we understand their motivations for working? Monetary and like payment for work are often only the starting point. The basic contract of employment exchanges time for pay. However, this does not ensure that workers provide valuable or meaningful time for pay. People provide value and meaning to endeavors that yield a psychological reward. For a salesperson, the commission is not a representation of cash-for-time—it is a trophy. Each individual salesperson is different and understanding their idiosyncrasies will allow us to craft a work environment that ensures they deliver to their potential.

A starting point with pastoral thinking is recognizing that monetary rewards must be in place and in line with expectations. But, to obtain maximum utility from resources, we must demonstrate concern for the aspirations and motivations of our subordinates.

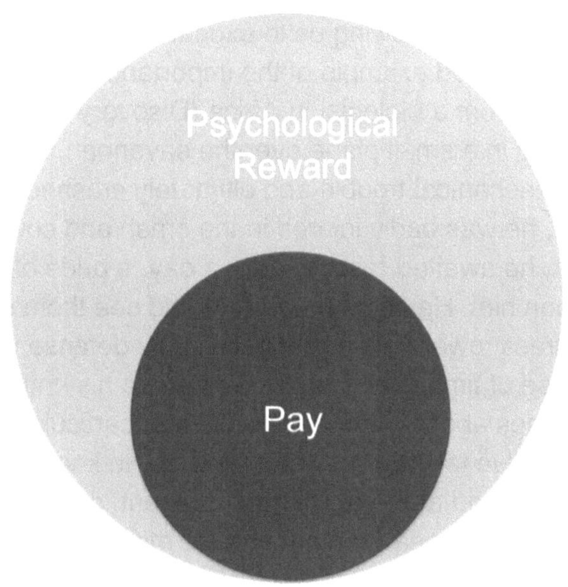

Figure 7 - Pastoral thinking takes into consideration not only pay but also the psychological rewards of employment.

The Junior Executive will understand that monetary rewards are a bare minimum of compensation and that pastoral care must be a fundamental part of their leadership persona.

TIMING

Timing requires subtlety and a deep understanding of normative movements of resources within an organization—that is, understanding the timing of when resources move from place to place in relation to an initiating decision. To understand timing is to understand how our presence at certain times and places affects outcomes. Make a move to the appropriate place too early and we will potentially miss out on more important opportunities. Move to the appropriate place too late and we will not have enough time to establish our competence and excellence for the opportunity. Get our timing right and we will find ourselves in a whirlwind of activity as events take shape, allowing us to execute at the right place and right time. A very good example of the importance of timing comes via an anecdote from a biologist in Africa (Disovery Channel, 2010). As he was flying in a small plane over the savannah, he experienced mechanical trouble and ultimately crashed. Unfortunately, he was badly injured in the crash and could not walk. Finding cover, he awaited rescue. After a day, a pride of lions happened upon him. He could hear them and see them stalking through the grass toward his position. His only defense was an educated sense of timing. Having lived in Africa his entire life, he knew a few things about the behavior of lions, particularly how they approached a kill in terms of risk and reward. He knew that if a lion attack were disrupted at the exact right moment, the predators would abandon the endeavor. That precise moment is when the attack is at the highest potential—just after the lions have committed but just before they pounce. As the tension built and he sensed two lionesses reaching this exact point, he screamed and banged a stick against the airplane. This startled the lionesses to such a degree that they panicked and ran away. The precise action in the right place and time had a life-saving effect.

We must not confuse timing with luck. Luck is the brute force calculation of probability against infinity. Luck is a quantity that we seek to reduce with timing. The degree to which we can reduce pure chance is a good measure of our sense of timing. The best way to think about timing is to break it down into two principal aspects: time and place. Timing is being in the right place at the right time. How can we address this in a disciplined and reliable manner? It may help if we consider each aspect separately:

> **Place**: Proximity is the greatest predictor of success in a particular endeavor. If we want to catch a fish, we must spend time by a body of water containing fish. If we want the highest priority projects, we must spend time with the group and people who decide which projects go to which people. Understanding place in our organization will require a deep understanding of the undocumented channels of power and

communication. A low-level engineer might not be privy to the strategic direction of the company, but he or she may be a resource on the most important projects. Understanding why they were chosen and who made the choice is critical to understanding place. Are resources pulled off existing projects for higher priorities? Or are resources pulled from the bench? Once we have a clear understanding of how the organization makes decisions with regard to place, we can maneuver ourselves into the right position. This is particularly true for growing organizations. Which projects are likely to expand new lines of business? Which executives are heading up the most important projects? Understanding place means that we understand that we need to be proximal to the individuals and teams assigning work that supports our goals.

Time: Comedians understand that even a great joke mistimed is a bomb. Knowing when to be at the right place is a skill that requires a lot of experience and thought to hone. Further, it requires great vigilance and a broad intelligence network to gain the most useful information. We must have a clear understanding of the decision-making cycles of our organization and when to begin "being" at the right place.

Our timing skill will reduce our reliance on pure chance. Luck will always have some level of influence but it need not wield the greatest influence. Our understanding of the movement of resources in our organization following an initiating decision will provide intelligence that we can leverage to be in the right place at the right time.

The Junior Executive will be mindful of their place in time in relation to the movement of resources in their organization and leverage this information to seize opportunities as they arise.

CROSS-DISCIPLINARY THINKING AND HUMILITY

We should consistently be asked why we are reading and studying subjects not related to our particular field. This curiosity truly marks those who will achieve executive leadership. Although confidence has been addressed in a previous chapter, it helps us here as well.

Confidence must be tempered by humility to avoid hubris. Hubris in this sense means unsupported confidence in our ability to over-deliver in a particular domain. If we are experts in our domain, then we must understand that this expertise is true at the present time and not necessarily true of the future. This specific version of over-confidence is a significant hurdle to advancement that will hold back a majority of candidates. We must have humility in assessing our expertise and bring ideas from other domains into our own—much like robotics engineers use bio-mimicry to enhance their designs. The ability to interpolate factors greatly in our fitness for executive leadership.

In order to become a candidate for executive leadership, we must be masters of our particular domain of work: marketing, engineering, sales, finance, operations, administration, etc. However, it is very likely that our rival candidates are also masters of a similar domain. A decision could be made on some incremental domain metric that shows one candidate to be better than the other—but in decisions of this sort, simple performance measurement is not usually the deciding factor. Typically, some other factor is at play. For example, an honest and fair question may be raised by the promoting executive as to whether or not they "like" one candidate better than the other. This is not a strict measure of performance or domain expertise, but it will have a great impact on the decision. Excluding sycophancy as a tolerable trait, these "other" decision criteria are often out of our control and subject to a million other factors. Thus, a better differentiation strategy must be employed—one that not only demonstrates an existing advantage, but also a better long-term performance edge. Best is a strategy that both justifies the decision to promote one over the other and stakes a confident long-term bet on a candidate's ability to perform excellently and consistently confer advantages.

One of the most effective strategies for demonstrating a differentiation advantage is the intelligent pursuit of a program of cross-disciplinary study and thinking. The most direct benefit of this approach is non-linear innovation. The particular implementation of cross-disciplinary study is not important from our perspective. It can be as simple as a reading list or as involved as a volunteer position. When we demonstrate innovative thinking as a result of cross-disciplinary study, we prove to senior leadership that we are not only experts now but that we have the capacity to develop and evolve as thought leaders in the future.

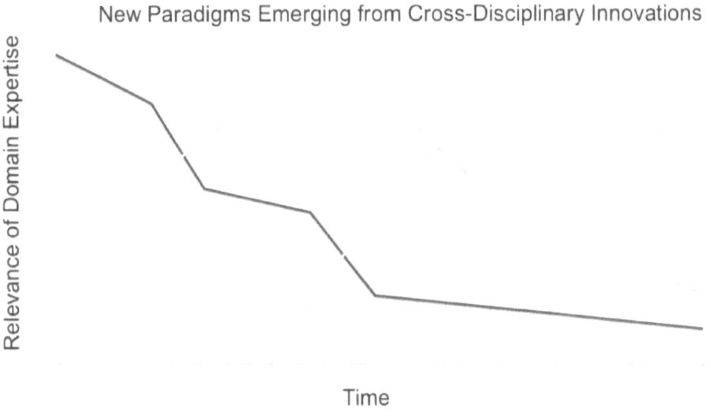

Figure 8 - The relevance of our domain expertise erodes as new paradigms emerge from an ever-changing environment.

The Junior Executive will acknowledge the transitory nature of expertise and pursue a course of cross-disciplinary study to ensure their position as a thought-leader in their domain.

INNOVATION

We can spend years reading the best literature and thinking on innovation, and should pursue new insights on the topic throughout our career. However, as the purpose of this book is to prepare us for a role as an executive, it is critical to spend time on the core of the concept to grasp its importance.

Despite the guidance of those who would make a career out of this one topic, the approach to innovation is straightforward but difficult to implement. Innovation is important for executive advancement because it represents the ability for betterment. If an executive is innovative, then they have the ability to make the product of the organization better—in potentially non-linear ways. This is a critical attribute of a successful organization and is the root of most differentiation strategies. For innovation is not limited to "new" products or services. Rather it encompasses the betterment of all facets of an organization: how mail is handled, how customers are treated, how policies are developed, how meetings are run, how operations are managed. All forms of betterment require leaders who are innovative. So what is innovation?

Innovation is the **robust unconscious automation of function**.

This sentence is a bit opaque, so we will decompose it. Function refers to any non-static state of a subject (i.e., change). Sorting mail is a function, as a pile of mail is changed into groups based upon meaningful criteria. Driving a car is many functions combined. So, we focus on the idea of a function. Innovation requires changing an aspect of a particular subject and thus changing how the function associated with that subject is executed. In this light, the carriage return of the first typewriters was an innovation. Automation is relatively straightforward, but unconscious automation is more complex. Many functions are automated and many combined functions are automated as processes. But, a majority of automated functions require conscious action to initiate and manage the automation.

Advancements in the telephone provide a good example. Initial rotary phones required physical action to generate tones that could be translated in switchboards to initiate, broker, monitor and terminate call circuits. An incremental innovation was automation of tone generation through digital dial tones. Instead of relying on physical, rotor-generated tones, new phones automatically generated the applicable tone at the push of a button. A further, combined innovation was the introduction of automated dialing—pressing a button to dial a stored number (one button for many tones). These innovations demonstrate unconscious automation. Rather than consciously managing the function of physically generating tones to initiate a call, we simply push a button. Thus, our mental and physical processes are freed up for other tasks—the core benefit of innovation. There is one final qualifying word to be examined. Robustness means the reliable operation of a function. Unless the unconscious automation of a function is robust, it is not truly innovative. Our conscious thought processes are not freed by the innovation unless we can implicitly trust that it works as expected. Once this trust is gained, the innovation yields its value. Users are freed from some function that required their conscious attention and can now focus on other value-creating activities.

One of the best examples of innovation in the technology product space in recent years was the initial launch of the Research In Motion (RIM) Blackberry. Prior to this device, it was possible to wirelessly synchronize and send/receive e-mail, notes and calendar events. But it was technically challenging and highly prone to failure. Thus, few people tried to integrate this feature into their lives. RIM succeeded in innovating because they created a product that delivered robust unconscious automation of wireless e-mail and calendar synchronization. In most analyses of the RIM Blackberry's success, focus is given to the security model or the strength of the integrated hardware and software design, et al. These were contributors to their true innovative feature, to be sure, but not the core innovation. When one used the RIM Blackberry, no conscious thinking was required to receive the benefit of the service. As long as the device was powered, it robustly delivered the synchronized data. Users were free to address other problems and leverage the device's benefits. It was incredibly innovative and launched RIM as a hugely successful company at the time.

A note about innovation in an organizational setting:

> The "not invented here" problem besets many organizations—no new functions are integrated unless they have been developed in-house. This is not necessarily a matter of pride or hubris. Rather, it is often a cognitive block. Without having gone through the process of inventing something, most people cannot process how to integrate it. That is, unless they have gone through the component build-out of a particular product or service as it addresses pain-points, they cannot understand how to properly use it.
>
> One way to address this block is to expand the scope and depth of engagement for all team members of an integration project. Rather than invent from nothing, the "invention" is the clever integration of the outsourced product or service.

The successful executive candidate will decompose all relevant functions in their domain and look for opportunities to innovate using this core concept. What functions could benefit from robust unconscious automation? Delivering on this question is an absolute requirement for consideration as an executive. This is one of the core criteria for senior leadership to determine if a candidate will provide significantly leveraged benefits to their organization. Anyone who ever struggled to understand the outsized compensation for executives would do well to understand this. Leveraged benefit matters, and innovation by executives and their teams is precisely how it is delivered.

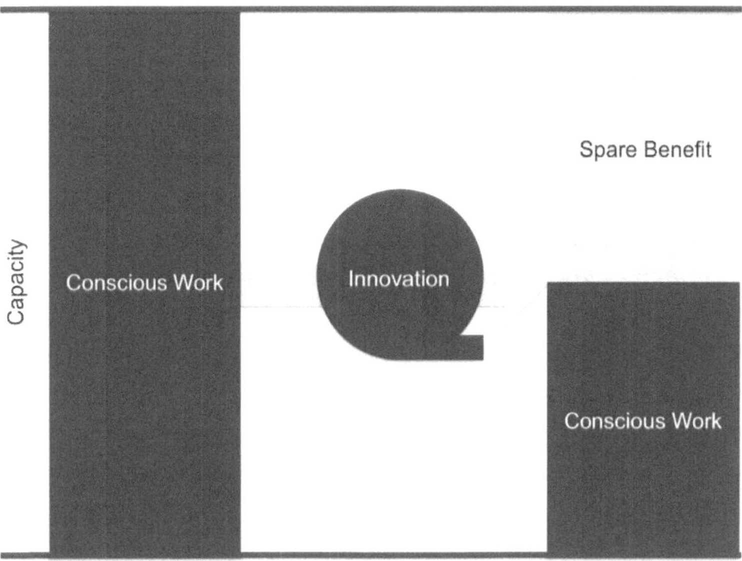

Figure 9 - Innovation frees capacity from conscious work, which provides a leveraged benefit.

The Junior Executive will innovate through robust unconscious automation of function in all areas.

FAILURE

A lot has been said on the concept of failure, specifically regarding our understanding of the fallibility of individuals and the feedback it provides for improvement. The majority of arguments are centered on semantic dissection of what we understand as failure. A central argument in this vein: "A fear of failure yields a symptomatic condition that stymies innovation, creativity and rapid growth." What inevitably follows is a call to embrace failure, and various methods of embrace are then put forward. There is certainly some truth to this argument. But, as with all hyped management concepts, the successful executive should not buy into it. The purveyors of these hyped concepts take a discrete, simple behavioral aspect and try to create a management method out of it. This does any consumer of their thinking a number of disservices. First, it oversimplifies a single concept as a lever that can yield outsized results. Second, it generates a lexicon of jargon that only serves to obfuscate the core truth. A basic behavioral aspect is not a magic lever. With regard to failure, the behavioral trait is simple: people who are punished for honest mistakes have a disincentive for taking risk. So, as a leader, we should learn one and only one lesson from failure: Do not punish for honest mistakes. Adhering to the tenet noted above is certainly a good idea for a leader, but it will not yield outsized results.

Our concerns here are understanding what failure means, and learning how to genuinely demonstrate leadership to both those who follow us and those who would promote us. We will not try to define failure again, other than to say that a failure is an outcome that did not meet objectives. From a long-term organizational point of view, success or failure on a discrete basis is not that impactful. What matters is where value is generated. For an executive, in the majority of circumstances, value is generated through the struggle required to make an endeavor a success. Thus, rather than rapid, finite experimentation (Failing Fast) or minimal resource allocation (Positive Failure), the organizational benefit is not based on discrete outcomes.

It is better to think of failure as friction, stymieing success. Using sailing as an example, we see that the approaches above amount to lazily substituting one large rudder movement for many small rudder movements. True leverage of friction makes continual rudder adjustments, while also redesigning the sail, strength-training the crew, adjusting course assessments and planning the next port of call. The successful executive organizes resources and processes under their purview to conduct perpetual experimentation across all functions. In this perspective, discrete success or failure is irrelevant. The friction generated by perpetual experimentation and adjustment will mature a team and organization in such a way that friction itself will yield indirect benefit. A key challenge for us is to determine how to develop and manage an organization in a way that leverages the benefit of friction.

So what exactly is friction and how does it relate to the concept of failure as discussed so far? Friction is often related as a negative—something that slows or erodes. However, friction has a much more important attribute—it excites. Think of how a match is lit: The friction of particular atoms taking and giving electrons yields an excited chemical reaction. This chemical reaction builds to a spark and a burst of energy is released. In the same respect, friction in the organizational context is the taking and giving of ideas, often in an excited state, that can build to a burst of creativity. As with a chemical reaction, the environment must be controlled. We cannot easily light a match in the rain. There are countless examples of this in politics, sports, business and science. A key takeaway from Paul Allen's memoir, "Idea Man: A Memoir by the Co-founder of Microsoft," is that Bill Gates would aggressively challenge all ideas. Only those that were debated convincingly with force would pass muster, sometimes requiring adjustment as a result of the challenge (Allen, 2011).

Thus, with regard to failure, we must establish an environment that promotes creative friction to yield the best outcomes. There must be evil geniuses, contrarians, passionate supporters, and all types of thinkers. The ground rules are simple: be honest, transparent and fair. It is up to us as the leader to enforce these rules ruthlessly and immediately. In terms of measurement, these questions are what matter: Have we created an environment that will yield the best and brightest sparks? Are the right people in place? Are the right tools available? Are the right incentives in place? Are the right goals and projects aligned? These are the challenges of managing failure holistically. Success or failure of the discrete goal or project will not be determined by one-off workmanship. Rather, it will be a product of the environment in which it was attempted. We must establish a track record that demonstrates the ability to craft an environment conducive to leveraging friction.

The Junior Executive will acknowledge failure as a normal consequence of creative friction.

PHILOSOPHICAL DEPTH

As a leader, we will find ourselves in the often-unenviable position of serving as a source of inspiration and certainty to our staff and colleagues. It is a basic truth that most people lack confidence in how they conduct themselves on a day-to-day basis. Thrown into new situations or even familiar situations that they are not presently prepared to deal with, they will do one of two things: Shut down, or grasp at a mental model for guidance. The first is irrelevant to our discussion, as it speaks to the individual and not to the leader. The second, however, is important. We have certainly asked some form of this question at some time in our life: “What would X do in this situation?” It is human nature to ask this, often consciously, but it extends deeper into the subconscious. Often the question is less circumstantial and more holistic: “How does X deal with this stress?” Or “How does X think that allows her to manage this complexity?” Or “What behavioral rules and signaling does Y use to manage conflict among his subordinates?” If we are honest, we realize that this is part of the learning process and something all people do both consciously and subconsciously. With this in mind, we need to analyze what searching for a mental model means for the executive as both a candidate and as a leader. For once we are an executive, we will become X for many people in our sphere of influence.

How we answer the questions above educates much of this book and focuses us on the self. This internal source of power, then, is a fount of inspiration and certainty that others will look to for assistance. In general, we refer to this as philosophical depth. As always, this material is not dogmatic but practical in nature. The particular sources of philosophical thinking are not that important. A survey of comparative anthropology provides ample evidence that, at the heart, most philosophical systems arrive at the same answers. The critical tasks, then, are to read, think, talk and write about the great philosophical questions. Our study of past and present philosophical thought will eventually provide a basis for an internal model of reality and our place in it. For example, if we study the life and thinking of Siddhartha or Jesus (among others, real or as metaphor), we see that a hero's struggle occurs within all people to some degree. This knowledge provides the basis against which we can evaluate the aspirations and goals of those around us. It provides a model for interaction that is considerate of these goals. We must create an environment that allows our subordinates to craft and pursue their own quest, in which their colleagues are encouraged to assist them. For practical purposes, this typically means that we give our subordinates freedom to lead projects or initiatives that provide them opportunity to achieve a tangible prize (authorship of a paper, release of a piece of software, arranging an event, etc.).

To the same end, if we study Confucius or Socrates we learn the basic truth that time will go on regardless of our actions, so our actions must have meaning in the present (e.g., the sun will come up tomorrow, so we should not lament a minor setback). Both of these thinkers had a great deal to say about what it means to be centered in the present and intellectually honest about our place in time. If we can internalize the basis of their thinking, the contemplation will engender not only rule sets and argumentative models, but will provide an enhanced basis for our own critical analysis. This basis for critical analysis frees us as leaders and individuals from temporal morass: What is the array of possible outcomes from this action or this direction? Regardless of what we decide, the sun will come up tomorrow. Thus, the best course of action is to evaluate the decision given all available information and make the decision now. Of course, this must be tempered by other considerations, but as a basis it gives us confidence that we can and should make decisions in the now. Few leadership qualities are as important as the ability to act with confidence in the now. For intelligent and thoughtful leaders, philosophical depth provides the basis for making decisions and moving forward. As others see in us the ability to do this, they will be inspired and use this knowledge as a source of security themselves. For the junior executive, it is imperative to internalize these philosophical truths and base our actions upon them.

If we study Lao Tzu or Martin Heidegger, we understand that infinite possibility provides the opportunity for willful action but only as the result of both effort and providence (e.g., we cannot harvest a crop until it has grown). As will be discussed in Chapter 3 regarding the calculus mind, a philosophical understanding about the role of the infinite in our daily lives is critical to creating integrated and complex courses of action. When considering both Lao Tzu and Heidegger, we see that the infinite is total possibility of action and outcome, but that within this total possibility, Will has a place. Concrete outcomes within the infinite are the culminating point of various causal threads of thought and action. We can act to influence these threads to achieve desired outcomes, which cannot be guaranteed, but must be worked toward. We see that the subconscious also has a part to play. As we identify desired outcomes in the infinite, a conscious plan can be formulated for a thread of actions that will arrive at that desired outcome. Subconsciously, our actions will be influenced to arrive at this desired outcome as well. The key is to realize that providence dictates that the path is never straight. Only through our sustained effort to course-correct can the desired outcome be achieved. For the executive, it is critical to internalize these truths and create plans that incorporate both providence and effort. It is this planning and our reactions to circumstance that will provide confidence to those around us and inspire them to follow us.

If we study William James or John Dewey, we understand that for the most part, practical matters are the only matters and we should ground our efforts in what can be done. In the context of organizational growth, we see that lofty goals should be striven for, but not at the expense of efficient operations. We must first understand and work to alleviate the constraints on efficiency. It takes an enormous amount of effort to compel individuals to do what we ask of them, and enhancing this ability within our team is of paramount importance. Having a philosophical basis for understanding this will provide the executive with confidence in the face of competing considerations. For executive success, it is critical to avoid hyperbole in endeavors and ensure that the operational environment is as conducive to efficiency as possible. This focus will provide certainty to our colleagues that practical matters are being handled appropriately.

It is easy to lose ourselves in philosophical contemplation. The successful executive will be humble enough to recognize that many brilliant thinkers have spent an enormous amount of time pondering life's big questions. Their knowledge and learning is free to use and is a great source of leverage. The successful executive will not only study these thinkers formally, but will continue to contemplate them and adjust internal models for decision-making and analysis. Philosophical depth is a critical concept to understand and must be integrated into all aspects of organizational life.

The Junior Executive will use philosophical depth as a well of strength and inspiration in their decisions and serve as an example to their subordinates and colleagues.

EXISTENTIAL UNCERTAINTY

Many of the topics in the book refer to the importance of responsibility and accountability. It is important to also look at the basis of these concepts and give thought to the foundation upon which all decisions and actions are based. A successful executive must be able to state, "I know that I am free to make decisions and that my actions are my full responsibility." This seems melodramatic, but it is necessary. Existential uncertainty is a struggle for everyone, and few, if any, are actually able to resolve it. Most assuage themselves through living by example.

For the executive, or any position of leadership, there is a gravitas associated with decisions. To make them effectively, honestly and with a clean conscience, we must be able to acknowledge our responsibility for making them. It is for this reason that executives are given responsibility: trust that they understand the gravity of their authority and trust that they will take responsibility for the decisions they make. No legitimate executive denies the responsibility and accountability of their role. Yet any honest person has doubts about their place in the world. This is natural and important, but it must be properly acknowledged for what it is—an unanswerable question. There is great benefit in examining our place in the world, but that search must be separated from the role of the executive. Existential uncertainty, as a source of conscious inquiry and thought, must be compartmentalized away from decision-making and discerning centers of thought. When staring into the void, one cannot decide what to have for lunch.

What does this mean in the context of the executive role? It means that we must do the work required to truthfully state "I know that my actions are concrete and my full responsibility." Certainty that the actions we take matter and matter greatly is a necessity. The role of the executive is to make decisions that affect other people in complex ways. In this sense, our decisions unequivocally matter. The successful executive will believe this and live it on a daily basis. The decisions we make will be made with full acknowledgement that they are the best decisions that could be made in our common circumstances.

The Junior Executive will acknowledge their insignificance in the universe and the irrelevance of this fact to their personal responsibility.

PRIDE

One of the biggest challenges in an executive role is understanding the impact of pride in others and us. In particular, the challenge is to grasp how our underlying sense of pride is fed and how pride is expressed in our daily actions. To be successful in the executive role, we must examine the impacts of the many types of prideful expression and develop a healthy model for how they should be expressed.

The negative attributes of pride are tempered by maturity and confidence, both of which are expected of an executive and must be cultivated. Objectivity is critical to understanding the impact of pride in our work. By removing the self from consideration, pride is no longer tethered to the incremental tasks and outcomes of compositional work. Rather, it is tied to the overall outcome, where it is appropriate.

In the context of the executive role, we look to St. Augustine of Hippo's definition of pride as "the love of one's own excellence." Under this definition, pride is a logical consequence of the performance required for an individual to be considered for the executive role. Thus, pride is found in substantial quantity at the executive level. Individuals who have excelled throughout their careers will have a substantial amount of pride. Of course, there are many other sources of pride for an individual, which may or not be beneficial. But they do not enter into our ordered examination of the organization. What are the various ways pride is expressed in the individual within an organization?

Good: Pride in one's work has a bar-setting effect. If an individual delivers a certain quality of work and has earned accolades for this work, the pride derived from those accolades will set the bar against which all future work is measured. In this way, their work will be of an increasingly higher quality. Additionally, pride in one's work provides a strong basis for the accountability and responsibility that an individual will need to be successful in roles higher in the hierarchy.

Bad: Pride, as it affects the ego, can have a substantial negative impact on an individual's work and is a determinant of an individual's potential for success in the executive role. It manifests in several ways:

> Control and Domain Knowledge: Because pride is tied to the level of achievement an individual has attained and provides a bar against which subsequent efforts are judged, it is easy to fall into a mode of behavior whereby all tasks within a particular domain must be controlled and that all knowledge within a domain must filter through the individual. This is the trap of micromanagement. There are plenty of studies showing the damaging effect of micromanagement on productivity. It is simple enough to state here that true leadership relies on the excellence and outputs of subordinates. If they are not allowed to control their own domains, we will never leverage their abilities and will be overwhelmed by the complexity of our role. The successful executive will check their pride by delegating control and domain knowledge to appropriate subordinates.
>
> Over-Confidence: Past performance is no guarantee of the future, but it is a very common fallacy to carry forward projections on a linear growth curve to outsized ends. If our pride has rendered us unable to share credit for our success with appropriate parties, we will have an inflated sense of ability. This is a recipe for disaster. There are several implications. First, it can lead to a situation of over-promising and under-delivering. Second, it can lead to a failure to acknowledge the efforts of others. Finally, it will lead to an

inability to admit a lack of understanding. This is the most pervasive expression of pride in the executive ranks, and the most deleterious to productivity and efficiency. On a day-to-day basis, over-confidence will serve to cloud communication, delay information, confuse others and damage the personal integrity of an individual in the eyes of others. There is substantial competitive pressure to behave with over-confidence at the executive level—particularly if a competitor does so successfully in the short term. But like all bad behavior, over-confidence will eventually trip up our competitors. If senior leadership allows over-confidence to continue, then the individual essentially becomes a tool for their internal political machinations.

Failure and the Cover-Up: An individual with an immature sense of pride does not handle failure well. If we have a mature attitude toward the objective nature of the goals and work involved, we will understand that failure is a necessary component of creative friction. The culture of an organization has a substantial impact on how failure is handled and how pride is expressed in relation. However, if an individual is unable to admit failure, a cover-up will inevitably follow. There are many and varied examples of this in private and public life. In all examples, the damage associated with admitting failure is a pittance compared to the damage caused by the cover-up, when it is inevitably discovered. In the organizational context, a cover-up typically results in finger-pointing, hiding evidence, and much trouble. All of this is extraordinarily wasteful in terms of both organizational resources and personal integrity. As individuals, our first instinct is to not admit failure, so as to protect our ego-tethered pride. This is a base instinct that is not appropriate for the executive role. The successful executive will objectively evaluate the performance of their work and admit failure, before immediately moving on to remediation and lessons learned. Senior leaders who do not appreciate this level of integrity and behavior should be avoided at all costs.

Pride is a difficult emotion, inextricably tied to how we view ourselves in the world. In the context of the organization, pride must be seen objectively and maturely. The successful executive will not tether their pride to day-to-day tasks or interactions. Rather, they will derive pride from higher-level goals and the overall performance of their team and the organization. All other expressive attributes will fall in line. The successful executive will demonstrate maturity and a practical understanding of the limits of individuals and teams to craft strategic operations grounded in controllable functions and realistic performance. They will monitor and modify work with the same level of maturity to achieve long-term and higher-level goals.

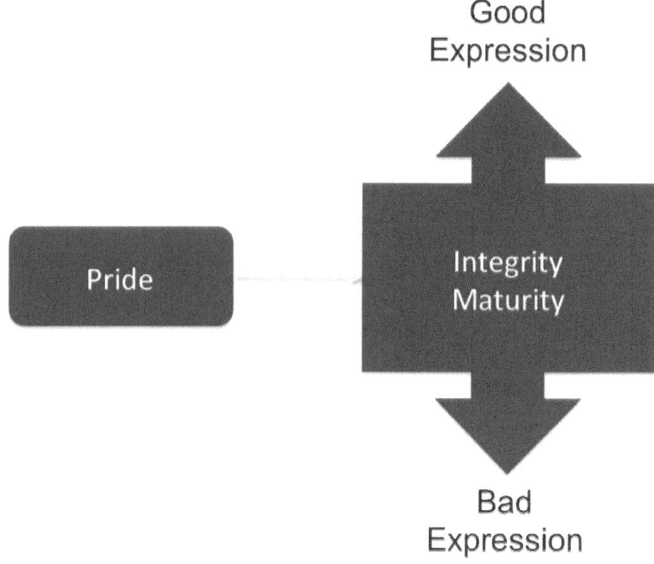

Figure 10 - The expression of pride in our work is determined by our level of integrity and maturity.

The Junior Executive will acknowledge the influence of pride on their actions and mitigate by focusing on outcomes.

Chapter 3 Execution Clarity

"I look like the you I turned into."

-Rachel Whiteread

SELF INTEREST

Every executive must read the work of Ayn Rand, if for no other reason than that our peers will have read her work. At the least, "The Fountainhead" should be read. If Rand's philosophy strikes a chord, then we may find the experience inspiring and uplifting. If it does not, then we will have a good understanding of what inspires many individuals who earn their way into an executive position. We will not cast judgment on the merits of Ayn Rand or Objectivism (her philosophical model), but seek to explain their precepts in the organizational context and underline why they are important. Further, we will highlight what the executive will need to understand as they interact with men and women who knowingly or unknowingly align with Rand's outlook.

Randian self-interest refers to the idea that all people do and should focus all their efforts on the betterment of themselves and their position. There are many arguments as to why this is a dubious position. However, these arguments are straw men based on the supposition that Randian self-interest is pathological. That is, the pursuit of self-interest infers that success comes at the unexamined expense of others. Upon reading "Atlas Shrugged," we see the opposite presented—Randian self-interest is the refusal to subjugate ourselves for the betterment of others. That is, we are not free to subjugate others because we all should be free from subjugation. Randian self-interest is neither pathological nor antisocial, and acknowledges an underlying truth about humans: We are imperatively beings of and about the self.

So how does Randian self-interest apply in the context of the organization? It starts with the assumption that rational self-interest is a good thing in comparison to altruism or communalism. Obtaining a higher education is pursing rational self-interest. Obtaining a higher education in a discipline in which we are uniquely suited for excellence is an even better example. In a rational sense, this does not result from the detriment of others. Borrowing money to fund this higher education aligns with Randian self-interest in that the individual's betterment is enabled and the individual is otherwise unencumbered. Obtaining the funds through dubious means does not align, in that the risk of jail does not lend to the betterment of the individual nor does the deficit of goodwill created by cheating or tricking others. Dubious means will lead to consequences in either the short or long term. Giving money to charities that support local education and crime prevention is fully in line with Randian self-interest. Our local economy and environment are direct influences on our self-interest. Within the organization we see that in the framework of Randian self-interest we look after our own betterment by bettering the environment around us and the individuals with whom we interact.

What does this mean for the executive? On a personal level, it invites introspection into individual motives and alignment of goals and actions with our moral and ethical codes. In dealing with others in our organization and society at large, Randian self-interest provides a basis for an alternate approach to interaction and work. For example, a common persuasive approach to requesting funds for charity is to highlight the plight of those in need. Out of pity or compassion, an individual may provide money for this charity. Given the track record of organizations using this approach, it seems to have some success. However, this appeal likely does not work effectively, if at all, with a person who has a strong sense of Randian self-interest. This may seem callous, but in this context the following holds a truth: Another's "need", by itself, is not a call to action as it presents no impact to the target individual's self. Of course, in the broader context, the "need" of another does have an effect on the individual.

Their need may cause them to turn to crime, which destroys the environment in which the target individual lives. Need may cause people to forgo education, which deprives the economy of a trained resource and thus decreases the overall economic environment in which the primary individual earns their living. The need of another does impact the individual self. To interact with a person of strong Randian self-interest, the executive must understand how to present that fact in a rational manner. Rather than asking for money based upon the "need" of the charity, ask for money to better the circumstances of the needy. For example, if we provide money for after-school programs for middle school children in our neighborhood, it will decrease the amount of graffiti and drug use in our neighborhood. Both aims are served; at-risk children have their "need" satisfied and we pursue our self-interest. It is critical to understand this type of self-interest and to tailor our leadership approach to accommodate and leverage this knowledge where present.

To a greater or lesser degree self-interest lies at the heart of all of us. It must be acknowledged. By understanding the dynamics of those with a strong sense of self-interest as exemplified in the writings of Ayn Rand, we gain a better understanding of ourselves and our colleagues.

The Junior Executive will acquire an understanding of the philosophical and psychological basis of Randian self-interest.

PRACTICE

"There are some things you learn best in calm, and some in storm."
-Willa Cather

There is a secret weapon available to anyone seeking advancement: practice. Much like any sport or other skilled activity, success is based in preparation for performing the appropriate actions at the appropriate times. For the novice, or those who do not practice, everything is a scramble at best and a complete rout at worst. To understand the power of practice, we need to think logically and fairly about the working environment of the executive level. Does it make logical sense that in gaining more responsibility and more accountability that the job would become easier? Does it make logical sense that current executives do not have to operate at a high-level of competence at all times? The answer to both questions is no. If we make the logical assumption that the job of an executive is difficult on a daily basis and that those who have attained that position are working at a high level of competence, then we can conclude that a person entering this environment with no experience will be at a substantial disadvantage. This is exacerbated by the fact that there are very few training opportunities for executives. The irony here is that newly promoted executives are expected to know what to do and what senior leadership expects of them. A substantial and historically steady failure rate in new executives highlights the challenges of this situation.[1] Yet, there are also many successes. What are they doing right? Some may have a natural talent or their position may afford some protection from error. But for the majority of successful new executives, the key to their success is an acknowledgement of the challenge and studied practice to address it before promotion.

One of the most consistent lessons we hear from athletes who move from collegiate competition to a professional league is that

[1] An internal study by executive search firm, Hendrick & Struggles, found an average failure rate of 40% for newly placed executives (Masters, 2009).

everything is faster, harder, and more complex at the pro level: literally stunning, as the transition often causes a new player to freeze up. They do not freeze up because they are deficient in some traditional sense. Their hard work and talent were sufficient to reach the professional leagues.

They freeze up because they are presented with a situation that is new to them, but not to those around them. This asymmetry is substantial enough that it changes the frame of reference that this new player bases their decisions on. Without a solid frame of reference for making decisions one of three things happens: the player guesses right, guesses wrong or freezes. This analogy holds true for professionals moving from the managerial ranks (or elsewhere) into an executive role. The context of the game is fundamentally changed; the boundaries and rules have changed; the stakes are much higher; and the other players and competition are bigger, faster and smarter. Again, one of three outcomes will happen.

Of course, this analysis is too simple. If we focus on the positive outcome, guessing right, it would follow logically that something could be done to gain more confidence in the basis for a right answer and increase our chances of guessing right more often than not. Practice is the right course of mitigation in this circumstance, but not for the obvious reason. It is not practical to prepare for events of which we do not yet have a clear understanding. Attempting to create scenarios based upon discrete events will be a wasted effort. Better, we can gain an understanding of the high-level operation of our organization. Are we in operations with a retailer? Then supply chain is a critical function. How many vendors do we have in rotation? How is their performance tracked? Who are the main points of contact? What are their internal politics? How are they managed from a financial perspective? Who provides forecasts? How is funding arranged internally? What is the duration of the current contract? All of these questions will help establish "what" must be practiced if we are to take on an executive role in this function. If we are a manager in this division, do we maintain an internal Profit and Loss? If not, why? That work will be expected of us in an executive role. Any uncertainty stemming from an absent frame of reference will compound the challenges of the new position immeasurably, and we will make bad decisions or freeze up.

So, is the point of practice to prepare ourselves for all contingencies when we take a new position? Yes and no. The key point of practice is that it resolves the newness of the situation and provides a basic frame of reference for making decisions. With this frame of reference in place, we can focus on the real challenge of the new position: freeing up our conscious processes for actual learning and rapid, on-our-feet thinking. If we have been running an internal P&L, then taking on a departmental P&L means extending that skill set to a broader scope. Rather than focusing on what to track, we can focus on verifying the data and understanding the contextual importance of the reports generated. Furthermore, we will likely know what reports need to be generated; and even better, we'll be able to speak about them in an intelligent manner. If we have been operating our managed group as an internal cost center, we will understand the friction caused by payment paperwork delays. The benefits of practice are many-fold.

- We will be able to get some sleep. By having a higher-level grasp on the day-to-day functions of our new role, we will be able to relax and avoid a general feeling of dread.
- We will impress senior leadership. For a senior leader, there are few worse mistakes that promoting the wrong person into an executive role.
- We will impress our staff. For a staff member, there are few worse circumstances than not having any respect for or faith in a leader.
- We will establish a solid frame of reference for achievement. Moving into an executive position confidently is critical to success.

Practice is not a prescription for generating scenarios and playing them out on a one-off basis. It is a thoughtful modification of our existing position to simulate the environment of the executive role we are pursuing—living it full time. The successful executive candidate will modify the way they execute their current role to simulate the environment of the executive role. This will be extra work. But it will not be in vain. Very few people exert the effort required to practice effectively. This is both a testament to the challenge and a huge opportunity for differentiation in the contest for promotion. The executive role is a trusted position and carries significant responsibility. Senior leadership will rate highly the individual who has "practiced" for the job and demonstrates the ability to prepare for uncertainty. Done properly, practice is a secret weapon that few undertake and even fewer have the discipline to follow-through.

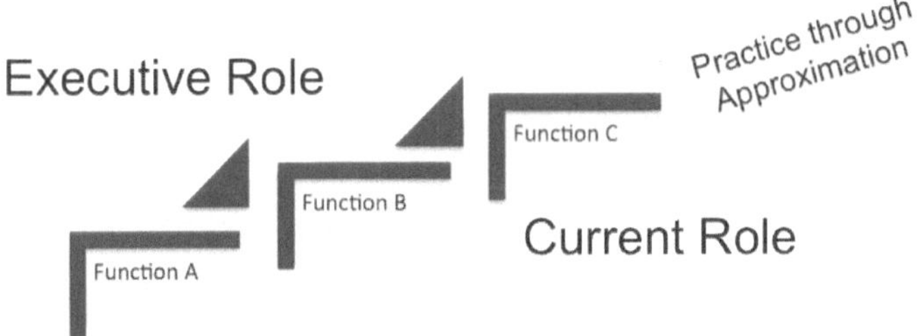

Figure 11 - Practice in the organizational sense requires research to map functions and approximate work.

The Junior Executive will modify their working environment to simulate the higher position they seek in order to practice for that position.

FEAR–LOVE BALANCE

There is a great deal of business literature and thinking around the importance of Love versus Fear in the relationship between leader and follower. Typically, the balance between the two emotional poles hinges on the underlying motivations of staff and the emotional incentives offered by leadership to adjust those motivations. If the staff is better motivated by Love, then the leader should provide emotional incentives that encourage a more endearing relationship and thus increase staff motivation. By the same logic, if staff is better motivated by Fear, then the leader should adjust their behavior and provide emotional incentives to the staff to encourage a more Fearful relationship and thus increase staff motivation. But this line of thinking, in truth, only seeks a course of action favoring a projected emotion, be it Love or Fear. The reality is far more subtle: There is no Love or Fear relationship between a leader and follower—at least not in modern, liberal societies. The reality is that Fear underlies all of our relationships with everything outside of the Ego. Love is superficial at best in the organizational context and is reserved for the self and nearest relations—family, close friends, and pets. So, if Love has no real application in the organizational context and Fear permeates all of our relationships, do these notions apply at all to how executives motivate staff?

To examine Love in the organizational context amounts to examining the non-Fear based aspects of an organization. That is, the aspects of the organization yielding positive feelings for the individual involved. This will vary among different organizations and is generally a direct reflection of the work conducted and the culture. For example, the positive aspects of a police station will be generally different from those of a day-care. However, there are many underlying commonalities that generally align with held beliefs around human rights and dignity. Are staff members free to execute their job functions and exercise their full responsibility and accountability? Are they respected and provided opportunity to be heard?

Are they compensated fairly? Are they working an amount of time that is consistent with their expectations? Are they working on projects that are aligned with their goals and interests? Is there opportunity for advancement? Is there a safe environment to air grievances? Is there tolerance for collegiality and fun?

These are the considerations with regard to Love that matter in the organizational context—anything else runs the risk of appearing gimmicky. From this perspective, it is absolutely critical that the executive ensures that the working environment is aligned with commonly held beliefs around human rights and dignity. Additionally, it should be noted that silliness, joviality and material reparations are not substitutes for meaningful compensation. Paying a high sales commission will not compensate for an environment where salespeople are not taken seriously. A successful executive will not establish a Loving environment or strive to endear themselves to their teams—this sort of environment only exists in families and friendships.

What of Fear, then? Fear is a far richer territory to examine in the organizational context and has far subtler applications. The core underlying fact that must be understood by all aspiring executives is that Fear is an ever-present emotion that is the basis for the majority of decisions made by individuals on a day-to-day basis. For example, when considering whether to jaywalk, we will weigh which of the following we are more fearful of:

- Being hit by a car
- The scorn of onlookers
- A police citation
- Being delayed on our journey

There are, of course, positives associated with some decisions. But regardless of how a decision is evaluated, the calculation is based on Fear. With this understanding, we see that the choice between being feared or loved or finding some balance is a false choice. As we have discussed above, Love is not a real emotion in the organizational context under practical circumstances. Fear is far more applicable. As executives, we are either feared or not feared. Bluntly, a successful executive must be feared. The important consideration is by how much and by whom. Our staff must have a fear of us based on the fact that we can fire them. If we do not have the authority to fire our staff, then we are not executives. If our staff members do not have a fear of us based on the fact that we can fire them, it will affect every action they make in the course of their job—all negatively, for us. But this rule must be examined a bit more deeply.

To have the power to fire someone at will is far different than the power to fire someone with cause: Only those lacking integrity fire individuals without cause. Here the relationship aspect of Fear becomes far richer. The executive should neither believe nor project the notion that they would fire someone at will—but having the authority to do so is critical. Constraining ourselves from using it is also critical, as this establishes the boundaries within which our staff can adjust their behavior.

Demonstration of this authority can come in any number of measures. In general, it will be assumed until tested. The act of hiring is a strong indicator of the authority to fire, and this is generally enough. How the executive demonstrates this authority will send a strong message and will further affect the Fear-based math used by their staff and others in the organization. It cannot be overstated how sensitive this demonstration is to interpretation, culture and inference. We will not prescribe how to demonstrate this authority, except to say that thorough comprehension of this book will provide a basis for success. The successful executive will give a great deal of consideration to the question of Fear in the culture of their organization. Fear will affect every aspect of the relationship with staff and the soundness of the decisions that their subordinates make on a daily basis.

The Junior Executive will understand that Love is a proxy for dignity and fairness in the organization, and that they must focus on how they are Feared by subordinates and colleagues.

PRESENCE

Creating an appropriate attitude toward Fear in an organization has a lot to do with the concept of Presence. Presence, in most respects, refers to the emotional impact of our physical presence on a group. Every single individual in a group has an emotional impact on the psyche and interactions of the other individuals within the group and the group as a whole. If the CEO is in a meeting, the emotional dynamic of the meeting is substantially changed. If a man joins a meeting otherwise attended solely by women, his presence will have a direct impact on the emotional makeup of the meeting and how others conduct themselves (and vice versa). It is critical for the executive to understand that the mere presence of an individual, no matter their role or personality, will have an effect on the meeting or group. In the group setting, this means that the executive must be sensitive to the degree to which each individual involved changes the dynamic. This consideration will provide valuable insights into the health of the organization and how work gets done. Being sensitive to the impact of individual presence will allow us to better shape the experience for everyone—in pursuit of our goals and those of the organization. It is important to understand how much the presence of specific individuals will fundamentally alter both the content and consequences of any endeavor.

Given this understanding, how is the executive perceived in terms of presence? The question may seem shallow or inconsequential, but that could not be further from the truth. Although it is possible to be successful without a strong presence, it is not likely. For the successful executive, it is far better to understand presence's natural equilibrium and how it might be adjusted, if at all. A great deal of self-awareness is required for this task. Practically, many leaders look to outside help to understand how they are perceived in the organization—360° reviews, coaches, peer reviews, etc. These techniques may be successful to some degree, but the bulk of the analysis can be done through introspection and attention to normal interactions. The most basic concept to understand with regard to presence is that it is a manifestation of our control over our environment. It cannot be faked or feigned convincingly among intelligent people—in fact, manipulation will have a significantly deleterious effect.

Creating a stronger presence is about owning the legitimacy of our position. Do we believe that we deserve the role of executive? Do we have the skillset, experience and leadership qualities necessary to deliver value to senior leadership and our Board? If not, we will have no real presence in any executive situation. Presence is about being fully engaged in all aspects of what is happening in the moment and in control of our reaction to the surrounding environment. It has little to do with arrogance, dominance or control over people or resources. These traits are harmful in any context.

There are many benefits to understanding presence in the organizational context—but it potentially requires a change in how we think. How can we be fully present in the moment when we face multiple, overlapping and converged long-term considerations and distractions? This challenge is really a culminating point of cognitive friction. How can we be fully aware in the present and still process what is happening as it relates to our longer term concerns? The current consensus in the literature typically advises for a superhuman talent to manage these considerations in real time or to slow down the proceedings or to block out future considerations from our thinking while in the moment. What really happens at this point of culminating friction is that we either make a bad call or stall. That is, we do not capitalize on the situation because we lack presence.

So, we say that having presence means implicitly believing in our legitimacy within the organizational environment. Given this belief, we should have the freedom to be in the moment. Our subconscious will provide a basis for real-time decision-making that is founded in our role in the organization and the execution of our strategy. This freedom and the confidence that manifests from this foundation will yield true presence.

The Junior Executive will understand that all individuals will demonstrate a level of presence within a group and that they must cultivate a strong degree of presence based upon a confidence in their legitimacy and a focus in the present.

PERSISTENCE

An old joke: Two hikers are walking through the wilderness when they come upon a bear. The bear is startled and appears to be about to charge them. The first hiker panics and looks around for the second hiker, who has already started to run away. He yells, "Where are you going? How are you going to outrun the bear?" The second hiker yells back, "I don't have to outrun the bear, just you."

Persistence is the ability to outlast setbacks until a goal is reached. There are two aspects of persistence that are bounded by their measurement: subjective and objective. Persistence in the subjective aspect is measured by our performance in relation to others. Persistence in the objective aspect is measured by our performance against objective goals that we have laid out for ourselves that do not consider the performance of others. In the joke about the hikers, persistence is measured in the subjective aspect and relates to who is first to fall under the bear's claws. Here we will evaluate both aspects, but always focus on the core, underlying truth of the matter: Persistence is a manifestation of the enduring will.

In the objective aspect, persistence is the ability of the individual to overcome obstacles and setbacks in pursuit of a self-stated goal. Learning to speak Mandarin in a year is a self-stated goal. Persistence is the ability to overcome the fact that we were too busy with work last week to study and felt an impulse to quit. How we persist is not important: That we do it is. When presented with the decision to pick up the book upon our return from work, we will experience several corrosive feelings: despair at having not maintained our focus, regret for missed opportunities to study during the week, fear of falling short of completing the study program, exhaustion at the idea of continuing the study when we have a busy work life, and anger at the goal for burdening us. Persistence requires us to acknowledge these corrosive feelings. Importantly, this is not a deflective thought to the anticipated, positive outcome. Rather, it is an acknowledgement of the truth of these feelings and the determination to continue despite them. We persist in this manner not just because we desire the goal, but because we will not be deterred by corrosive feelings. This perspective is critical to ensuring persistence in objective contexts.

The measurement of meaning for success or failure is within us. There is external acknowledgment of our persistence, but it has no real meaning other than that which we, as an individual, have attached to it.

Thus, persistence in the objective means that we have the ability, independent of external influences and outcomes, to overcome setbacks; not pulled across them by our desire for the positive outcome, but pushed because of our will and our determination. By this meaning, the successful executive will be persistent in the objective aspect.

Whereas objective persistence is measured by our ability to not be deterred from our goals, subjective persistence is measured relative to others. The underlying truth is consistent—persistence is a manifestation of the enduring will. In the subjective aspect, it is not calculated against ourselves but against others. Although this seems simple, it is the culmination of many other factors in our social environment. If persistence in the subjective aspect is relative, how is it measured? At the most basic level, it is measured by the acquiescence of our competitors. The vast majority of people do not have the capacity for true persistence. They will fall under the corrosive feelings discussed above and realign or abandon their goals. Why they fall out is irrelevant; that they fall out is what is important. We see this in many industries as economic cycles periodically make conditions worse for success. For example, if we look at the real estate market we see that as market conditions demonstrate significant liquidity and high demand, many individuals will enter the real estate brokerage business. As market conditions sour and liquidity dries up, buyers dwindle and sellers retrench, persistence becomes important. Those who can persist and survive, if not thrive, during a downturn, will gain share in the dwindling market. This is critically important for cyclical markets. On the upturn, the persistent will stand atop a substantial barrier to entry and can leverage their market share as the market itself grows. How they persist during the downturn is not as important. That they persist is what is important. For it is through persistence that our competitors self-select themselves out of the competition. As the conditions for success become more difficult and additional sales require more work, other real estate brokers will fall out. They will find other, easier ways of making money. This is the first and biggest cull.

A second cull will happen as those who have stayed are tested on their ability. Those with less ability relative to others will not be able to secure enough business. In this analysis, persistence does not mean that we were pulled to our goal by desire. Rather, our will pushed us to persist through trials that caused our competitors to fall out—we endured what others could not and become a success as measured by survival. Persistence in the subjective context is not pretty. The manifestation of enduring will not only provides a basis for goal attainment, but is also self-perpetuating. As we persist through trials and setbacks, competitors will see this as a barrier to entry. The successful executive will persist at all costs in the subjective context and will demonstrate strength of will. They may or may not outrun the bear in a race, but they will outrun the competition.

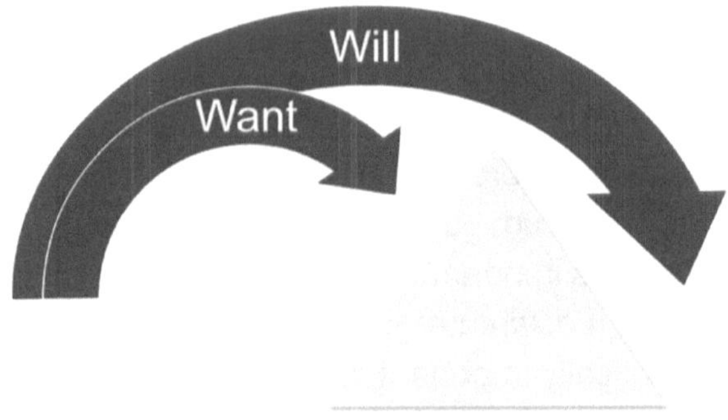

Figure 12 - Success through persistence is proven through strength of will and not from strength of want.

The Junior Executive will persist in the face of both objective and subjective trials.

CALCULUS MIND

The successful executive will have a deep and intuitive understanding of calculus. This is true less from a math practitioner's standpoint (although there is certainly much to be gained from this as well) and more from a conceptual standpoint. Calculus is the study of change. More practically, it is the analysis of rate of change and prediction of the resultant consequences. This is the underlying concept that makes an understanding of calculus critical in the organizational context. An analogy is relatively straightforward—as job responsibilities expand up the hierarchy in an organization, so does the complexity of calculation. Thus, we see that working on the shop floor, answering phones or delivering mail is arithmetical in nature, while first-line supervision is more algebraic. For example, as a first-line supervisor at a retail bank branch, we know that if we have four clerks and they can process 10 customer transactions an hour and they work a 7-hour day (30 minutes for lunch and two 15-minute breaks), then we have the following labor resource calculation:

4(clerks) X 10(transactions) X 7(hours) = 280 (transactions/shift)

This is a very straightforward calculation and is the foundation of most resource planning. In fact, despite ERP software marketing statements to the contrary, this is the level of math that is typically done on a day-to-day basis. As we move up and expand our scope into the organization, and the market as a whole, we see that this level of calculation is extremely limited. At the executive level of the organization we begin to see requirements for integrated calculations.

To carry on with our example: as the executive in charge of branch operations, the complexity we face is evident. Resource constraints multiplied by the number of branches, marketing strategy implementation across the branches, growth goals, cost-cutting goals, employee churn rate, competitive maneuvers, IT integration plans and issues, new product sales and retirement of old products, new regulatory reporting and compliance procedures, internal politics and more must be factored into calculations.

All of these present significant challenges for leadership, individually and in concert. If we know that Branch 1 has a clerk churn rate of 5% monthly and Branch 2 has a clerk churn rate of 10%, we must put in place strategies to equalize staff levels at these two branches.

But how is this affected by a 7% annual overhead cost reduction goal? Or, by the fact that the 10% churn at Branch 2 was caused by the opening of a competitor's branch location nearby? Is this a blip on the radar, or are there long-term implications? What are the succession, training and transition procedures in place to handle this rate of churn? Can the staff at Branch 2 accommodate the new requirements for monthly audit reporting? Can they accommodate the new online banking system changes that the IT department is rolling out? With a linear mindset, we would likely conduct discrete calculations on each of these particular questions and attempt to draw some higher-level conclusions. Plans may change or they may not, but they likely cannot be modeled in any meaningful way. This is a point at which executive candidates succeed or fail. A calculus mind moves the analysis to a more fluid and integrated level. The target dates of the IT rollout matter, but more importantly, what is the velocity of the IT rollout? What is the impact of the rollout in terms of hours of training and the implementation curve? Can the implementation curve be integrated into the existing branches' current churn rate? If we know the implementation curve of the IT change and the churn rate of an individual branch, this gives us a recruiting trajectory target. We know that we need to recruit at a net 7% headcount increase rate for several months to overcome these impacts and deal with the new competitor's branch location.

As we can see from the simple example above, linear calculations and algebra will not suffice to manage the complexity of the executive role. With a calculus mind, we see how functions can be mathematically assigned velocity, trajectory, mass, etc. It is not necessary to have a command of applied calculus to model out the actual equations for this integration (although it certainly can help). The key is to fundamentally understand the integrated rates of change associated with each of these functions and develop strategies to manage them as an integrated whole. Other chapters in this book will cover practical applications of this (portfolio management, measurement, operational tempo management, etc.). There are multiple techniques and tools for leveraging this understanding of calculus.

The successful executive will acknowledge that raw arithmetical horsepower will not allow them to handle the level of complexity required at the executive level. Higher-level mathematical thinking that considers rates of change in the various functions and most importantly, provides the flexibility demanded by probability in a very uncertain world, is necessary. The ability to model integrated functions on the run will provide a level of understanding that will substantially differentiate the executive candidate.

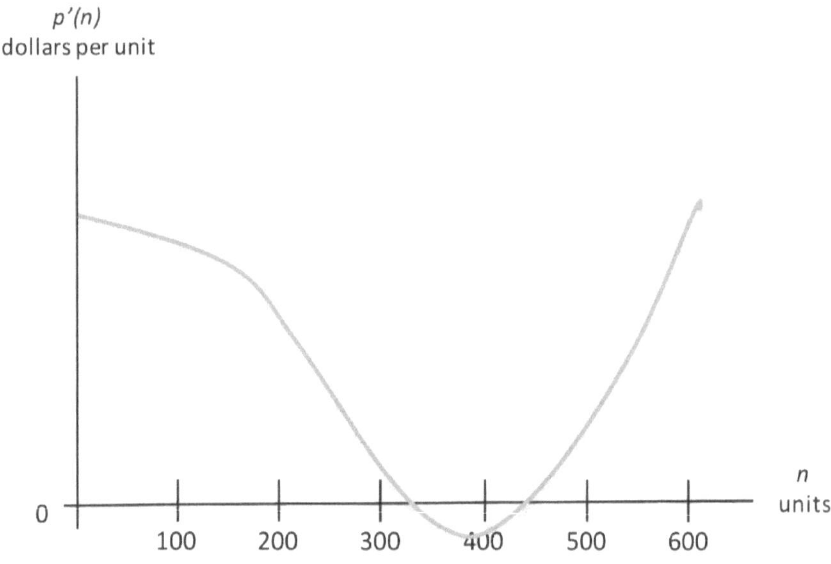

Figure 13 - Using calculus is necessary to leverage multiple rates of change for solid decision-making.

The Junior Executive will have a strong understanding of applied calculus.

PERSPECTIVE

More than any other level of the hierarchy, the executive level requires us to adjust our perspective in relation to our work. At lower levels, we will view our relation to our work as a value judgment of our involvement. If we like the work, then we will have a positive value judgment of our involvement in that work. But at lower levels, our involvement in that work may not be completely of our own volition, and the work itself will likely be presented to us. Thus, we have the choice of applying our effort to the work presented or not. At the executive level we will be the source of work. That is, we will define what work is to be done. Rather than having projects or work presented to us for our involvement, we will generate work and projects for presentation to colleagues and subordinates. As such, our perspective in relation to the work shifts significantly. This change in perspective is often difficult for newly appointed executives and is one of many ways that individuals fail in the role. There are two main reasons for this failure: residual resentment and immaturity. It is easy to find examples of individuals who carry resentment with them on a daily basis, particularly at the lower levels of work. In this context, resentment often arises from individuals lacking control over their environment (namely, subordinates receiving direction from their managers). Many books explain the roots of the phenomena and describe techniques that serve to reduce this resentment, all of which is very useful for managers. However, we are concerned here not with reducing resentment in subordinates, but with understanding the effect of resentment in the mind of the executive candidate. To a large extent, individuals do not like to be explicitly told what to do. Rather, they like to feel that they have control over what they do, when, and in what fashion. External forces that impinge on this internal desire are a trigger for resentment. In many respects, this resentment is an excellent source of motivation to perform better and achieve greater levels of control over work. But absent the ability to rise to a higher level, resentment can lead to destructive behavior. A person predisposed to this kind of resentment tends to have a skewed worldview, and perceive every interaction in the work environment diverging from the likely reality.

A person who resents the constraints of circumstance and authority will likely fail to internalize a change to their perspective that allows them to succeed at the executive level.

They will always feel like a subordinate burdened by a higher authority. Resentment is then linked to immaturity. It is a lack of understanding of the fallibility of others and the complexity of both the work and the organization. It can also exist as a lack of understanding of the freedom of action that is granted to an executive to either succeed or fail. At lower levels in the organization, success or failure is judged against the tasks and circumstances assigned to an individual. At the executive level, success or failure is judged against the projects that an executive creates and drives. This change in perspective requires maturity on the part of the successful executive candidate.

Resentment occurs in any number of situations. Maturity helps us to understand the context in which resentment occurs and provides a basis for a change in perspective. Like any growth activity, overcoming resentment is a struggle. There is an additional aspect to resentment in the organizational context: resentment at not getting something. This is essentially the flip side of the type of resentment discussed above. Rather than resenting being dictated to or directed in our scope of work, this resentment is triggered by our not receiving guidance or resources. Very often, it is referred to as a "setup for failure." It is a response to what are often circumstances that no one has the power to change. This resentment is likewise often tied directly to immaturity. It is a passive-position statement that obviates responsibility for a task because the individual does not have the tools to complete it. Of the two types of resentment in the workplace, this one is more often found at the executive level. It is not necessarily a block for advancement into the executive ranks.

We must note that under certain circumstances it is wise to stop a project that is under-resourced. But those situations are not under our scope of discussion. We are focused on the resentment of the individual who is not handed everything they want at the right time to complete a task or project. Like the first type, this manner of resentment will not allow us to make the perspective change required to move up to the executive level.

Resentment is viewed as an immature attitude and a liability in candidates for promotion. As has been discussed in many other chapters, the executive role's core purpose is to take total responsibility for their domain and grow it. A person who demonstrates the symptoms of resentment at not being given something cannot be trusted or relied upon in that role.

In an organizational setting, maturity is required to understand the circumstances surrounding any discrete situation and to adjust planning in accordance. This is the executive perspective. The successful executive candidate will spend a great deal of time and effort maturing as an individual to ensure that they can contextualize external constraints and circumstances. It is this perspective that will allow them to achieve the freedom of purpose needed at the executive level, and positively benefit the organization as a whole.

The Junior Executive will be sensitive to their basis for perspective and ensure that it is free of resentment or immaturity.

ASSET MANAGEMENT

This book provides insights across many subjects related to the executive role. Many of these are admittedly abstract. But, the topic of this segment, asset management, is very concrete and speaks directly to the question of why the executive role exists.

Unlike most roles further down the hierarchy, the executive is charged with growing the enterprise: increasing revenue, scope of operations, scale of products and services, competency of excellence in delivery, etc. We are not looking for incremental growth. While it is nice to add revenue to the business and reduce operating costs, growing the fundamental capacity and competency of the business is what matters. For example, if Sales earns a new account, this is great but does not generally affect the corporate valuation or provide a basis for leveraged growth. By the same token, if Facilities identifies a lighting scheme that reduces electrical bills by 10% across the organization, this is also great but does not materially affect the value of the organization. As an employee in the staff of a particular group or division, our scope of responsibility is typically limited to these types of discrete events that impact an existing line of business or organization function. However, at the executive level, we have the scope of responsibility to not only ensure that these discrete events happen, but to build an environment for such events to happen without our direct involvement. In any type of organization, the executive role exists to not only ensure proper maintenance of established scopes of work but to also find new ways of working that can be leveraged into the overall value of the organization.

Essentially, this means building intangible assets that provide a basis for total organizational value and a platform for leveraged growth. In the realm of industry and the private economy, we might be talking about new lines of business or new processes that yield leveraged benefit. In the public or not-for-profit sectors, we might be talking about new competencies for training or processes that yield more efficient use of funding. Across all organizations, the executive must work to build assets. As an existing executive or an aspiring one, we understand that within our purview as an executive, we must establish both a scope and plan for asset building. This will be a central focus of our efforts as an executive.

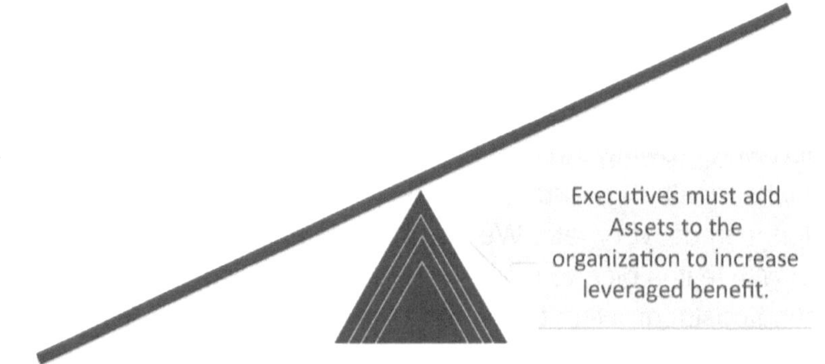

Figure 14 - The executive role exists, in part, to add assets that can be leveraged for the organization.

The Junior Executive will view competencies and processes as assets that enhance the value of the organization and focus effort on developing these assets for leveraged benefit.

RISK MANAGEMENT

How we handle risk will be an important determinant in our advancement and our success with senior executives. As has been covered in other chapters, providing clear situational guidance to all stakeholders in our work is absolutely critical to their trust in our abilities. This is particularly true with regard to risk. As with most topics we cover, there is ample expert thinking around the topic of risk management. In fact, many organizations and all large ones have specific roles in their senior management ranks that deal exclusively with risk. The successful executive must contextualize the role of risk in their organizational domain to determine the appropriate level of attention.

Risk management is a discipline that can quickly overwhelm any initiative through both FUDD (fear, uncertainty, doubt, distraction) and paranoia. This is the opposite of the intent of proper risk management, particularly in an open, honest organization. Risk management, at its heart, is the imaginative survey of potential problems that may arise in a project or in operations. It is a clear-eyed evaluation of what decisions should be made in reaction to risk and its possible impacts. The intention is that these decisions will provide a clear path to progress in the project or operations in full consideration of the apparent risks. Although we will discuss a general theory of risk management, we should make a clear initial delineation as to what is a risk, for the real challenge with risk management is to focus our time, effort and resources on addressing the right risk.

We will avoid discussions around corporate risk: business continuity planning, disaster recovery planning, etc. Although these are critical to overall corporate risk management, they are beyond our scope of discussion. We differentiate between external risk and addressable risk. External risks will be excluded from our risk management strategy at the executive level as they are either typically not addressable in practical terms, or addressed at a corporate level and demonstrate constraints as corporate policy. Force majeure events are a good example of external risks. Risks to organizational survival or to market conditions are typically external risks. Although external risks may well be risks to the work at hand, there is essentially nothing that can be done about them at the micro-level or within an individual executive domain. That is not to say that external risks should not be considered on an organizational level. But from a probabilistic standpoint, external risks are extremely unlikely and effort spent addressing them would be wasted. Given that, how should the successful executive manage the risks that can be addressed?

There are different risk management methods, many of which are excellent and any of which can be used. Whether a particular method is used or not is unimportant for this discussion, except that the method should be underpinned by the following: Addressable risks are understood to be within the control or influence of the individuals and entities involved in the work. This can be either on a program, project or running operational basis. There are three components of any risk that should be considered: source, impact and approach. All of the components must be controlled by the risk-management work of the executive and team. If a package must be delivered by a certain day to a certain location, the source of the risk is uncertainty about the shipment. At a deeper level, we see that the risk is based on an assumption that the shipment would take a particular amount of time. The stakeholder assumed that the shipment would arrive on time and so the true source of risk is the assumption. By extension, if we made a domain decision that we only ship with a certain carrier or via a certain class of shipment, that decision would be an additional source of addressable risk. Any risk management method must use as the source of risk those assumptions and decisions that are made through the course of the work and planning. Our tempered confidence in these assumptions and decisions will yield a likelihood of the risk turning into a problem.

The next component of risk management is assessing the potential impact of the risk. In the running example, what would happen if the shipment were late? If the shipment is a donor kidney slated for transplant in a dying patient, a delay of one day could be a matter of life and death. If the shipment is a box of gaskets to a standing buffer stock, a delay of one day could have no impact. Once the impact and likelihood of the impact is understood, an approach can be implemented to deal with this potential impact. Generally, there are four practical approaches: mitigation, avoidance, acceptance, and transference (Dorfman, 2007). The source and impact of the risk will dictate which approach is most appropriate, which will provide a framework for the time, effort and resources that we apply to managing the risk within our domain.

Risk management is an important feature of the executive role. Excellence in managing risk not only demonstrates maturity and reliability; it also provides a basis for senior executives to make sound decisions in larger domains and thus benefits the organization as a whole.

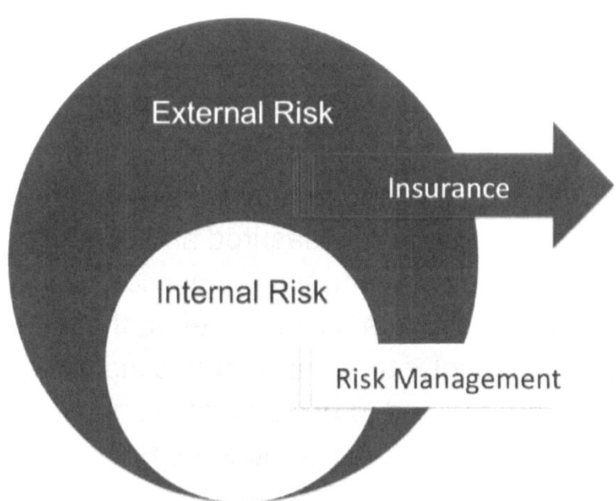

Figure 15 - Risk management and associated work is applicable to Internal Risk.

The Junior Executive will establish a pragmatic and efficient risk management strategy that provides a framework for managing addressable internal risks and insuring against external risks.

PROJECT MANAGEMENT

It is absolutely essential that an executive candidate become expert at project management. Not project management as a discipline, but project management as a way of thinking. There is an entire industry built around project management (pmi.org is a good example). Professionals within this domain should be included in our teams, but we do not need to be an expert practitioner. Rather, the successful executive will be an expert at managing workflow through the use of project management principles. At its core, project management is the controlled execution of discrete tasks that yield measured performance. It is a way of thinking that allows for robust decomposition of complex work into manageable activities that can be defined, estimated and resourced to ensure predictability in delivery. Additionally, it encapsulates effort and time into concrete costs and outputs. At the executive level, this approach is important for three reasons: goal alignment, reporting and measurement.

Executive candidates across all organization types must manage complexity: multiple work streams across diverse teams, high-frequency delivery in a single team, greenfield work, etc. This complexity must be monitored, measured and controlled within a reliable framework. Project management provides this framework by encapsulating work in discrete scopes of effort that can be decomposed into particular tasks assigned to individuals. These assignments are aggregated to understand resource utilization (over or under) and when work can be completed. For operational purposes, this is critical for managing resources and expectations of other stakeholders in the work. For planning purposes, this information is required to understand resource and operational capacity. How do we know that we need more people if we cannot measure how much our current staff can do? Without a solid framework for managing work and resources in place, we are essentially guessing, which is insufficient at the executive level.

As an executive, we will have organizational goals that the entire leadership team is tasked with achieving. It follows that our team goals must align and support higher-level organizational goals. Once our goals are established, a plan for achieving them must be put in place. Each goal can be achieved through one or more projects that will yield the goal success criteria. If the goal is reducing shipping costs by 10% over the course of a year, a project can address that goal, with a discrete timeline and deliverable. We can measure this project over the course of the year and adjust, as necessary, to ensure appropriate resources have been allocated and that expectations stay in line with current reality. The same holds true for the goal of opening a new chapter of a charitable organization in a different city. The desired outcome is clear and resources can be applied to execute the necessary tasks. Over the course of the year, we adjust resources and expectations to ensure success. In this manner, higher-level goals are decomposed into subordinated goals that are tied to discrete projects. This alignment ensures that the organization operates within a framework that is directed toward goal achievement in a controlled and efficient manner.

Once goal alignment has been achieved within a project framework, the status of those projects can be reported in a consistent manner. Much of the discipline around project management is directed toward standardization and consistency in reporting. Thus, if our organization were involved in software development, we would know that there are five phases of work before a software development project is complete. If reporting is standardized and robust, we can see clearly how each project is doing in relation to overall goals. For example, Project 1 may be 50% complete with phase 2, while Project 2 may be 50% complete with phase 1. Across the portfolio of projects, this relative information is extremely powerful for efficiently managing resources and expectations. It is predicated upon standardized and robust reporting. The successful executive will establish a simple and extensible reporting mechanism for all projects in their portfolio. There are many different methods of doing this—some better suited to particular organizations than others. The key is to ensure that the method provides confidence in the reporting available. Without reliable reporting, no higher-level planning or work can be conducted effectively.

Strong reporting means that the status of work on our projects can be measured, and measurement is what allows us to demonstrate excellence in our work. At the project level on an operational basis, reliable measurement is how we ensure that work is completed as planned and that outcomes are delivered as expected. For example, if we know that phase 2 of a technical manual publishing project requires two technical writers for one month, we can measure their performance to determine if we are ahead of or behind schedule. This information provides a basis for adding more writers, extending the deadline or reducing the resources required. Measurement is what allows us to justify decisions that affect the incremental and overall outcomes of our projects. For the candidate, demonstration of this discipline is required for advancement to the executive level. For existing executives, expertise in measurement is essential to ensuring that complexity is managed in a disciplined and controlled manner and demonstrating sophistication sufficient for advancement to senior leadership.

Project management is a deep and powerful discipline. Its concepts, techniques and methods contained allow leaders to control the work completed by their teams and to deliver the maximum output with the minimum inputs. The successful executive does not need to be an expert practitioner of project management, but rather an expert in leveraging the underlying concepts. Further, it is strongly suggested that our team include a project management expert.

The Junior Executive will use project management methods of reporting and measurement to ensure goal alignment and operational excellence are delivered within a project framework.

PORTFOLIO VIEW

Regardless of industry, one of the key differentiators between a manager and an executive is their respective level of view on the work done by the organization and in each domain. As a general rule, some managers have a portfolio of work, while all executives have a portfolio of work. If the executive candidate does not have a portfolio of work, this should be the first order of business.

By definition, a portfolio is a higher-order organization of work. From lowest to highest, the hierarchy is as follows: task, activity, work stream, phase, project, program, portfolio, department or domain, organization. Of course, some organizations have fewer levels; some have more and some interchange names and levels. But the list above is typical. A portfolio should represent the simple rollup of lower-level, salient metrics and reflect clearly the goal structure of the organization. At the least, every executive should have a “cost” and a “revenue” portfolio. Beyond that, the need for portfolios depends upon the type of work conducted.

The portfolio is a tool that provides a concise and candid view of how the executive is affecting the higher levels of the hierarchy and often the organization as a whole. As every candidate should know, the higher up the chain, the less time an executive has to pore through minutiae to tease out information. Thus, portfolio reports provide inputs to higher levels used in making decisions that affect not only our domain, but also all others in the organization. As an exercise in executive leadership, continual optimization of portfolio performance will hone our ability to quickly get to the root cause of an issue or opportunity. Further, a portfolio view provides a substantial basis for goal alignment with higher levels of the organization.

Portfolios provide a framework within which goals can be decomposed and applied to discrete programs or projects temporally for analysis and achievement. For example, a cost portfolio could consist of all cost reduction initiatives currently in process and planned for our domain. If a domain goal is cost reduction of 10% for the fiscal year, then this goal can be decomposed across the portfolio components, typically programs, to yield the desired result. Further, new initiatives can be undertaken in the portfolio to cover gaps as they arise, or take advantage of opportunities to over-deliver. Common metrics are then applied to these existing and new programs to measure performance throughout the temporal constraint of the fiscal year (weekly, monthly, quarterly, etc.). From a reporting point of view, as the year progresses, granular progress (or lack thereof) among the various portfolio programs can be rolled up to provide a clear measure of portfolio effectiveness in achieving the top-level goal.

This clarity of effectiveness is critical, not only from the perspective of providing candid and clear information to senior leadership, but also from the perspective of action. With clear metrics on aligned portfolios, we have the opportunity to mitigate risk, flag issues and seize opportunities. Mastery of portfolio management is an absolute requirement for advancement. The portfolio organizational component will be expanded upon in later chapters, as it provides the framework within which most other executive functions lie. Resource management, quality assurance, reporting, risk management, delivery, process management, etc. are all founded within the framework of the portfolio.

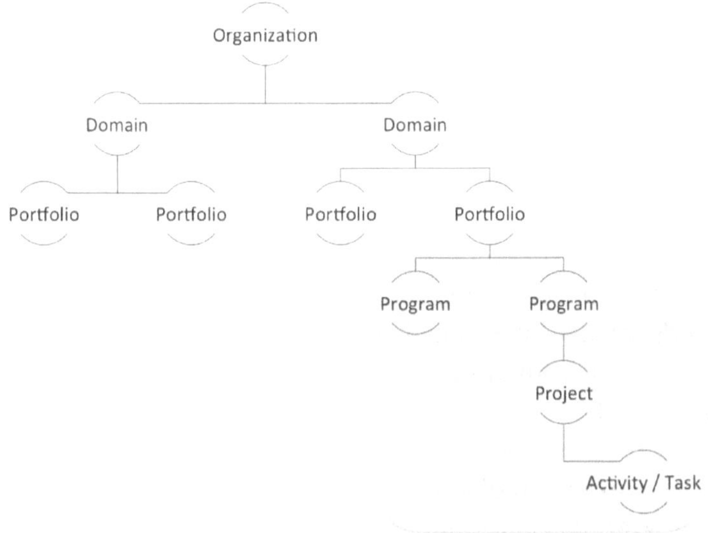

Figure 16 - Portfolios of work leverage lower-level tasking for domain- and organization-level benefits.

The Junior Executive will organize all domain activities into portfolios that can be led by lieutenants.

DISCIPLINE

There are many ways to think about discipline. In this book, we review modes of thinking and acting that can help us attain an executive position. At some point, these ideas must be put into practice. How this is best done comprises the discussion around discipline. What we are concerned with is in two parts: the daily application of will to ensure that a prescribed course of action is executed consistently, and the surge of will required to break through difficult periods. In this latter part, discipline can be viewed as “going to the well.” Of course, both parts are founded in the same source: the will to power. The difference requires us to discuss the application of will on our external environments and what steps need to be undertaken to develop this ability—in short, developing discipline. We will avoid the debate around “nature vs. nurture” and simply state that everyone has a certain degree of willfulness and this can manifest in many different ways. The very fact that we are addressing these subjects indicates a substantial will to power—the meek do not pursue an executive role. Suffice to say that an executive candidate will have an adequate will to power that can be cultivated, or reigned in as the case may be, into a reliable source of discipline. With regard to the two aspects of discipline, we will lead with the assumption that the first part (the daily application of will) can be developed consciously and the second (the surge of will) manifests itself from the subconscious as confidence in our abilities is internalized.

The daily application of will to ensure that a prescribed course of action is executed consistently is an absolute requirement for success as an executive. It is the very definition of discipline. True change and true progress are only achieved through discipline over time. This is particularly true at the executive level, for a number of reasons. First, the workload at the executive level is substantially larger and more difficult than at lower levels. The best way to approach this daunting truth is to address the workload in a consistent, intelligent and disciplined manner. A higher-level disciplinary function is to ensure that workload optimization is implemented consistently. Do we clear our e-mail inbox daily? Do we respond to all correspondence within 24 hours? Do we provide clear, concise and actionable guidance to our subordinates? Do we apply strict attention-to-detail in our communication, work outputs and documents? Most importantly, do we do these things every day? If so, then our application of daily discipline is well-honed and will serve us well as an executive. If not, then we need to implement discipline immediately. We will not go into a specific plan here. However, we will discuss the root cause of why discipline is typically not implemented.

A lack of discipline is fundamentally rooted in misalignment between what is considered imperative and what is considered discretionary. From this perspective, we see that imperative tasks, as ordered by the Maslow hierarchy (Maslow, 1943), are typically conducted in a disciplined manner—that is, we ensure that we eat every day and find shelter every night. Alternatively, every time an individual is faced with a discretionary task, they are forced to make a value judgment about the worth of that task against the expected effort, in consideration of their current physical and mental state. Therein lays the problem. We are often tired or busy or distracted. Thus, our current physical and mental states can very often yield an environment that is not supportive of disciplined action. How do we address this challenge?

Discipline in this context is first achieved by moving discretionary tasks into the same mental model as imperative tasks. The choice of which discretionary tasks will move should be dictated by our higher-level goals and the timelines associated with them. If we have decided to run a marathon in six-months, then the tasks associated with training must be moved from the discretionary mode to the imperative. This movement requires will. Through the prism of achievement, we see which individuals have the will to make these adjustments. Having the will to implement and develop our personal discipline is an absolute requirement. As a successful executive, we make the decision to employ our will to conduct our work and life in a disciplined manner.

The second part of our discussion on discipline is an examination of a higher function of discipline, essentially a meta-condition deriving from consistency in the first part. This is the discipline to not quit. When events and circumstances are building hurdles to our achievements, do we have the discipline to fight on? In other contexts, this may be referred to as "going to the well" and it requires significant confidence. This confidence is grown and nurtured through the disciplined approach to our work as noted in the first part. John Elway was a successful professional quarterback in the National Football League during the 1980s and 1990s. Of all the quarterbacks of his era, he was the most consistent in his ability to pull the team through what seemed to be overwhelming circumstances to achieve victory. When behind by 20 points with only 5 minutes left in the game, he would establish a plan to 21 points and then execute flawlessly. His success as a leader was reliant on the team's ability to execute in a disciplined fashion. These feats were the direct beneficiary of the confidence both John and his team had in their abilities and their disciplined approach to playing the game. They would have been unachievable otherwise. If we do not prove to ourselves that great things can be achieved through disciplined action, we do not have the faith or confidence in our ability to lead through times of crisis or trials—nor do others. This is a basic truth of discipline and a demonstration of the higher order benefits.

As an executive, we must have the tenacity to demonstrate discipline on a daily basis. Not only will all real achievements be reliant on this, but also our ability to overcome hurdles and lead through crises will be entirely dependent upon it.

Figure 17 - Moving discretionary goals to imperatives is accomplished through discipline.

The Junior Executive will employ consistent discipline in executing imperative goals.

Reading List

"Ways of Seeing" by John Berger
"The Hero with a Thousand Faces" by Joseph Campbell
"Acres of Diamonds" by Russell H. Conwell
"The Story of Philosophy" by Will Durant
"Being and Time" by Martin Heidegger
"Siddhartha" by Hermann Hesse
"Man and His Symbols" by Carl Gustav Jung
"Thus Spoke Zarathustra" by Friedrich Nietzsche
"Anthem" by Ayn Rand
"The Fountainhead" by Ayn Rand
"Rebellion" by Joseph Roth
"Tao Te Ching" by Lao Tzu
"Musashi" by Eiji Yoshikawa, Charles S. Terry and Edwin O. Reischauer

Justin Saye

The Junior Executive

Chapter 4 Context

COOL, CONFIDENT, UNFLAPPABLE

"Courage is resistance to fear, mastery of fear - not absence of fear."

-Mark Twain

The executive role requires a relatively serious disposition. This is not to say that there is no place for levity or fun; rather, it is to say that the executive must have a serious attitude toward work to set an example. A balance must be struck: Too lax and things fall apart, too intense and everyone burns out or runs away. There are many aspects to this, but we are concerned with the default posture of the executive. Regardless of a tendency toward one extreme or another, an underlying trait of successful executives is unflappability. Day-to-day negative feelings and circumstances conspire to hinder achievement of our goals and influence our posture toward our work and our team. It takes courage to resist, yet this is required of the executive. As an executive, we must project an unflappable demeanor.

Remaining cool and confident in all circumstances serves to calm and objectify the environment; this is crucial for several reasons. Fundamentally, the executive sets the tone for how subordinates will behave. We will not often find an unflappable executive with a lot of loose cannons on their team, unless they are tools for other internal, political purposes. Everyone around us takes cues regarding the acceptability of their behavior in light of ours. Thus, it is crucial that we maintain an air of unflappability.

For our subordinates and colleagues in other organizations and companies, maintaining an unflappable attitude will serve a number of purposes. For our subordinates, it will signal that there are no personal vendettas tolerated and that we will be neither rash nor petty in our judgment. For colleagues in other organizations, it will signal that we and our team can be trusted to prioritize work effectively and manage difficulties in a mature manner. If we are calm, things must be under control. Fear, panic and ambient neurotic behavior are contagious and infectious. It is crucial to our working relationships that they never enter the team psyche.

We should never underestimate the constant scrutiny that we will be under from both our organizational competitors and our superiors. Both will be looking for signs of weakness, but for different reasons. For our competitors in the organization, they will constantly be looking for weaknesses to exploit for their benefit. A cool, confident and unflappable demeanor is a brick wall in this context. It will serve the dual purpose of thwarting their attempts to demonstrate weakness in us as well as showcasing their weakness of character, should they pursue a campaign against us. Most importantly, it will provide a source of comfort for us as we are beset by them. People who do not belong in the executive ranks due to merit will often find a path through subterfuge and disingenuousness. Their desire for the rewards of better position can tempt them into dishonorable behavior. An unflappable attitude is the best defense against these types of individuals. It will prevail in the end as these types weed themselves out.

For our superiors, there is enormous value in having an unflappable subordinate. Those individuals at the highest levels in the organization are not superhuman and when they assign functions to individuals in their teams, they must be able to trust that these functions will be executed efficiently and effectively. An unflappable persona is a very good indication that an individual can be entrusted with such functions. Sit through any senior leadership meeting and it is clear the distaste that senior leaders have for the hot-tempered, the doomsayers and the whiners. We should mention that there is an especially strong distaste for cockiness in this context in that it indicates immaturity and a lack of real confidence.

As we review the relevancy of an unflappable persona, we need to focus on one final aspect: objectivity. There are varied and striking personalities in any group of people and this inevitably leads to substantial conflict, which can easily bring work to a halt or skew the outputs substantially. One of the most important phenomena associated with an executive's unflappable attitude is that it will serve to objectify the work at hand. Removing the Id from team-based work is absolutely critical to enjoying the leveraged benefits. This will be expanded upon in later chapters. Although objectivity in work will not result solely from an unflappable persona, it cannot be obtained without one.

The Junior Executive will maintain an unflappable persona.

METHOD

A basic truth: Human beings have fixed mental processing capacity. That is, there is only so much that we can think about at one time. Yet there is a vast field of knowledge to be examined and tasks to be completed. This leads to a problem that no one is free from: There is more happening than we can process.

To address this, we look toward automating lower-level tasking to free up more cognitive capacity for higher-level tasking. In a business context, front-line managers or high-achieving contributors are often able to rely on raw intelligence to effectively execute (at middle-management levels and below, this is often sufficient). In practice, what this means is that individuals can re-contextualize every new situation and determine a new or derivative path to handle it independently. Within a discrete task set, this approach is sufficient and can even be useful in that situations can be evaluated in different ways to yield new insights. However, outside of their discrete domain, individuals who do not have a global method for approaching problems will typically experience one of three outcomes: freeze, fail, or get lucky. None of these are desirable or sustainable. The successful executive will have a standard modus operandi (MO) for how they address new situations in their work and for how they automate their lower-level tasking to allow for higher-level thinking.

When driving a car, if we do not automate the lower-level tasking of continually adjusting steering, throttle, brakes, etc., we will be unable to look down the road to anticipate new scenarios or heed present circumstances. In the context of work, having an MO for addressing new situations and for automating low-level tasking allows us to both pay attention to the present and look forward to the future. This is critical at the executive level. In the vast majority of circumstances, we will be presented with scenarios without clear precedent in our experience. How we address these new situations will determine whether we succeed, and will also demonstrate to senior leadership that we have the maturity, flexibility and capacity to handle the executive role. How is a productive MO constructed? There are shelves of books on the topic, but we can highlight some core fundamentals.

Much like our method for handling known situations, our MO for new situations gathers information, makes inferences and estimates, evaluates stakeholders and likely outcomes, etc. All of that is necessary, but at the executive level there are greater expectations. First, as an executive we must be able to conduct our typical analysis in the context of multiple domains and potentially the organization as a whole. The executive must be sure that internal changes are integrated into the wider organization and external changes are integrated into their domain. A solid method for decomposing new situations and generating a planned approach is called for here. However, the successful executive will demonstrate two additional facets that separate their MO from competitors and colleagues. First, they will have a ruthless investigatory approach to determining the root cause of a new situation. Finding the root cause(s) to any situation is the first step in gaining control of the outcomes associated with it. Once the root cause has been established, the standard MO is typically sufficient to deal with it, with one exception. The executive will integrate a Monte Carlo dimension (purposely including a factor for randomness) to their MO with regard to new situations. It is absolutely critical that executives maintain varied interests and study in topics and domains outside of their norm. Study of seemingly unrelated topics will allow the mind to draw broad meta-conclusions about interconnected truths in those domains. By developing this skill, the successful executive will be able to insert new situations into a mental framework based on the interconnected nature of human experience, but that has a substantial variability to it. This variability is the Monte Carlo dimension (Eckhardt, 1987).

This, more than any other aspect of the executive's MO, will differentiate them from the competition. While others are hampered by insular thinking focused on intra-domain methods, the successful executive will cross-apply methods from multiple domains. This is not simply the act of mimicry from one domain to another. Rather, it is a way of thinking that opens a problem or situation to novel solutions. This, coupled with an environment that values experimentation, creates a daunting competitive advantage for the focused executive.

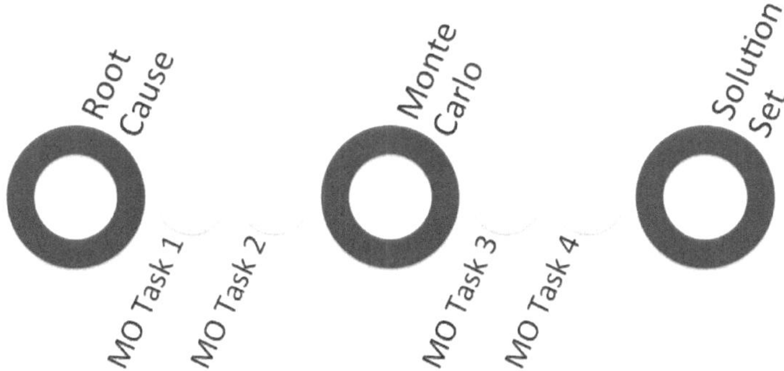

Figure 18 - An established MO will contain not only the method for scenario handling, which may vary, but will always include Root Cause and Monte Carlo components.

The Junior Executive will establish a reliable Modus Operandi for handling new scenarios by ruthlessly seeking root causes and introducing volatility into their solution set.

INTENT

One of the major challenges at the executive level is ensuring that others within the organization fully understand the work and roadmap of their team. This is critical for senior leadership, the board and peers, all of whom must understand how they will interact with our teams and how to integrate our roadmap into their own. Complicating this challenge is the fact that the degree to which planning is a collaborative affair varies across organizations. But we have a proven approach to this challenge: projection of intent through collaborative planning. Optimal team and organizational collaborative planning devolves decision-making authority to the lowest possible level. The US military's transition from large-scale, dual-theater orders of battle to small-scale, micro-theater orders of battle is a great example. In the former, orders could be dictated down lines of communication and reports sent back as a manifestation of the decision-making structure. That is, fewer decisions were necessary and the time required to implement those decisions longer. However, as the geopolitical situation has changed, so too have the types of conflicts and engagements that the military must handle. In this new situation, many decisions are required across many lines of communication and with very little time to implement. Thus, the only rational course of action is to devolve decision-making authority to lower levels in the hierarchy to ensure that decisions can be made in a timely fashion. But the overall mission is still prosecuted within a hierarchy of decision-making and authority that has not changed substantially. How does the US military handle this? An excellent tangential study of this transition and the underlying concept appears in Gary Klein's book "Sources of Power."

The effective execution of devolved decision-making requires two key items: a well-trained lower cadre of personnel and a clear method of communicating intent from leadership. We will leave the first item for discussion later and focus on the second. Given the post-modern economy's extraordinary complexity and speed, the successful executive must convey intent with high fidelity to their team to ensure that decisions and work can proceed in a timely manner. A good example of this concept is the maxim from George S. Patton: "Never tell how people how to do things. Tell them what to do, and they will surprise you with their ingenuity" (Patton, 1947). This concept has been covered in many other organizational books and studies, but they often skip over the key point. Decentralization of decision-making authority does not relieve the executive of responsibility; rather, it elevates the burden to a higher level of management. No longer is the executive concerned with discrete decisions about minutiae. Now they are concerned with how effective their intent has been conveyed to ensure that the higher-level goal is being achieved. Communication of intent with the highest possible fidelity is a trait of the successful executive. So how is this accomplished? Klein's "Sources of Power" gives a good initial accounting.

Klein argues for a simple approach to intent. Intent must be conveyed in a manner that allows for internalization of the content on an intuitive level—a story. He argues that the narrative form is hard-wired into our psyches to allow us to organize a lot of disjoined information into a coherent guideline for making decisions. To this end, the successful executive must establish a simple narrative among their team that will serve as a template for conveying intent. For this purpose, any dramatic analog will do: a movie, sports, etc. This is the power of the statement "what would Jesus do?" It allows the audience to internalize the intent of the question into a common narrative. Within this narrative, intent must be broken down into its constituent parts. A hierarchical deconstruction is often insufficient. However, by addressing the constituent parts in the narrative, the intent is conveyed in a manner that the audience can internalize. Klein identifies seven components of intent.

- Purpose of the work: What is the high-level goal that is being addressed by this task? How does this support our goals as an executive and the organization as a whole? Why should our subordinates care about or put priority on this work?
- Objective of the work: What is the expected outcome of the work that is being conducted? What are the specific exit criteria of the work? What should everyone visualize internally as the artifact of completion?
- The sequence of steps: This should be limited to six or less. These six (at most) steps should represent the logical steps required to complete the work or maintain the operation.
- The rationale for the plan: This is a statement that identifies the unique circumstances in space and time that justify the work to be undertaken.
- Key decisions that have been made: It is critical that the audience understand what has already been decided and is off the table for further consideration.
- Anti-goals: What are the discrete outcomes that are not desired? Can they be represented by one or two specific, artifact-based outcomes? This is often just as important as identifying the desired outcomes, particularly if there is a possible confusion of priorities.
- Constraints or other considerations: The audience must understand if there are boundaries to what action they can take and what decisions they can make. This will avoid wasted effort and frustration.

These components, if delivered within a commonly understood narrative, provide the clear parameters of intent. These parameters create a basis for devolved decision-making and confer all of the benefits of such.

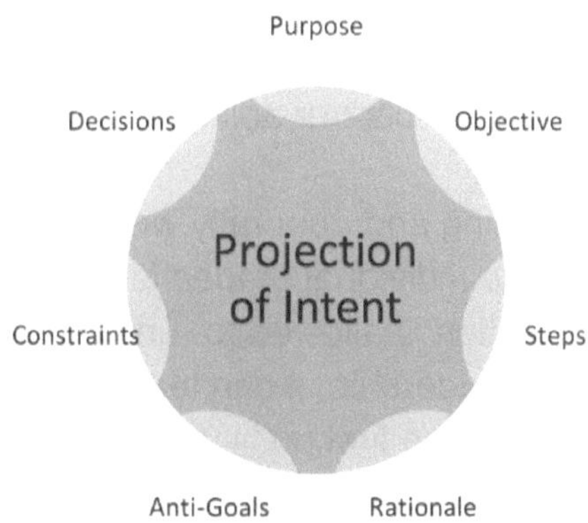

Figure 19 - The successful executive projects their intent throughout their teams to decentralize decision-making.

The Junior Executive will ensure decision-making is handled at the lowest possible level by clearly and intuitively conveying their intent to subordinates and the broader team.

CANDOR

The competitive environment associated with achieving an executive role can be extraordinarily ruthless. This is necessary for many reasons. The competitive environment outside of the organization is also ruthless and difficult, so executives must be vetted in that context. Also, there are often many qualified candidates for the executive role, which necessitates some sort of competition to determine the most appropriate person for a role. Further, the decision to promote one person over another is very difficult—far better for senior leadership to allow individuals to self-select themselves out of competition. As has been discussed previously, many of the underlying reasons behind individual behavior in organizations are based in fear. Fear of conflict or failure or missed opportunities all play a part in the reasoning behind many organizational cultural norms and behaviors. Of course, there are positive motivators as well; but, our expectation is that these are self-evident and do not need to be discussed here. This chapter is concerned with how fear affects our ability to demonstrate candor.

Competition is a good thing and generally works well in ensuring that the most appropriate individual or idea is implemented. However, when competition is allowed to run unmanaged or worse, manipulated, by senior leadership, it can lead to negative cultural attributes. Candor is often the first positive attribute that is thrown aside in unchecked competition. We are all familiar with the negative connotations associated with a culture of "yes" men and women. Candor is a quality of expression that is frank, open and sincere, rooted in practicality and avoiding sentimentality, hyperbole and manipulation. In a culture that is tilted in favor of fear-based behaviors, candor can be a death sentence. Even in relatively positive cultures, candor can prove difficult. Bad news is always hard to deliver, but candor is absolutely critical to the efficient operation of any organization. Without candor, decisions are based upon ill-informed, altered, or manipulated information. The resulting outcomes are not efficient nor are they aligned transparently within the organization.

Some may see an opportunity here in that many decisions are made behind closed doors and as the result of back-room deals. But in reality, most in the organization will know this, and that knowledge destroys trust in leadership and tramples morale. It is only the naïve who believe that deceit is an acceptable long-term strategy in any organization. At some point in time, all deceits are revealed and the perpetrator loses everything as a result. Given this, we understand the successful executive candidate must express candor. It can be difficult, but it is absolutely required. So how is candor expressed appropriately?

Contrary to most dramatizations, candor is not some emotive exhortation, and certainly not a wet-blanket contrarianism. Rather, candor is the honest and sincere acknowledgement of reality and the practical analysis of the positive and negative outcomes of an action. Further, it is delivered in a timely manner. As Tom Hagen said in "The Godfather," "Mr. Corleone is a man who insists on hearing bad news immediately" (Coppola, 1972). The successful executive will enforce candor among their team as well. From the executive perspective, candor should be demonstrably expected and rewarded. Lack of candor should be demonstrably punished. Two other cultural norms should be established:

> Decisions: In an organization that values and demonstrates candor, decisions are made in a manner transparent to all stakeholders. This can be challenging, particularly in organizations that punish minor failures and bad news. Regardless, decisions can be made transparent in any organization. This transparency is useful on two levels. It demonstrates to the stakeholders that they are respected enough to share in the information used to make a decision and it necessitates a level of rigor in weighing a decision that will hold up under scrutiny. Both of these culminate in a situation whereby stakeholders can buy into the decision. Those who do not will have done so with the same information as everyone else. This level of rigor should be implemented at the executive level such that all decisions are documented and evaluated openly. Candor in this sense is laying all the known facts on the table and having an open discourse about them.

> Owning Information: A corrosive trait seen in many cultures, particularly organizations involved in knowledge work, is an attitude of derision toward individuals who admit to not knowing something. It is childish and damaging to organizational efficiency. The symptom of this trait is individuals pretending to know information and faking their way through discussions on a topic. In these situations, the original communication on the topic is a complete waste of time and there is substantial added waste associated with covering up the lack of knowledge and substantial

> resentment that obfuscates cooperation in the future. Typically, this trait appears in individuals lacking the critical thinking skills required to openly debate topics; rather, they rely on school yard bullying. On the surface, it can be a daunting task to take this on. But much like in the schoolyard, openly calling out the bully on the topic generally puts a stop to it. We must never give in to bullying nor engage in it. The successful executive must own their understanding of information and ensure that their subordinates, stakeholders and peers do as well. This is a simple and effective way to ensure candor in the organization. But it can be emotionally difficult.

There are of course many books on the importance of candor. Like all of the concepts we cover, the specific implementation of the concept is up to the individual. But the core truth of it must be internalized.

The Junior Executive will demonstrate candor in their daily communication and encourage the same within their team and across their peer group.

HERO VS. LEADER

The narrative for our life derives from our internal interpretation of external events. And, we are all necessarily the heroes of our own narrative. We may consider ourselves an outsized hero for the forces of good, or a troubled hero or a hero beset by circumstance. In groups and society at large, this often presents a problem as individuals struggle to empathize with others. The scope of that issue is beyond this book, but we are concerned with how this basic point of view affects the executive in interactions with subordinates and peers.

This heroic narrative is directly manifested in how people view their performance at work. In those individuals who are high achievers we see the heroic trait is particularly close to the surface. Success at this level builds an individual's sense of self-sufficiency and confidence in the face of challenges. In a quantitative view, this type of achievement is compelling to senior leaders evaluating the fitness of a particular individual for advancement. Yet we all know of strong individual contributors who are wholly ill-suited for positions of organizational authority. Rather, individual achievement is merely one of many criteria that senior leadership will evaluate in determining who will be promoted to the executive level.

How do we measure an individual contributor's ability to adjust their internalized hero point of view to include higher-level goals? This ability allows that individual achievement is still important, but it is no longer measured in discrete contests; rather, it is measured as the aggregate achievement of the team. This includes both subordinates and peers. This point of view adjustment can be terribly difficult and is often a barrier to advancement for many otherwise excellent candidates, for several reasons:

> Heroic achievement is intoxicating: Despite realignment of much of our education systems, achievement is measured on an individual basis. This will likely never change as individuation is part of the development of our psyches. Regardless of how we hope individuals may realign their internalized priorities, we all center on the individual point of view, especially high-achieving individuals. The reason is relatively simple: heroic achievement is highly rewarding. This is true at all levels from the biological to the psychological. The challenge for the successful executive is to remove the reward link from individual hands-on work and attach it to the output that is achieved by a team under their direction.
>
> A leadership skillset must be learned: There are risks associated with transferring the egoistic attachment of reward from the individual to the team scale. The individual may not fully transition the attachment or implement it poorly.

But the skills required for the transition can be learned through dedicated study. Many people are not able make this transition, but it is required for the executive role.

We often do not choose our teams. Too often, people are justified in their belief that team-based work is an excuse for others to get a free ride. This can be particularly scarring for high achievers. As they pour mountains of effort into tasks, they can develop a strong resentment of others who cannot equally contribute or who choose not to equally contribute. This lack of control over the efforts of others can serve as evidence of the waste associated with teams. However, this is a fallacy. As the best coaches in sports and best leaders in other organizations will attest to, everyone is capable of contributing such that the overall effort benefits. The challenge is to learn how to motivate and integrate individuals to work at their capacity so that the overall effort is multiplied. It is not an easy task, but the successful executive will understand that all individuals are capable of contributing and will ensure that their leadership style is inclusive.

The successful executive will transition from a heroic point of view to a leader point of view. There are challenges to this from a biological and psychological perspective. It requires the individual to be self-aware and flexible in their thinking. Individuals who are not able to transition from a heroic to leader point of view will either not achieve the executive rank or will fail once they do. Organizational history is littered with examples.

The Junior Executive will be a leader, not a hero.

ORIGINATION

All organizations have a process of origination. The successful executive will understand and integrate the concept of origination into their working life. There is a fundamental step-change in the nature of work that is conducted at the executive level in relation to subordinate roles. One of the characteristics of this step-change is the concept of origination. Origination is the manifestation of a scope of work from an abstract state to a concrete one. Executives are responsible for introducing new scopes of work and initiatives. These new scopes of work may be within an existing domain (expanding charters, new geographic markets, etc.) or may be within entirely new domains. The actual steps required to introduce this new work are not all that different, regardless of domain experience. There are phases of feasibility, analysis, evaluation, engagement, integration and operationalization.

For the executive, there are two aspects of origination that need to be understood. The first is that communications from an executive are directives for action. Executives must communicate with the understanding and expectation that it will result in action. So, when we communicate as an executive, we are engaging in the act of origination. When an executive sends a memo indicating that office supply expenses are too high, it is a call to action for the team. This is a significant responsibility and ripe territory for errors and confusion, which is why the second key aspect of origination for the executive is temperance.

One of the biggest mistakes an executive candidate will make is to act in a cavalier manner with regard to origination. Having enjoyed success in subordinate roles, given their decision-making style and scope of authority, they misunderstand the true nature of the executive role and the consequences that attend to every decision. So, we see individuals who may have been successful in off-the-hip decision making at lower levels continue with that style when promoted. Previously, their decisions and their consequences were bounded by their particular domain (in most cases). But the executive environment is geometrically larger and so are the consequences. This is true for a number of reasons, but primarily due to origination. At lower levels in the hierarchy, individuals operate within originated scopes of work. That is, they are bound by existing operational processes and defined outcomes. The consequences are limited to the bounds of the originated work. At the executive level, the work has not yet been originated and so is generally boundless. It is the responsibility of the executive to establish the bounds within which the work will be conducted. It should be clear that off-the-hip decisions in this context can result in disaster. The initial communication from the executive is the originating act, and its importance in an organizational context cannot be overstated.

So, if we understand that the executive call-to-action is the act of origination, how is this tempered? As with most topics, there are myriad methods for tempering the origination of new work within the organization. The organization itself may have existing processes that can be leveraged for this purpose. However, we should do at least the following:

> **Documentation**: The written word is the source and record of all that we do in organizations. Direct speech is important and powerful, but it lacks permanence both in a legal and objective sense. When a new scope of work is originated, it must be documented in a clear and concise manner. All known information about the context of the origination must be documented to provide a historical record of justification. Further, documentation organically provides the basis for growth of the complexity and scale of the originated work. Without a documentary basis, the work cannot grow beyond the individual or core team behind the origination. From an executive standpoint, we must ensure that originated work has a solid documentary basis for growth and adjustment.
>
> **Estimation**: Truly original work is without direct precedent. Thus, there is little historical basis for confidently understanding the impact or consequences of its origination. A key function of the executive and their team is to ensure that robust estimation provides a rough framework for

expectation management of the wider audience. The estimation must be organic and revised continually as the work takes shape and is influenced by internal and external forces. Further, it must be comprehensive and provide expectation guidance for positive and negative consequences of the origination. The successful executive will ensure that a robust system for estimation is in place and undertaken for all originated work. These estimates must then be contextualized and communicated.

Reporting: Feedback is the single most important feature of any original work. As there is no precedent, there is little intuitive sense for how the original work is progressing or being received, in the short or long term. Without clear and timely reports, there is no opportunity to adjust, and any honest executive knows original work will require significant adjustment. There are many techniques available to implement a robust reporting regimen. The existing organization may have a framework that can be leveraged. At the least, it must be the following:

<u>Timely</u>: Reports must be delivered as frequently as practical.
<u>Comprehensive</u>: Reports must include all key data points.
<u>Approved</u>: A delegated authority must vet and approve all reports.
<u>Database Ready</u>: Reports should be codified to ensure that they can be consumed by systems for higher-level analysis.
<u>Flexible</u>: Report formats should be malleable to shape to new situations.

The successful executive will be responsible for origination, which requires intelligence and diligence to manage. Although there are many discrete methods for managing origination in the organization, there are two core aspects to understand: the power of the call to action and the need for temperance. Origination directly connects to the performance measurement of the individual in the executive role.

The Junior Executive will acknowledge the responsibility of origination and implement a policy to manage it with temperance.

POSSIBLE AND PROBABLE

One of the more difficult changes required in the move from manager to executive is building confidence in uncertainty. A refresher is required on the nature of confidence. It is not the headstrong belief that we know the right thing to do at the right time at all times. Rather, it is the belief that despite any circumstances, we can find a way to achieve success. Confidence of the first type is cockiness, which has no place at the executive level. The successful executive will avoid it at all costs. Our concern here is confidence of the second type: a belief that despite any circumstances, we can find a way to achieve success. We will examine confidence per this meaning.

There are myriad inputs that yield confidence: applicable skill and toolsets, historical examples of success, relative achievement in our particular domain, belief in ability, and mature assessment among a peer group. It is part of this last input that we are concerned with here: mature assessment. As a demonstration of confidence, mature assessment holds paramount importance. A confident person will reasonably and maturely assess the information at hand in regard to any decision. In particular, they will acknowledge what they know and do not know, both in the concrete and abstract sense. This allows for the qualification and quantification of risks and outcomes. More importantly, it provides opportunity to align knowledge and expectations among the team. This is essential for the team to operate effectively, both from a performance perspective and a trust perspective. If all parties in a team know the level of knowledge of other members of the team, they can use this information to direct their internal assessments for resource utilization and to optimize their own activities. If we have a team member who has all of the knowledge required to ensure GAAP compliance for our audit project, then the remaining team members and team leader can focus on other areas of knowledge. However, if this team member has overstated or misstated their level of expertise, then the project will have an un-quantified risk and potential resource drain. Even worse, if other team members doubt the level of knowledge of this team member, they will be forced to duplicate and waste resources to overcome a perceived, but un-quantified, gap in knowledge. Both outcomes negatively affect performance. They are also the result of a lack of confidence leading a team member to pretend to knowledge that they did not have. This is a typical situation in many struggling organizations. The successful executive will never pretend to have knowledge that they do not actually have. Rather, they will implement a strategy to deal with knowledge gaps in a mature and reasoned manner. How is this accomplished?

As noted in the beginning of this book, it is important to be a domain expert. The successful executive will be expert in their particular domain of knowledge. Further, they will acknowledge the impossibility of knowing all things—even partially. The successful executive will acknowledge openly and honestly any gaps in knowledge. Finally, they will establish a strategy of classifying unknowns (both understood and assumed) in terms of their potential impact. The successful executive must classify unknowns in terms of their possibility and probability. This classification establishes the boundaries of likelihood for particular impacts. At a higher level, it establishes the basis for confidence in our ability to complete the work or project. Further, it is a long-term toolset that allows us to conduct feasibility analyses of new opportunities. So how are potential impacts separated into possibility and probability?

> **Possibility**: Possibilities are typically of two types: unimagined impacts and impacts that are highly unlikely. Possibilities are events that are rationally feasible given our understanding of the parameters of the project but are highly unlikely, thus not typically requiring an allocation of

resources. For example, if our project is to build a house in an area with no history of earthquakes, an earthquake is possible but not likely enough to allocate resources toward mitigation. A lahar (mudslide caused by an earthquake) would be an even more unlikely and potentially unimagined. In many circumstances, this would be an outcome that would not even be considered given the unlikelihood of its occurrence. From an analytical perspective, it is sufficient to merely acknowledge the possibility. Possibilities should be brainstormed and mapped against the work or project to understand the potential impacts on the project from a broader, holistic range. With regard to confidence, establishing a large subset of possible impacts builds a belief that enough potential impacts have been considered and the plan for success has a greater chance of success.

Probability: Probable events are those that have a reasonable likelihood of occurring and should be resourced. Probable events should be generated across a matrix that denotes both the impact and the likelihood of occurring. Probable events are only fully understood by an honest assessment of the current circumstances that acknowledges both the known and unknown impacts. A trap laid for many executive candidates is a lack of confidence in their own abilities that leads them to pretend to knowledge of probable events. The successful executive must be humble in the face of uncertainty and acknowledge gaps in knowledge. This is particularly relevant for probability. In order to have confidence in the individual or team's ability to handle uncertainty, we must acknowledge all probable events and plan to mitigate the impacts.

An honest understanding of probability and possibility is key to confidence at the executive level. A mature acknowledgement of the fallibility of the individual and the limitations of intelligence is required for this. The successful executive will be humble in the face of unknowable complexity.

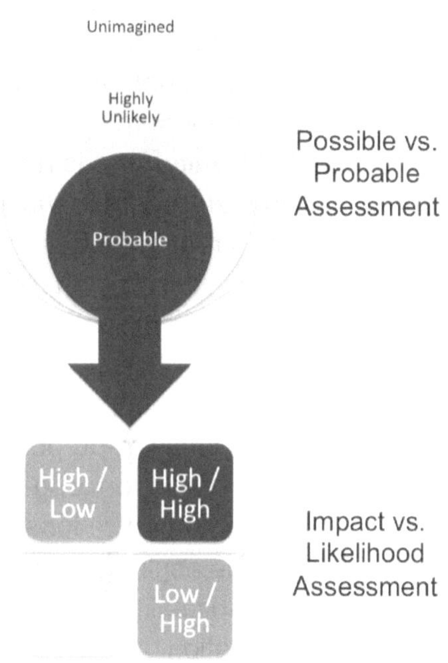

Figure 20 - Confidence is supported by the two-part assessment of circumstances as possible or probable.

The Junior Executive will ground their confidence in a mature analysis of the possibility and probability of impacts to their work and projects.

INDIVIDUATION

Depending upon our particular demographic, our organizational loyalty will hover somewhere along a spectrum between freelancer and life-long employee. It is typically true that older generations of workers have greater organizational loyalty than younger generations. And this trend tends to hold true across different cultures and markets. These are generalities, but they highlight a key point of consideration for the aspiring executive. Free agency is not an attractive trait in executives. Because the executive rank holds substantial trust and responsibility, the senior leadership and directors of an organization must have confidence that the individuals entrusted in this role are loyal to the organization. However, organizational loyalty is not often rewarded, nor is it often a wise long-term strategy. The modern working environment is not well suited to the concept of loyalty. This is not to say that organizations are callous in their regard to the individual. Rather, it is an acknowledgment that entrenched organizations no longer have the margins and overhead available to ensure that underperforming individuals can be carried. Further, organizations in the modern era do not have the same perception of invincibility as in previous ones. That is, organizations more quickly fail, fall behind competitors, merge with others or are completely re-purposed—all of which lend to an environment that does not support long-term loyalty. The executive rank demands strong organizational loyalty, but the modern era punishes it. For the aspiring executive, navigating this effectively demonstrates our suitability. A major aspect of this question is the role of individuation.

Individuation is the process of sentient separation from the surrounding world. In a psychological sense, it is the process by which an individual comes to understand that their thoughts are their own. A subsequent expression of the individuation process is an innate understanding of the relationship between discrete individuals. If we consider the organization itself as an individual, we see the question of loyalty as not one of unquestioning fidelity to an entity, but as discrete relationships between individuals.

Very often relationships between individuals are based on reciprocity. In this sense, a promotion to the executive level is a significant gift that must be repaid. This makes the relationship between the individual executive and the organization relatively straightforward. The organization provides rewards, both tangible and intangible, with the expectation that the executive will provide benefits in kind. Loyalty in this context is not a blind fidelity but a reciprocal relationship between two individuals. If the executive fails to provide the expected benefits, then they can expect to lose the rewards. Likewise, if the organization fails to provide the expected rewards, then they can expect to lose the benefits brought to bear by the executive.

It is incumbent upon the executive to fully understand the benefits that are expected from the relationship. The majority of the attributes and expressions of these benefits are covered in this book, but every organization is different. The rewards, too, must be evaluated and understood to fully weigh the value of the relationship. Once we understand both the stated and unstated benefits and rewards of the relationship, we can evaluate this particular relationship in relation to others. How will this relationship impact our relationship to our spouse or partner, children, or other organizations? All of these are important considerations. From a career perspective, it is critical to conduct one further evaluation. As in many relationships, the attractiveness of the parties is very often greatly influenced by their attractiveness to others. That is, scarcity drives up prices. So, we must evaluate our loyalty in the relationship against ensuring that we are still marketable and attractive to others. Given the rise of social networking, a strategy must be implemented to ensure that we are not only delivering the expected benefits to our organization but that we are also connected with other organizations. Every circumstance is different and a balance will have to be struck on a case-by-case basis. However, from both a promotion perspective and an ongoing value perspective, our current organization must believe two things: We are loyal to the organization and will deliver the promised benefits.

If the organization fails to deliver the expected rewards, there are others who would jump at the chance to work with us. Abuse of this point is covered under other topics, but the danger should be clear. A relationship where one party is continually negotiating for more benefits or threatening to leave is doomed.

This is an extension of the psychological process of individuation.

We are our own person and must establish mature relationships to ensure that our goals are achieved. We can only do this through relationships with others. The successful executive will conduct a thorough evaluation of their individuation and establish a strategy to ensure that their relationships with organizations are mutually beneficial and not guaranteed.

The Junior Executive will maintain a mature relationship with the organization based upon reciprocity and respect of the individual.

EXPERIMENTATION

"Knowledge has to be improved, challenged, and increased constantly, or it vanishes."

-Peter F. Drucker

The transition to the executive role can be daunting. A great deal of time will be spent fighting fires and adjusting to new responsibilities. This is a crucial time in the evaluation of our fitness for the role. New executives tend to do one of two things: tread water until they get comfortable in the role, or come out swinging and make sweeping changes. Neither of these are successful strategies. Treading water is a safer strategy and may buy some time, but eventually it will fail through entropy. The role and the environment are constantly changing, in part and in whole. Relying on a strategy that requires us to "wait and see" before initiating any changes will result in being perpetually behind the power curve. At the other end of the behavioral spectrum is to enter the executive role with a strategy of radical change. The pitfalls of this strategy are numerous—making changes without fully understanding the new context within which we should view them is doomed. Sweeping change is a neutron bomb to an organization. There are scenarios that call for it, but not typically at the junior level. Rather, the successful executive will understand that they can neither wait until they are comfortable in the role to begin changes nor shock and awe the team with immediate, sweeping changes.

The successful executive must instead initiate a culture of experimentation that allows for iterative and parallel changes to be executed and evaluated in a controlled manner. This approach has many benefits but several preconditions. The first precondition is that we must be able to handle multiple, iterative initiatives at the same time with an eye toward an end goal. Many chapters in this book cover concepts and ideas that can assist here (Calculus Mind, etc.). The reality of the executive position is that we must simultaneously learn and adjust to the new role while also initiating change. How can we change what we do not fully understand? A strong approach is to establish a culture that designs work flows for experimentation. Experiments should be tracked at a report level and directed by the executive toward team goals. There are several considerations:

- Team level goals must be unattainable through current modes of operation.
- Team members must have enough authority and initiative to establish experiments in their domain.
- There must be enough slack in the team-level delivery schedule to accommodate experiment failures.
- All processes must be backstopped to ensure continuity of operations.
- There must be executive-level controls in place to ensure operational tempo and delivery: reports, projects, meetings, metrics, etc.
- There must be incentives aligned with delivery.

Essentially, higher-level experiments can be generated to ensure that multiple pathways are undertaken to modify performance and ensure team goal achievement. This takes a great deal of discipline and message enforcement. Experimentation can be exhausting and demoralizing if it is not managed in a positive manner. It is critical that failures are forgiven and successes are celebrated.

There are many benefits to approaching the executive role from the viewpoint of experimentation. Initially, it requires a disciplined analysis of the underlying processes supporting the work of the organization. This is true not only within the domain, but also as it interrelates with other domains in the organization and externally. If the executive is promoted from within a particular domain, they will typically have the benefit of an intimate understanding of the existing processes. If they are coming into the domain from the outside, then this approach provides a disciplined and efficient framework for familiarization. Regardless, the executive role requires an analysis of the particular domain with a new perspective. Additionally, a culture of experimentation requires that subordinates within the particular domain take ownership of their role in the group. This is critical not only for their level of commitment to the job but also for the team-level benefits of their expertise. Toyota became a quality powerhouse by pioneering this philosophy. As each individual feels responsible and accountable for their particular domain of work and encouraged to experiment for improvement, they are able to implement incremental changes that aggregate to significant gains at the team and organization level.

From the executive perspective, this incremental experimentation provides point-solution benefits that can be rolled up to team-level goal achievement. It is not easy to create this type of culture if it does not already exist in some fashion. However, the direction provided by this concept of experimentation is the best strategy the aspiring executive can use to ensure early and sustained success in the role.

The Junior Executive will establish a culture of experimentation to incrementally improve performance from day one.

PROCESS

From a process standpoint, complexity is very often initially necessary to demonstrate that a new idea will work in the physical world and can be executed in a controlled manner. That demonstration may be a far-fetched Rube Goldberg machine or a highly decomposed process flow. Understanding this, we see that complexity is not necessarily a bad thing, but it does present a challenge for the executive. All work that is conducted by our team can be described through processes. These processes must then be rationalized given all of the constraints demonstrated by our environment. That is, we allow and acknowledge complexity before optimization to ensure that the expected output of the idea is delivered. Process is the discipline we use to initially deliver ideas to reality.

Process as a general concept has two core purposes: assurance of minimum standards and performance optimization. If we look back to the material presented so far, we see that assurance of minimum standards is tied to the idea of backstopping all work and that performance optimization is tied to goal achievement. For the aspiring executive, it is critical to establish a mindset that decomposes all work into underlying support processes. This skill not only allows for the rapid integration of new ideas into the existing organizational processes, but also allows us to rapidly diagnose issues in workflow as they arise. With this mindset, then, we can see how process is integrated into the organization to yield its two core purposes:

> **Assurance of Minimum Standards**: A majority of processes are developed for this purpose. When a new idea is presented to an organization, the process by which it is delivered will often be unknown. Thus, there must be minimum standards that all new ideas meet with regard to workflow and delivery. In order to satisfy these minimum standards, the current processes that underlie work in the organization must be understood, documented, measured and controlled. For example, if our

organization is a library, then there should be a process for handling returned books.

1. A book is placed into the "Return" bin.
2. Every two hours, a librarian collects returned books.
3. The ISBNs of returned books are scanned into a central repository system.
4. The system prints out stack locations and tags the books as "Out for Restock."
5. The books are loaded onto a stocking cart.
6. The librarian restocks the books in their appropriate location.
7. The librarian tags the group of returned books as "Available For Checkout."

This process is simple and likely slow, but it delivers several benefits:

- All books are accounted for in their current state.
- All books are replaced in their correct position in the stacks.
- All returns are processed on a periodic basis.

From a process point of view, the assurance of minimum standards is achieved and the basic work (presenting books in a controlled manner for borrowing) of the organization is backstopped. As a new executive, one of our initial imperative duties will be to fully document all processes and conduct an analysis to ensure that minimum standards are met. This documented process becomes our baseline for evaluating new ideas in the organization. Further, this framework will establish the basis for all workflow reporting.

Performance Optimization: As we know, a key function of the executive is to grow, expand, and substantially improve their respective domain. Assurance of minimum standards is a prerequisite and means to this end. But it is through optimizing the performance of processes that gains are made for the organization: faster delivery times, more efficient use of resources, greater margins, more value delivered. This can only be accomplished if a solid and comprehensive measurement system is in place on existing and proposed processes—understanding how new ideas and optimized processes will yield benefits. Once this is in place, the successful executive will use controlled experimentation to find ways to optimize any existing and new processes. Again, there are myriad methods for executing this type of optimization: Lean, Six Sigma, TQM, etc. Our particular circumstances will dictate which is most appropriate. The critical consideration is to ensure that our organizational and team-level goals are tied directly into underlying support processes so that they can be impacted by a regimen of experimentation. To continue the example above, if our new goal is to improve our book availability ratios, we could initiate experiments and measure their impact. We could add a new control metric into the process to dig deeper into the problem. If we asked library customers to self-scan the books upon return, then we would have a clear understanding of the actual time the book is in the "Checked Out" state. Experiments could then be designed to affect the length of time that library customers keep the books "Checked Out." Additionally, it would give us better insight into how long it is taking to restock books. Given this information, we could design experiments that increased the frequency with which the librarian collected the returned books and restocked them. We could design an experiment that distributed our return repositories to place them closer to their stack location. The results of this could then be monitored through our existing process controls. Assuming positive results from one or more experiments, we have direct guidance in how to optimize our underlying process to improve performance. This seems relatively straightforward, but in organizations of any level of complexity, process requires discipline and hard work. And it is a pervasive, tangible asset that all executives will use to impact the organization and ensure that they are delivering executive-level value.

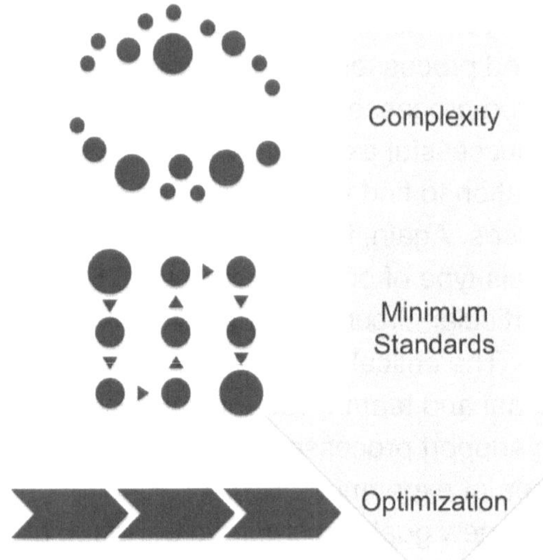

Figure 21 - Process is necessary for organizing work to move from complexity to optimal performance.

The Junior Executive will ensure that all underlying processes are understood, deliver minimum standards of quality and support a framework for performance optimization.

ASSIDUOUS

As an aspiring or newly promoted executive, we will be at a disadvantage. Few in the organization will be rooting for us. The senior leaders who promoted or hired us will have high expectations for our performance and may have an ambient anxiety about our future potential as a threat. Our new colleagues will immediately view us as a threat to their power base, incorrectly or not. Subordinates or others at a lower hierarchical level than us will be a mixed bag: jealous of our promotion, genuinely happy for our success, eager to solicit favors or indifferent. Of course, there are varying levels of intensity of these points of view, depending on our history within the organization. If we are brought in from outside the organization, then there will only be the most cursory of justifications for the points of view mentioned above, but they will still be there. If we have been promoted from within, there will be much more context for any given point of view.

We cannot hope to control the opinions of others. Rather, we can control our actions and the context in which opinions are formed. If we carry an assumption that most people are predisposed to good (not to say predisposed to saintliness, but to pursue a path of peace) then we see that we have the ability to control the environment and many of the circumstances that color their relative point of view. It is important to remember that everybody is consumed with concern about themselves and their own particular circumstances—solipsism is a state of nature. As an executive, we can control the environment and many of the circumstances that influence our daily work and the creation of perceptions in others. To further this point, we see that our inability to control the opinions of others coupled with a general predisposition to peace-seeking behaviors provides the framework within which we can influence perceptions of us.

So, what does this mean for us practically? It means that all individuals, in a given culture, will generally tend toward the path of least resistance that ends in peace. As an example, if we arrive at the office early every single day and leave late every single night, we thereby control the environmental conditions within which others form an opinion of our work ethic. It is far easier for even our greatest detractor to admit that we have a solid work ethic than to concoct some theory that is easily disproved by the available evidence. They will likely remain a detractor, but the goal of this is not to change an individual's opinion; rather, it is to control the environment in which they form that opinion. If we are assiduous in this task, virtually all detractors will eventually quiet down.

How should the aspiring or newly promoted executive go about doing this? There are many different methods. In this case, the successful executive will be assiduous in their duties in the organization. It may sound simple, but it is challenging to implement and maintain. There are many benefits of this type of behavior (and some negatives); but at the core, it establishes a contextual environment within which perceptions and opinions of us will be formed and influenced by organizationally relevant criteria. If we perform excellently, then our detractors' true feelings are laid bare. As noted, there are many methods of demonstrating assiduousness in the organization. Any are fine as long as they address the two core concepts:

> **Root Cause**: The ability to drill down to the root cause of any issue, problem, symptom, etc. is rare and highly valued in any organization. The particular method by which individuals implement this will vary person to person. But we can rely on the unerring truth of causality. A source of waste in any organization is the work done to address symptoms (or noise, if you will) associated with an issue. The successful executive will ignore the noise and look for the root cause of a symptom. This skill can be practiced at any level in the organization. The key is having a clear understanding of the underlying processes of the organization. How does the money flow? Who vets information for decision makers? What are their underlying motivations? What is the specific, discrete action that must be taken for a decision to be made: form signed, e-mail sent, check cut? How do the organizational processes truly work? How does work initiate? Who are the stakeholders in getting work started? Who are the stakeholders in signing off on completed work? What is the technological landscape of the organization? Where are there manual process points that should be automated? If we look back to our previous example about a library, we may see that our librarian assistant turnover rate is high. Exit interviews may indicate

that they feel overwhelmed with administrative overhead and are not able to give enough time to customer service. If we are assiduous in our investigation of the root cause, we may find that the real problem is that our intake process is too manual and is causing a backlog of restocking work. This root cause is yielding symptoms within the group that is causing the problem of assistant turnover. Rather than addressing other aspects of morale or workload, we can apply the simple fix of automating the intake process. This relatively elegant solution then yields the resolutions necessary for assistants to feel greater satisfaction in their jobs. This is an oversimplification, but the underlying truth should be clear. The work required to assiduously investigate the root cause of any issues will generate a more elegant and efficient result. Root cause analysis and execution is a high-order skill that will demonstrate the fitness of any executive.

Attention to Detail: More than most fundamental behaviors, attention to detail is the best defense against organizational assassins and detractors. The first object of attack from our detractors is often the main purpose of our work, as an advocate for the organization. If we are assiduous in attention to detail in our work, our detractors are forced to acquiesce this point. Failing in a frontal assault, they will fall back to sniping. It is at this point that attention to detail provides several important defenses.

Preparedness is one of the most important. As has been mentioned by many creators in the past, creation is hard and criticism is easy. Criticism is seductive to many people, because it brings easy attention and often yields quick results. Preparedness is the best defense to criticism. If we are working on releasing a new product, the attention to detail we apply to analyzing and preparing the business plan will be critical as it is demonstrated to our colleagues. There is of course often a real benefit to critical analysis of

> proposed action. The goal here is not to suppress all critical analysis of our planning. Rather, it is to address all critical analysis of our planning through preparedness and leave our detractors with no other recourse than to either acquiesce or to expose their true feelings. In either case, preparedness reiterates that the successful executive's best defense is to control the environment in which the perceptions and opinions are formed. By demonstrating world-class attention to detail, we will create an environment that exposes negative attribution.

If all snipes can be addressed or shown to be baseless, then there is no peace-seeking justification for harboring a negative opinion. Of course, there are competitors and detractors who will refuse to change their opinion. Again, assiduous attention to detail and root cause analysis are the best bulwarks against this type of behavior. Individuals who are incapable of following a peaceful path will eventually damage themselves sufficiently to remove them from contention. The successful executive will acknowledge that the opinions of others cannot be controlled, but that the environment and circumstances under which they form opinions can be influenced. Assiduous attention to detail and root cause analysis are the fundamental skills that influence the environment and circumstances.

The Junior Executive will be assiduous in demonstrating the skills of root cause analysis and attention to detail.

CREDIBILITY JUDO

Many people mistakenly believe that when they achieve the executive rank, that they will immediately enjoy a certain level of gravitas and power. This is fundamentally wrong. For the most part, all relevant measurements of gravitas and power are relative to our associated peer group. In relation to our previous role and peer group, a promotion is of course an elevation of power. But this measurement is no longer relevant to us. In relation to our new peer group, we are low person on the totem pole. It is critical to remember this when thinking about our engagement strategy with the executive team. Our promotion or hiring represents a change to the collegial power map and thus will likely cause a significant amount of maneuvering as the existing executives seek a new equilibrium and pecking order. This adjustment is unfortunate and stressful, but inevitable. As the junior executive, we will be at a substantial disadvantage during this process. We will lack a contextual understanding of the existing relationships as well as the necessary organizational capital to justify any perceived or real power projection within the executive team. Further, we will initially lack the executive-level perspective that the other executives have with regard to any organizational pitfalls or bad assignments. For senior and existing executives, a reshuffle is a great time to offload unpleasant ancillary duties, accounts, personnel, etc. However, as any third-party political candidate in an election can testify, there can be substantial power in weakness—particularly if the goal is not the top job.

Depending upon how well we are networked with individuals in other domains before joining the executive team, we may have a dossier of intelligence on those domains. Many times, this will be information that is filtered or otherwise unknown to the domain executive. This information, coupled with our position as a weaker executive in a reshuffle, can be used as a type of Judo to ensure that we are not placed at undue disadvantage or railroaded. The founder of Judo, Jigoro Kano, tells us that "resisting a more powerful opponent will result in your defeat, whilst adjusting to and evading your opponent's attack will cause him to lose his balance, his power will be reduced, and you will defeat him. This can apply whatever the relative values of power, thus making it possible for weaker opponents to beat significantly stronger ones" (Kano, 2005). As the junior member of an existing executive team we will be the weaker individual. The successful junior executive will avoid direct confrontation, instead relying on core values and intelligence to put their opponent off-balance. Of course, the degree of application of this is directly related to the circumstances of the executive team. If it is a supportive and friendly environment, then a position of initial weakness need not be disadvantageous; rather, it is merely the starting point in a new learning experience. However, it is far more pragmatic to acknowledge that the environment may not be entirely supportive and friendly. Thus, the successful executive will prepare assiduously for the new environment.

If we continue with the analogy above, we see that the key to Judo is the core of the body. In this same respect, we must have a core from which to leverage our will in a particular contest. The core of any executive lays in integrity and credibility. As the Judo masters use their core muscles to leverage stronger opponents into defeat, so must we use our established credibility to leverage our opponents into defeat. This is not to say that a confrontational attitude is always useful. But when an existing executive attempts to disenfranchise or otherwise place us at undue disadvantage, the effort will belie a lack of integrity. It is this lack of integrity that the successful executive will leverage their credibility against in order to topple the stronger opponent. The particular circumstances under which these contests will take place vary depending upon the organization and the individuals involved, but the core truth is the same.

Figure 22 - Like the core of the body in Judo, our credibility and integrity serve as a fulcrum.

The Junior Executive will use their integrity and credibility as a core for leveraged projection of will within the executive team.

Chapter 5 Organization

"Good leadership consists of showing average people how to do the work of superior people."

-John D. Rockefeller

Author's Note: It is better to raise the baseline competence of the entire organization than to focus resources on a few components. The organization will be more resilient and able to accept and implement advanced concepts. This is the reason why common-sense ideas appear to be rarely implemented. The organization is often not sophisticated enough to process them in concert.

VISION AND MISSION

As the scope of this book is limited to the concepts associated with becoming a successful executive, we will avoid philosophical discussion of an organization's vision or mission statement. But we are concerned with two aspects of these concepts: what vision is required of the executive and what to do if our organization lacks a clear mission. To clarify further, we are more concerned with focusing our planning energies on goal alignment and ensuring performance measurement at the executive level. By satisfying these very important and critical requirements we will be creating the same sense of mission that is intended by a mission statement, without the abstract noise. Further, an individual sense of vision is absolutely critical for the executive. A vision for the higher-level state of our domain that directly supports our goals (in the organization and our career) is also critical to ensure that we are cognitively aligned with the work requested of us.

Vision for an organization or domain is not the same thing as goal alignment. While goal alignment is required to ensure that our team's near-term tasking and projects provide the required outputs for goal attainment in a prescribed period, vision alignment is necessary to ensure that the future state of our team and domain is aligned to the future state of the organization. Is our organization's vision to be design and management-focused, while outsourcing much of the production work? In that case, it makes sense that the vision of our domain should support this by creating abstraction layers between the design and management of the work and the actual production of the work. This may mean greater automation of reporting, different job descriptions and types of employees, different locations, etc. The purpose of vision is to leapfrog near-term constraints and challenges to identify the Machiavellian "far bank."[2] It is to acknowledge that there are unknown threats and opportunities that can be overcome through our team's ability and confidence. Vision is a cognitive alignment of expectations and cultural norms among our team, and should be simple and clearly communicated among the team, in such a manner that all strategic and goal evaluations can be judged in relation to it. The successful executive will craft a vision statement for their team, ensure that it aligns to the organization's vision statement (if one exists) and ensure that both are clearly communicated to their team.

In organizations with no clear vision, the underlying requirement for the executive is the same: Define a vision for their domain and team. At this point, our guidance and discussion diverges from most of the mainstream advice regarding a vision statement. Rather than explaining how we do our work, our vision statement should explain why we do our work. No one wants to be a drone in the factory. Rather, individuals derive genuine value from their time in an organization and the key to success is to acknowledge and grow that value. The vision statement is the beacon that signals that value. If our organization is a charity seeking to reduce homelessness, our vision is not to obtain enough money to house

[2] In his book, "The Prince," Niccolo Machiavelli demonstrates that in order to attain greatness or achieve something beyond our understood capacity, we must aim for something that appears out of reach: "[we] should behave like those archers who, if they are skillful, when the target seems too distant, know the capabilities of their bow and aim a good deal higher than their objective, not in order to shoot so high but so that by aiming high they can reach the target."

homeless individuals; rather, it is to help homeless people take care of themselves. Our volunteers and employees do not work at our charity to secure a prescribed number of beds; they work at our charity to help desperate people regain the ability to make their lives better. So, as we identify this "Why" we see that the vision for the organization is not an efficient fund-raising machine or an effective real estate handler, but instead a team of highly effective and caring individuals who can immediately tailor an achievable, individualized plan for every homeless person who enters the door. That is "Why" the employees and volunteers work. "How" they achieve this and "What" is the output are clear derivatives of this "Why." The successful executive will take time to understand "Why" their subordinates work in their organization and their domain. We use this information and emotion to craft a vision statement that clearly addresses this and communicates it to our team. This is required, whether or not the overall organization has a clear vision statement.

The Junior Executive will craft and proselytize a vision for their domain.

ORGANIZATIONAL POWER STRUCTURE

Although it has been peripherally discussed in previous chapters, we will spend some time reviewing power structure in more detail in this chapter. There are many theories and treatises about organizational power structure: How best to build it; How best to navigate it; How to successfully change it. All of these are well and good, and we should study them. However, this meta-layer theory is not what we are interested in presently. The implementation of any particular organizational strategy will be unique to every individual in every circumstance but it will be underpinned by the same fundamentals—the organizational power structure. So, what is an organizational power structure? By design, it is a direct expression of the organization's purpose. For example, if the organization's purpose is to provide an open forum that allows tensions to be defused and peace promoted, the power structure will reflect this.

No one party will have too much power, and many parties will be empowered to temper any directives that could detract from the organization's purpose. Thus, we have the understood purpose of the United Nations. If the organization is a software company that is tasked with creating a single product and delivering it to a single market or customer, the organizational power structure will be markedly different. That organization's purpose is to create a finite product and deliver it to a customer, and so deductive decisions must be made in a directive manner and work must be executed in a logical progression toward delivery of the product. In this organization type, power is often relegated to single individuals or teams to ensure efficiency in decision-making and execution. The organization's purpose will necessitate its power structure. The degree to which a power structure aligns to the organization's purpose will dictate the effectiveness of the power structure. When a power structure is implemented inconsistently or disingenuously, there is opportunity for manipulation and skullduggery, which we will touch upon later. For the executive, the imperative here is not to judge the organizational power structure subjectively, but to understand it objectively with consideration of the reasons for its current state. This objective understanding will yield valuable information as we determine how to execute work within the organization. More importantly, it will yield critical information about how effective the organization is at a fundamental level and provide indications for its suitability for our individual success. A dysfunctional organization is of little use to us from a career standpoint.

In analyzing a power structure, proximity to the organization is helpful, and an executive who has been promoted from within will likely have greater insight than an external hire. However, an externally hired executive will have the benefit of interviewing the members of the organization during the selection process and will be privy to their insights in a less political environment, which very often yields more honest answers. Regardless of their origin inside or outside the company, the successful executive will evaluate the power structure of the organization to determine its likelihood for effectiveness and to understand how work will get done. There are many formal tools for conducting this type of analysis, but there are four basic components:

> **Purpose**: What is the core purpose of the organization? This will likely not be the mission or vision statements. Rather, it is a focus on the discrete outputs of the organization and their underlying media. If our organization is Coca-Cola, our core purpose is to make a profit on invested capital—sugared water is not the output, stock dividends are the output. Sugared water is the media by which this output is delivered. If our organization is Habitat for Humanity, our core purpose is to move homeless families from the street or shelters into private, self-funded residences. Houses are the media by which this output is delivered. There is an extraordinary amount of noise designed specifically to obfuscate many organizations' core purpose. The successful executive will understand the true purpose of an organization.
>
> **Structure**: Once the core purpose of the organization is understood, then the structure is evaluated to determine how efficiently it is built to deliver on this core purpose. The structure is often defined by the complexity of the supporting media. If the core purpose of the organization is to yield profit and the underlying media is sandwiches, then the structure of the organization is relatively simple. If the core purpose of the organization is to ensure continuity of commercial lines of communication in the South Pacific, then the underlying media will be projected military strength and the organizational structure will be vastly more complex. Every organization is different and each must be evaluated in depth. However, there are some general points of consideration. Are all structural components involved in delivery of the output? Do any structural components have unilateral veto power? Do any structural components have

the ability to stall work? Do any structural components have redundant functions? The successful executive will evaluate the structure of the organization to determine how effective it is in delivering on the core purpose.

Flow: Once the structure is understood, it is important to evaluate the flow of work that turns all inputs into outputs—not necessarily process, but flow. Even misaligned structures can have excellent workflow if the individuals involved are committed. Understanding workflow in the organization will yield several benefits. It will identify power misalignments (e.g., work held up at certain points). It will identify decision-making steps and individuals. Additionally, it will provide for an ongoing evaluative dataset for monitoring and evaluating the organizational power structure.

Power structures underlie all organizations. None are perfect and many are dysfunctional. As a junior executive, there will be scant opportunity and basis for changing the existing organizational power structure. We must work to truly understand our organization's power structure and how well it works to deliver on the overall purpose. After a thorough analysis, the successful executive can assess organizational fitness, potential roadblocks and pitfalls as well as opportunities for improvement. This information will allow the executive to modify engagement strategies, determine campaign initiatives, identify future problems with workflow and provide a firm footing for delivering on their responsibilities.

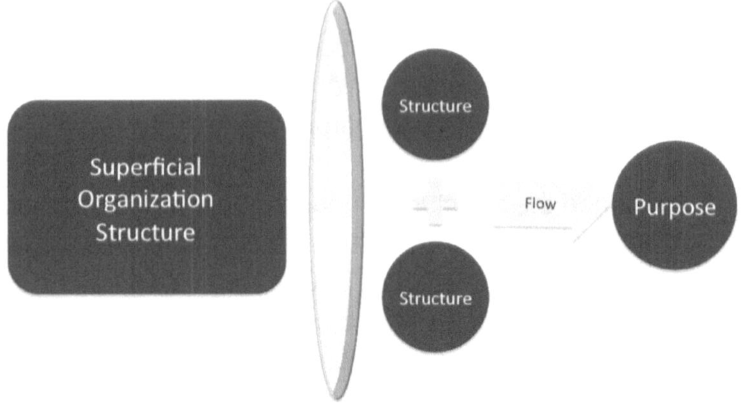

Figure 23 - The organization's superficial structure should be evaluated through the lens of purpose.

The Junior Executive will have a clear understanding of the organizational power structure.

SOCIOLOGY

It is fair to say that the meaning we assign to the vast majority of ideas and material things in our daily lives is derived from their relativistic value in a society. That is, the value that we assign to items is a direct reflection of the value that our social group assigns to them. This pervades both private and public life, and thus it becomes important for the executive to understand the role that the scientific aspects of sociology has on their working life. This topic is broad and deep—as such, we will limit our discussion to the importance of this concept in the life of the executive and some core aspects that should be considered in relation to the organization.

Previous chapters have briefly touched on the sociological impacts of the executive role and the impact that individual behaviors can have on others within the organization. In this chapter we are concerned with sociology in general and the peculiarities of the individual in a social context. The executive who heeds the concepts presented thus far will succeed in avoiding many of the social pitfalls that beset teams in an empowered organization: group think, bullying, etc. Further, the successful executive will deterministically assign both punishment and rewards to incentivize individuals to align value appropriately. Two key ideas are relevant here: sources of power within the sociological context and situational variability.

Sources of Power: As previously discussed, the models through which individuals in an organization make decisions are shaped by the culture of that organization and the nature of the work conducted. Thus, it is essential that the executive understand the sources of power in their organization and within their own team. The sources of power in a cancer research hospital are going to be much different than those in a hospital trauma ward. The meaning associated with specific behaviors and work tasks will vary in each sociological situation, in every organization and unique culture.

Situational Variability: Richard Nisbett and others have made a compelling case for the substantial influence of the variability of situational factors on the behaviors and actions of the individual (Nisbett & Ross, 1991). That is, individual behavior is mostly influenced by circumstances. This goes to the core of how we as people often incorrectly make sense of the actions of others—we extrapolate generalities from finite observations. In truth, people have general proclivities toward particular behaviors and those behaviors manifest in varying degrees dependent on situational circumstances. These biases provide a model for understanding the true source of an individual's behavior consistency—goals, as described by Nisbett and Ross. It then follows that by understanding and influencing the goals of individuals, we may be able to influence their behaviors in varying situations. The successful executive will understand the true goals of their subordinates and colleagues as much as

> possible. With this knowledge, we can guide their goals in line with our domain and the organization as a whole. Those who do not align are not a good fit for the organization. This exercise, if implemented in a disciplined manner, will achieve team alignment with the overall goals of the organization.

Sociology is a substantial domain of knowledge and research. Because we all are subject to the scientific principles of sociology in the organizational as well as personal contexts, it is highly recommended that we make the field a regular source of study. At the very least, we must master basic sociological concepts and how they can be used to better understand and influence the individuals within our organization to achieve excellence.

The Junior Executive will know the sources of power in their organization and understand the impact of situational variability.

BUCKSTOPPER

A recurring theme of this book is that an executive will only be successful if they demonstrate integrity and perform excellently. A majority of the concepts herein rely on these two points, and many of the negative attributes and behaviors covered source themselves in individuals failing to maintain their integrity or to perform excellently. As an executive, we will likely be privy to the inner workings of the management team and gain much greater insight into the true nature and motivations of those on the team. It should be stated that individuals who attain the executive rank through means other than the two traits noted above will often be solid practitioners of deflection and obfuscation. Our advice for all newly minted executives and those seeking to advance to the executive rank is to be extremely cautious in the early days, and to always judge individuals on their actions rather than their words. We have discussed personal responsibility in other chapters, but here we are concerned with the level of personal responsibility demonstrated by other executives and senior leaders within the company and the degree to which they either resolve or deflect issues. In the early stages of our new appointment and as a matter of policy, it is extremely useful to keep track of how individuals, particularly other executives, deal with issues. Do they take immediate responsibility for addressing them? Do they vacillate until the issue eventually lands on them? Or, do they "pass the buck" on a routine basis? An individual's behavior in this regard provides far greater insight into their personal integrity and drive for excellence than anything they might say. The successful executive will make a dedicated effort to objectively observe the behaviors of others in the organization to gain insight into their personal integrity and drive for excellence.

It must be noted that we will not be special or unique in our analysis. As a matter of human nature, it is often commonly known in an organization who is a buck-passer and who is a buck-stopper. As such, an even more important analysis is how much buck-passing is tolerated. Tellingly, tolerance of buck-passing is symptomatic of far worse problems. Buck-passing is indicative of a culture that does not tolerate "earnest" failure and is lacking in maturity. Buck-passing is indicative of a culture that is not focused on excellence or on the overall growth or betterment of the organization. This is evident in our second question regarding an individual's attitude toward new issues. If there is a tolerance within the organization for issues to bounce around, unaddressed, until the rightful owner is finally compelled to acknowledge it, we will likely see several underlying problems: apathy, cowardice, laziness, distraction, and under-capitalization—all of which should be red flags to any executive. Remaining in an organization that tolerates buck-passing will be a detriment to our overall career goals.

Achieving promotion to the executive rank is a challenge and ensuring that we are successful in that promotion requires an enormous amount of work and intelligent thought. It is critical that the successful executive understand the true nature of their organization and the empowered individuals within it. As a new executive, we will be extremely busy dealing with the work itself, our reports, and the other executives. This is a time of great opportunity and great risk. The successful executive will employ keen observation and empathy in evaluating their organization from an accountability viewpoint. One clear marker of a good organization or a bad organization is the attitude it holds toward "passing the buck."

The Junior Executive will monitor closely the level of tolerance for deflection in their organization and never deflect responsibility.

EXPECTATION MANAGEMENT

Expectation management is one of the most difficult concepts to implement successfully in any organization. This is particularly true for new executives. For this topic, we will avoid aspects of expectation management that would advise for manipulation of expectations and instead focus on forthright action. The pressure to perform at a high level is tremendous and there is great value placed on those who can perform as such. However, mature individuals understand that stellar performance often comes at an unforeseen cost and is likely to be abnormal. Thus, executives are often trapped in a difficult scenario. They are high-level performers who feel compelled to make bold predictions for their success in order to justify their promotion yet they may lack the experience to understand the complexities of that performance. We would grant the assumption that senior executives and directors value honest and reasonable estimates for performance. Other aspects of this concept are addressed symptomatically from this root.

Senior leaders have a strong preference for linearly tracking performance and surprises will only be tolerated in the affirmative and even then, only to a limited degree. That is, upset expectations cause discomfort. If we set expectations too low and then greatly overshoot, we may be judged to have been sandbagging and any future estimates will be overcompensated. If we set expectations too high and then undershoot, we may be judged to have been naive or in over our head. The latter is worse than the former. Given that we are likely new to the full complexities of our domain, this presents a difficult situation. However, there is an approach which acknowledges the truth of the situation and the general uncertainty of estimates and predictions. This is expectations management: a process whereby we set estimates, explain our reasoning and then methodically and frequently communicate incremental changes to those estimates as conditions warrant. There are three basic phases to any expectation management process:

> **Baseline Estimate**: For any tracking estimation of performance (products shipped, donations secured, reports published, etc.), there must be an initial baseline estimate that covers the agreed period, which is typically a fiscal year. The baseline estimate must include a complete list of constraints under which the estimate will be measured as well as the decisions made in relation to these constraints. The baseline estimate must demonstrate a Likely scenario, against which actual performance will be measured, as well as Upper and Lower Control scenarios. This level of planning acknowledges uncertainties in the domain both to the affirmative and negative. The Likely scenario is the estimate on which we stake our performance measurement. This scenario must take into consideration many aspects of the organizational culture and the senior executives who will be judging this performance. In general, it should tend toward the Upper in organizations that value stretch goals and acknowledge that it is generally better to shoot high and miss than to shoot low and hit. It should tend to the Lower in organizations that punish underperformance. The successful executive will set a Likely performance target that is achievable in the given context.
>
> **Adjustments**: Periodically, we must adjust and explain the tracking actual performance against this baseline. It is critical that this is done as frequently and as honestly as possible.

Overshooting targets is undesirable, but surprises to the negative can be damaging. By frequently communicating adjustments to the actual performance, we can demonstrate several things: reliability in conveying true information, intelligence by conveying changes in the commonly understood dynamics of the organization's market or function, and maturity by evaluating and learning on a frequent basis what is working and what is not working. In an honest and mature organization, a dedicated process of adjusting estimates is the only reliable method of managing expectations. The successful executive will include in their reports a dedicated section that addresses adjustments to the baseline estimate, which will allow senior leaders to adjust their expectations in kind.

End of Period: At the end of the period, a complete analysis of the adjustments made throughout the year must be conducted to glean out the major changes that should be incorporated into the estimate for the next year. Based upon this knowledge, a new baseline will be set and new assumptions made, and expectations will be reset for the new period. This is all relatively standard process and part of goal-alignment, but comprehensive and thoughtful execution is rare in many organizations. More often than not, new estimates are thrown together based upon hunches or cursory analyses and then a dance of confusion ensues through the following period. The successful executive will demonstrate honesty in their reporting, candor in the end of period analysis and confidence in the new estimate.

Expectation management is often reduced to maxims and machinations. But experienced executives will be able to see through such maxims or machinations and determine their own expectations. Thus, expectations cannot be managed in the basic sense. Expectation management does not mean manipulation. The successful executive will avoid oversimplified maxims or machinations and implement a process whereby they explain, monitor and adjust estimates for performance against overall goals—that is, manage.

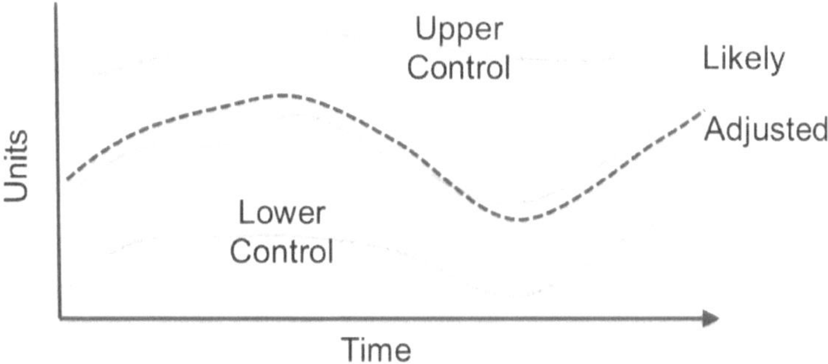

Figure 24 - Expectations are managed within a range of probability and adjusted periodically to reduce surprise.

The Junior Executive will manage expectations through honest analysis of available information, presented in a continually updated estimation of performance within control thresholds.

DEMEANOR

Every person is the hero of his or her own narrative—the good guy. So, even if a person does bad things, they typically rationalize them to align with a good guy narrative. People want the good guy to win, both consciously and subconsciously. By aligning the narrative of their behavior to good guy motives, they provide support for themselves and their actions. This is the mechanism whereby we generally act "good" and are able to move on without a soul-crushing load of guilt when we do things that are objectively "bad." This represents both an opportunity and a minefield. To navigate productively, we need to understand the effect of the good guy condition on the organization.

How is "good" measured and adjusted? If we frame the discussion in terms of Platonic Forms, we understand that there can be an optimal form for good behavior. The guideline for our behavior as individuals is our tolerance for how our behavior aligns with this form. In the organizational context, a variant of this form exists in some fashion. Of course, the general tolerance for behavioral misalignment varies widely across companies and cultures. So, within each culture we must evaluate the tolerance for variance from the general form. For example, if we say that a tenet of the form is to not express anger, but the culture within our organization has a relatively large threshold for variance from this tenet, then we may see common occurrences of swearing or outbursts. These eruptions are normal, but deviate from the commonly held form for appropriate behavior. Such outbursts produce a dissonance that can be leveraged to the advantage of the aspiring executive, with the added benefit of promoting a move of the culture closer to the form. When considering angry outbursts as variance from the form, a preliminary task is to understand and measure the degree of variance. Does the CEO swear in front of the management team? Does the CEO swear in front of the other employees? What about other senior executives? Are there emotional outbursts? Rude jokes? Bullying behaviors or other aggressive or passive-aggressive behaviors? How much is lying tolerated? What is the degree to which employees and managers engage in “cover ups”? A survey of this type will provide a solid foundation upon which to act. We should not be overly discouraged by what we find—humans are animals, after all. In the organizational context, this manifests in many symptoms of bad behavior. Our work here is not to judge but to understand.

So, what do we do with this knowledge? Is it worth anything? At the very least, it provides a basis for our decisions and interactions with others in the company. The better our understanding of the foibles of the culture, the more productive our decisions will be. Beyond this, we see a landscape on which we can begin to leverage the culture for the betterment of everyone and demonstrate our strength of character and integrity. The approach is to adjust our behavior to a point between the cultural norm and the form. Exactly where between norm and form will be based upon our analysis of the culture. How is behavior that deviates from the norm treated by others? Depending upon the degree of variance, the reaction could be indifference or alienation. We must behave better than the norm, but not so much that it is fully dissonant with the existing culture. In this way, we slowly ratchet the organization closer to the form.

Some well-worn advice on boiling a frog is helpful at this point. If we drop a frog into boiling water, he will quickly jump out. But if we put a frog into cool water and then slowly raise the heat, his internal temperature regulators will not register the difference and the frog will remain in the water even as it begins to boil. In this manner, we must provide cues to behavioral change that are not overtly dissonant with the existing cultural norm. Others will begin to follow in that direction—either consciously or not—because everyone values and craves "good" behavior.

On this path, we must methodically and sensitively modify our demeanor and public persona (attitude, verbal and written behavior, dress, etc.) to move from the cultural norm toward the form. The rate, degree and scope of change are all far less important than the fact that change is happening. It is the simple act of moving the culture toward the form that creates the value. Done correctly, this will engender faith among senior leadership and subordinates that we can be trusted, and are working toward the betterment of the organization. Among our competitors, it will be one more measure by which we are winning.

Figure 25 - Demeanor moves behavior closer to the form.

The Junior Executive will provide a model of good behavior and thus present a demeanor that provides freedom for others to move the organization closer to a form of excellence.

PERFORMANCE MEASUREMENT

Throughout this book, we have made references to performance measurement. It is worth noting that our approach to performance management does not rely on the standard time-based measurements. Repetitive tasks and jobs still exist and likely will for some time, but they are on a steep decay curve—much like agriculture in the early 20th century. Automation and intelligent systems are continually freeing individuals from repetitive labor. This is a wonderful trend from a progressive labor and humanistic perspective, but it presents a challenge for measurement of performance. Given this trend, our discussion of performance measurement will focus on knowledge work tasks and metrics. We will acknowledge trends in communication and toolsets that favor decentralization. Increasingly, there are no master, closed systems; rather, there are data that must be commonly understood, shared and consumed. Before addressing our specific approach for performance measurement, we should spend some time discussing the changing landscape and how to ensure that our mode of measurement acknowledges individual and systemic limitations.

> **Data**: Given the complexity, scope and breadth of the working world, there is no practical way for an executive to maintain an intuitive model of performance measurement. Traditional modes of working are ill-suited for globalization, attitude shifts regarding work-life balance, and an explosion in the variety of outputs. None of this should be a surprise, but the lack of flexibility in most performance measurement methodologies is a source of opportunity for the successful executive. In a constantly changing work landscape, the priority for measurement has changed from the reports to the data itself. It is foolhardy to imagine that we can create a system of reports that will be relevant for more than six months. If we focus on a robust system of collecting data points that can be modified as conditions warrant, our reports can be organic. Reports can be generated, automated, and modified to support experimentation to

better understand the performance of our teams. By acknowledging that the reports we design today will be irrelevant in six months, we are freed from a shoehorned measurement system incapable of making performance better. The successful executive will put their effort and resources into ensuring that whatever performance measurement system is put in place will have a robust framework for collecting chosen data points and presenting them in a format that can be manipulated at will. Once this is in place, we can seek out non-intuitive and forward-thinking strategies for improvement in a controlled manner.

This may be difficult in some organizations, and we should implement our own performance measurement system in the absence of an organizational tool. A simple spreadsheet will often do the trick if the data is available. In most organizations, performance measurement is a necessary evil that is required for pay reviews, hiring and promotions. We are not suggesting that we buck the system in this context. Rather, we are suggesting that performance measurement is a greatly underutilized tool for improving the level of output within our teams. In general, there will be a performance measurement system in place as a matter of HR policy. The successful executive will adhere to applicable HR policy and mold the outputs of their actual performance measurement system to enable this broader corporate system. There will be time later in our career to modify the corporate system.

In implementing our system, we must ensure that individuals have a stake in their performance measurement and that our system will yield actual performance improvement. For an individual in a modern, knowledge-based organization, there are three basic components to performance. However, we implement performance measurement within our teams, these components must be at the heart of it:

Goals-Based Targets: As we have noted, it is now

commonly accepted by psychologists and social scientists that individuals do not demonstrate consistent behavior or attitudes in their day-to-day lives. In fact, in any given situation on any given day, individuals demonstrate behavior that is wildly divergent from their "norm." This divergence is itself normal: Everyone does it, all the time. Rather than leading to chaos, this actually provides a great deal of freedom for the individual to accommodate changing circumstances and new realities. Richard Nisbett and others have argued convincingly that the actual range of this freedom of behavior is anchored and bounded by the goals that the individual has for the future (Nisbett & Ross, 1991). Thus, we see that a person who has a goal of passing an exam in two weeks controls their behavior in a manner that affords them time to study and learn the material, rather than go out to nightclubs. An individual who has a goal of losing weight will diet. An individual who has a goal of achieving a bonus will direct their effort and resources to attaining the bonus target. An individual who has a goal of designing a great computer program will research, experiment and put in the hours required to develop that application. The core of the matter is that as an executive, we can predict nothing about the performance of the individuals on our team unless we have a solid understanding of their goals. Everything else is noise. Any performance measurement system must be based upon goals to a large degree. In the organizational context, the challenge is to ensure goal alignment. The organization's goals should be supported by our domain's goals, which should be supported by our team's individual goals. This alignment must be guided by the executive to ensure that goals are directly causal. The successful executive will understand that the only constants in an individual's behavior are their personal goals and that these goals must be aligned to the organization's.

Projects-Based Monitoring: We have noted project-based methods often. This is because project management is a catchall concept that allows for an individual to apply discipline to a goal. The goal is defined and then decomposed into bits of work that can be achieved in a controlled manner in a monitored time frame. Resources are then applied to these bits of work and the goal is methodically achieved (or not). Given our discussion above regarding the changing nature of work and, by extension, the impracticality of traditional performance measurement methods, we see that the only practical method is to track performance through projects. For every goal, a project should be established to attain that goal. As an example, we could track the execution progress of a project to publish a research report. Has the research been conducted? Was the rough draft completed on time? Are the publisher's schedules in sync? Performance can be measured with data for any goal within a project methodology. The successful executive will ensure that all goals are supported and tracked through projects. The status of these projects then serves as the basis for performance reviews and goals forecasting throughout the measurement period.

Individual Control of Execution: One of the key concepts in this chapter is the idea that an individual's behavior is guided by their goals. It is important to emphasize that the goals are the individual's goals and not anyone else's. Despite what we or anyone else (including the individual) may hope, an individual's goals will drive their behavior (consciously and subconsciously). So, the individual must have complete control over the execution of the projects that support their goals. How else could we possibly measure their performance with any fidelity? The results of this measurement may yield a bounty of insights. Maybe the goals are great and the individual performance is great. Maybe the goals are wrong. Maybe the individual is not up to our standards. These judgments cannot be made without clean data. It is critical that the executive allow the individual to control the execution of their projects so as to truly understand the effectiveness of their team and to craft plans that will improve performance.

Performance measurement is an underutilized tool, often falling into disuse or acting merely as an HR compliance task. An executive who can make intelligent and effective use of it will be at a significant competitive advantage both within the organization and in the broader market.

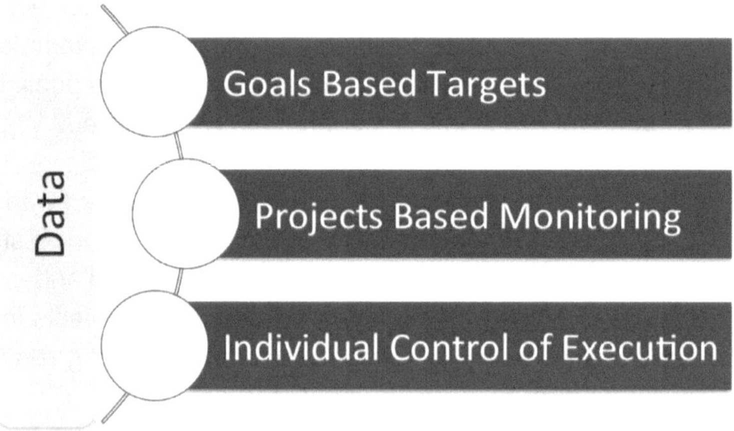

Figure 26 - Performance measurement requires a flexible approach to goal achievement and data collection.

The Junior Executive will implement a data-sourced performance measurement method to track an individual's execution against their goals.

ANTHROPOLOGY

The successful executive must understand how cultures are changing and in what directions they are likely to move. These are long-term concepts that require significant thought. And, if not integrated into our approach to organizational design and the control of work, we will find ourselves limited later in our career. A lack of anthropological understanding is how well established companies doom themselves to disruption and decline. This is not to suggest that we must earn a degree in Anthropology or be especially expert in the discipline. We must merely acknowledge that there is a great deal of insight that can be gained from an anthropological framework for evaluating events and behaviors in our organization and in the broader culture. This begins with an understanding of applied anthropology, or the anthropologic analysis of practical problems.

Applied anthropology enables a mode of thinking that is abstracted from the daily action to provide an objective analysis of the effectiveness of higher-level processes. Given the complexity of organizations, we will limit ourselves to a general approach that must be modified to fit our particular circumstances. The basis of our approach is twofold: place and value. Within these two ideas, we can establish a framework for analysis that identifies problems, questions, methods for evaluation and lines of experimentation.

> **Place**: Leaders must understand their organization's place in the broader culture. How did we get to this place? Is this place gaining or losing relevance in the broader culture? An excellent example is the newspaper publishing industry's demise throughout the early 21st century. Despite hopes to the contrary, the industry lost an enormous amount of relevance within the broader culture as a vetting agent and distributor of general news. Executives who spotted the anthropological trend in the broader culture were able to implement policy changes that moved their organization's place. News Corp was one of the few organizations to sense the change and move their place, successfully transitioning to a new mode of news vetting and distribution.
>
> **Value**: The lesson of place holds true for value. What is the value that our organization delivers to the broader culture? Is what we deliver gaining or losing value? How did we build value in the first place? As the fundamental drivers for value

> appreciation change, so must the value levers. A classic example of this is IBM's value in the business computing industry in the 1980s and 1990s. As the fundamental drivers of business computing moved away from mainframe systems and to more distributed systems, the value delivered by IBM was losing relevance. Sensing this trend, IBM senior leadership moved the company quickly and firmly away from hardware and into services. The company thus found new value levers that were aligned with broader cultural trends.

The executive must sense, test and anticipate changes to place and value. What is the framework for this? If we understand our organization's place and value in the broader culture, we can begin to decompose their elements and analyze trends in order to anticipate changes. In applying anthropology, we can fall back on the standard method for evaluation that is used across many disciplines: identify a problem or question, put in place a method for analysis, initiate a method for collecting data, and run experiments. Applied anthropology is well positioned to take advantage of the increasingly rich data sets available for mining and analysis via social networks and the Internet in general.

The Junior Executive will understand applied anthropology as a discipline and implement analyses that evaluate the place and value delivered by the organization in the broader culture.

ORGANIZATIONAL ARTIFACTS OF CONTROL

There is much theory available that provides detailed analysis and recommendations on the various artifacts and methods of organizational control. We have covered aspects of these theories as they apply to the specific challenges of the executive role. In this chapter, we will briefly cover the topic in general, as expressed through artifacts like titles and temporal compartmentalization. A general theme of this book is highlighted in this chapter: Old modes of working are no longer applicable to the new and anticipated work outputs and fully normalized integration of geographically and culturally diverse workforces. Many existing artifacts of control demonstrate a hindrance to organizations at the leading edge of leveraging the new ways of work. First, let us review the purpose of organizational artifacts of control and then evaluate two cases in relation to our role as executive.

Organizational artifacts of control exist to level-set workflow. One of the most important infrastructural supports an organization can have is easily estimated flows of work. Regardless of what our organization does with regard to outputs, the only way that it can continue as a going concern is to estimate the flow of work that will occur in the future. The organizational atmosphere must be controlled in order to accurately estimate workflow. Newly formed organizations lack this atmospheric control and must create it. They do so through organizational artifacts of control. They establish working hours, titles, reports, etc. that provide an atmosphere in which everyone within the organization can commonly and intuitively understand the flow of work and make judgments about the future. As an exercise, let us review examples of organizational artifacts of control and how they apply to workflow.

> **Titles**: Titles are very important in organizations, despite periodic fads to the contrary. Titles provide a map to the flow of work in an organization. It is important to note that actual work may not adhere to the titular structure of the organization, and is not necessarily meant to. But a titular structure should provide the general framework through which work flows. If work begins to flow outside of the titular structure beyond an acceptable threshold, then changes to that structure may be necessary. Very often, titles are co-opted beyond their fundamental use. Take for an example multiple layers of middle management, in which these layers are often established to satisfy HR concerns about losing senior and experienced people. If we understand that the titular structure is in place to allow for workflow and to

provide indicators to the collective atmosphere about the future flow of work, we can see that added complexity and confusion in that structure would be detrimental to both functions. The successful executive will ensure that the titular structure in their domain is efficient and supports an understanding of present and future workflows.

Temporal Compartmentalization: Time keeping is a relic of past modes of work such as manufacturing and hourly or piecework outputs. It remains in place only because no other granular method of quantification of labor cost is readily available. This is true of all compartments of time keeping: active hours, vacation, sick leave, etc. All of these aim to provide an easily tracked and estimable base for understanding the current and future flow of work. But hour-based outputs of work are becoming less relevant and necessary as technology changes how labor is implemented.

We are consistent in pressing for new ways of thinking about how individuals are managed in an organization and temporal compartmentalization is an excellent example. The blurring of the lines between personal and work time is inexorable. An example is found in a Dilbert cartoon, wherein the eponymous character argues that his lunch break should be extended by the amount of time he spent in the shower thinking about work (Adams, 1995). This highlights the impracticality of hourly time keeping. The successful executive will recognize that both they and their subordinates will work on the projects that they are interested in with little regard for formal business hours. Effective leadership relies less on hourly work and more on measured outputs. Will we get more value from requiring our subordinate to be in the office eight hours a day for two weeks to finish a report or by simply agreeing on a target of two weeks for the report to be finished? It is imperative to enforce personal responsibility on our subordinates and cull those out who refuse. In our experience, subordinates who have a high degree of personal responsibility and are treated well will have the report done in half the time. The accounting of the amount of hours that they spend in the office or at a desk is irrelevant. The successful executive will demonstrate a full understanding of the flow of work in their organization by flexing the boundaries of temporal compartmentalization to yield more work in less time.

Organizational artifacts of control are necessary, but over time these controls can become dogmatic and lead to inefficiencies. The successful executive will refuse to accept these artifacts as dogma and will instead focus on efficiency of the underlying flow of work. This understanding will lead to more effectual artifacts of control.

The Junior Executive will ensure that all organizational artifacts of control are focused solely on the efficient flow of work.

COMMUNICATION

Communication is the universe in which an organization exists, the manifest expression of all of our individual and group-based thoughts and behaviors. In this chapter, we will address several aspects of communication in the organization and how our strategy of communication should be conducted.

As noted, communication is the manifest expression of our thoughts and behaviors. If we are angry, our communication will express that anger, although not always directly. We may suppress that anger and indirectly express it in some other way. But our goal here is not to address communication in this broad sense, but rather to acknowledge its vast complexity and seek a simple strategy that supports our success as an executive. To that end, the only rational strategy is to establish a baseline, default style of communication. The successful executive will communicate in a direct, clear and timely manner in all instances.

Direct and Clear: The successful executive will limit supplementary information and discussion as much as possible and ensure that their core message is clearly stated and closed to broad interpretation. This is more difficult than it seems, particularly when we consider the importance of intent as discussed earlier. Direct and clear communication requires courage and a strong sense of responsibility. One of the best ways to determine if a person is unable or unwilling to take responsibility for something is the level of obfuscation in their communication. Obfuscation of communication is severely damaging to the organization. Imagine playing football against a team who had a clear understanding of who would pass the ball to whom and when, while your team did not know who was supposed to cover whom. In an organization, the effects of bad communication are not this obvious or this near-term—making for a greater challenge. Obfuscated communication can have subtle consequences which build slowly through ossification of bad practices.

An example: Assume that one unclear e-mail sent by an executive to a team of twenty requires ten phone calls and a follow-up e-mail to clarify. This one instance of poor communication (whether intended or not) could easily cause a delay of one to two hours. This may seem minor, but compound that across an organization over time and the delay becomes substantial. This snowball effect is one of the core reasons that small startups are able to move so much faster than large companies and why the levels of performance in large companies is so varied. At the executive level, such a communication problem could easily put our team days or weeks behind a competitor—more than enough to stall our success. So how do we communicate clearly and directly? In practical terms, through concepts covered in this book.

Show Candor: Openly acknowledge questions.
Be a Buck-Stopper: Take responsibility for the question and direct who will do what to address it.
Project-Manage: Apply deadlines and assign responsibility for ensuring tasks are done as necessary.

There are many other aspects to consider in communicating clearly, but these three must be done in every instance. We should note that there are significant cultural considerations that must be taken into account in relation to direct and clear communication. These should be considered as masks for the three concepts indicated above. That is, the successful executive will tailor their communication to the culture in which they operate while ensuring that these three concepts are at their core of their messaging.

Timeliness: Additionally, we understand that communication must occur as close to the point-of-action as possible. This critical point will take time and thoughtful practice to implement correctly. Messages communicated at the wrong time can be ineffectual and damaging in some cases. At the least, they will be inefficient. If we view the progression of the work in the organization along a timeline, we see that some messages would be more effective at certain times than others. A detailed planning memo sent six months in advance would be much more efficient if sent one month prior. It is our job as an executive to understand the impact of timeliness and control our communication for the greatest impact. This is challenging and takes dedicated effort, but will yield outsized benefits in efficiency and flow. A good example of this is a common scene in action movies wherein the main character is guided through an unfamiliar building by a colleague telling him which turns to make at the right time through an earpiece. When watching the scene, we see just how optimally he is performing—running full speed through unfamiliar terrain while making no mistakes. This is our goal.

The Junior Executive will address communication complexity through clarity, directness and timeliness of delivery.

VERBAL COMMUNICATION

Verbal communication is the real-time expression of not only message but also indicators for culture, emotional state and future intent. We will review the impact of verbal communication and its expressive relevance, as well as its use in cultural behavioral modification. To do this, we use two common scenes of verbal communication as lenses: meetings and interviews. But first, let us consider a less obvious aspect of verbal communication.

Because our words often betray underlying beliefs and behaviors, verbal communication has been proven to be recursively influencing. That is, if we speak in a positive manner, we tend to develop a positive demeanor. If we speak in a negative manner, we tend to develop a negative demeanor. The successful executive will evaluate the culture of verbal communication in their organization and their team to ensure that they have a positive aspect in all circumstances. This is not to say that we should spin away negative news or ignore critical analysis, but that negative results should never result in a judgment of the worth of those involved. For the successful executive, dedicated thought about the complex impact of verbal communication can help ensure a culture of growth.

One of the themes of this book is the value of removing noise from workflow. The positive application of verbal communication can greatly assist in that removal. If we look at two typical scenes for verbal communication, we can see excellent opportunities to apply this concept.

Meetings: Rarely are meetings viewed in a positive light. They are largely renowned as a source of frustration. There are many methods of managing meetings. Our particular organization's idiosyncrasies may call for one approach over another, and we will not recommend one, except to say a viable method must be based in the idea that meetings must be expressions of recursively positive verbal communication. The successful executive will enforce a policy that rewards positive verbal communication and ignores negative verbal communication. This is remarkably simple to implement. We will give positive verbal communication our attention, full stop. Punishing negative verbal communication, rather than ignoring it, is counterproductive. If we look at positive verbal communication in the context of efficient and timely execution, we see three relevant purposes for meetings: decision-making, status, and collaboration. In the best scenario, all three combine so that team members spend their time together actually completing work. As the agenda is progressed, it is incumbent upon the executive to ensure that all tabled comments are positive in nature. By enforcing this behavior and the discipline associated with the purpose of meetings, the recursive aspects of positive verbal communication will become the norm for behavior. Beyond the scene of the meeting, team members will engage a positive posture on a more consistent basis over time. In total, this positive attribution of behaviors associated with verbal communication in a public forum will modify the behaviors of those involved as a cultural effect. The successful executive will ensure that all meetings are focused on the decisions, status updates and collaborative work required to grow their team's capabilities through positive verbal communication.

Interviews: Much like meetings, interviews are established in the common culture as a scene of theater. This is due to the stakes involved and the highly subjective nature of the interaction. As with meetings, recursive attribution has a high degree of applicability. As we enforce positive verbal communication in our interviewing process, we complete the task of ensuring that negative individuals self-select themselves out of the team. Thus, the importance of having as many team members as possible interview with potential hires to ensure fit. Of course, this process is complex, but we are concerned with the basic idea of the interview. One aspect of the interviewer's role in the interview is evaluating their own personal assessment of the organization in order to evaluate the interviewee's suitability and vice versa. This analysis, if founded in negativity, will yield negative verbal communication. This will lessen the interviewer's commitment to improvement and will attract individuals who are already caught in a spiral of negativity. The interview process must be a source of positive verbal communication. Again, this is not to deny negative aspects, but to view them as challenges to be overcome through work and intelligence. Interviewers must convey this in their communication. It is strongly suggested that the executive personally involve themselves in group interviews to ensure that a positive verbal communicative tone is set for the future.

Verbal communication is critical for many reasons beyond the explicit message conveyed. Our words must be willfully positive to ensure that a culture of resilience and growth is supported by all.

The Junior Executive will influence verbal communication within their team and across the organization to ensure that positive messages are acknowledged and negative messages are ignored.

Chapter 6 Politics

ASYMMETRIES IN POWER

Because of inherent asymmetries in power, high-powered executives often do not acknowledge nor respect the authority of lesser-powered executives. To a certain degree, such dismissiveness is to be expected, as individuals must prioritize their attention and time to ensure that their goals are achieved. We are not concerned with the ethical or deferential nature of this attitude; rather, we are concerned with ensuring that as a junior executive, we will not be subject to this sort of treatment. Over time, it is career limiting. So, how do we deal with this situation as a junior executive?

In a military context, the analog of this phenomenon is an invading army who feels no pressure to engage the defending army as they march toward the capital. The invading army expects to secure their goal in spite of any action by the defending army. Such an outnumbered defending army has only one course of action: to legitimately threaten a full-force attack on the flank of the invading army (Clausewitz, 1993). The power in this strategy is based upon uncertainty. If the attacker avoids the defender and presses toward their goal, they will leave their flank open to attack that they are unprepared for and would endure far greater damage than otherwise. Conversely, if the attacker fully protects their flanks at all times in anticipation of attack, they will likely lack sufficient resources and momentum to attain their goal. The goal, then, is to avoid being overrun by forcing the invading army to forestall their movement and/or engage the defending army.

In the organizational context, the goal is not to destroy another executive, but to ensure that other executives acknowledge and respect our newfound authority. To that end, the successful executive must evaluate and understand the power bases of their colleagues. We have discussed in other chapters the importance of understanding the organizational power structure. As an expression of this structure, work and cash will flow through the various domains and departments of the organization. If we are in a functionally aligned organization, does our department control some resource or component that is required for delivery of the product or service? For example, if we are a newly minted marketing executive then we will likely have control over market messaging and associated budgets. If a sales executive is pushing hard to launch a new product, they may be tempted to bypass a marketing review and begin selling directly to favored customers. In so doing, this sales executive is signaling that the marketing function is not necessary and that the executive in charge of marketing does not have a sufficient stake in the success of the company's success. Given the asymmetries in power that are likely in place at the company, a full-frontal conflict is unwise for us as the junior executive in marketing. The better approach is to demonstrate the threat inherent in marginalizing the marketing function. In this example, resources are required to retroactively address the market messaging and outputs necessary to ensure that the new product's release is properly communicated and researched. These extra resources will not have been budgeted and may have to be pulled from other existing product messaging work. In short, marketing support for the sales executive's other products will be pulled. This is the threat of attack on the flank.

Carrying out this sort of attack will likely be damaging to all parties and the company in general. Furthermore, it removes the only source of power in this type of asymmetrical political situations: the threat of an attack that disrupts the aggressive planning of our adversary. Thus, it is crucial that the newly minted marketing executive make clear the consequences of dismissive conduct. This messaging is best done in a common forum, such as a product or sales planning meeting. By pre-emptively signaling the constraints on marketing budgets, the message is conveyed that a flank attack is likely if marketing is bypassed.

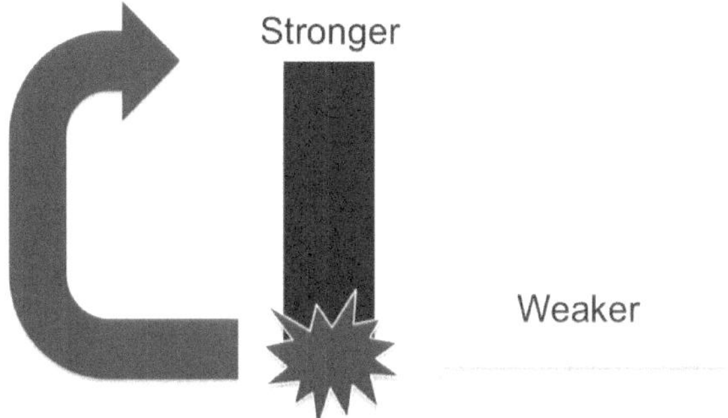

Figure 27 - Weaker executives can overcome asymmetries of power by creating a threat to the flank of a stronger executive and thereby command respect.

The Junior Executive will acknowledge asymmetries in power and signal clearly to their colleagues that they must be respected.

SCHEMES AND MACHINATIONS

Very often, executive team members will actively engage in strategic schemes whose purpose is to further empower themselves. Let us assume that schemes of this type are detrimental to the organization and other executives, including us. To further refine the scenario, say that the scheme itself is an adversarial approach to gaining power in the organization through means that may lie outside the schemer's particular domain. For example, a finance executive may engage in political schemes to wrest power from the chief executive in order to move into that position.

An excellent source of insight on strategic scheming is Carl von Clausewitz. His analysis of military strategy is easily applicable to the organizational context. In his analysis of how Napoleon Bonaparte addressed strategic machinations and schemes put in place by his adversaries, Clausewitz exposes the dangers of subtlety in strategic implementation. Essentially, Clausewitz highlights the fact that Bonaparte was a tactical genius and could be assured of victory in minor battles. Further, as strategic execution is, at the core, a campaign of minor and major battles, Bonaparte would shatter the strategic plans of every adversary who did not fully prepare for these minor battles. His adversaries, relying on machinations and schemes to dissuade him from a minor battle (e.g., threatening an attack to force Napoleon to commit to defensive positions so that they may maneuver a larger force elsewhere), hoped to progress a broader strategic goal. However, understanding the nature of the feint, Bonaparte would attack with the full force of his army, gaining both a tactical win and forestalling the strategic maneuver.

Thus, we see that a direct confrontation on a minor point can derail a broader scheme. This is also the engine behind the "broken windows" policing policy—by vigorously and consistently confronting minor infractions, greater crimes are derailed (Kelling & Wilson, 1982). This is an extremely important concept in the context of an organization and in terms of the junior executive. In fact, it is important for all adversarial situations and scenarios; but we find that it is most appropriate in terms of organizational politics.

Political schemes rely on the implicit approval of others. That is, a scheme can only progress as long as the other executives agree to move in the direction demanded by the scheme. One executive may pressure others to offset spending on a particular near-term project under their purview in order to allocate effort and resources to a broader strategic project—one that will accrue significant power to the scheming executive. That executive makes it clear that by pursuing our near-term project, money would be lost or some other strategic goal would be negatively affected. But surrendering on this seemingly minor issue will cost us the broader battle. As shown by Clausewitz, by yielding the minor tactical engagement, we give up our only possible successful course of action from a strategic standpoint. There may be some good reasons to delay our project, but we will carry the assumption that the offset is neutral. In this case, the only course of action is to pursue our project immediately and with the full force of our power. In this minor battle, we must be successful. Success in the minor battle demonstrates two critical points: we will not acquiesce to political schemes and we will execute our strategic plans in the only legitimate manner—strings of tactical successes.

Individuals who cannot obtain their ends through honest means perpetrate schemes. Individuals who employ schemes in their work life are relatively easy to spot—anyone in a position or applying for a position far above their capability level is a probable schemer. Individuals who refuse to acknowledge mistakes or seem mildly delusional regarding the level of their own competence are also candidates, as are individuals who express paranoid tendencies or who have a difficult time acknowledging the success of others. Why individuals behave this way is well beyond the purview of this book and subject.

Schemes are damaging at any time, but are particularly dangerous for the new or aspiring executive in a competitive contest. Given that schemes seem easy to spot, how is it that they persist in modern organizations? Generally, schemes require a level of disingenuous behavior that the majority of people are unable to identify with and understand intuitively. People who engage in schemes in the organizational context are sneaky and devote considerable effort to their designs. Their colleagues are focused on the business at hand and thus too distracted to see the subtle signs, which presents a challenge to the aspiring executive. If schemers are working diligently at their craft and we are working diligently at our legitimate work, we could be at a disadvantage. To combat this, the successful executive must implement a strategy to insulate themselves from schemers. Very often, schemers will be shrewd practitioners and implement subtle and long-game tactics to execute their plans. This is both an opportunity and a trap. As we assiduously attend to our work performance and our competitor attends to their scheme, their work performance will eventually suffer. To this end, we need only work to ensure that we perform excellently in our role. Over time, the schemer will begin to take bigger and bigger risks to either increase the impact of their scheme or move up the timetable.

Time is one way of countering schemes; a second tool is exposure. We must at all times promote and strive for open forums to review work, plans, progress, status, etc. These forums must occur regularly and involve subordinates, peers and superiors. Steering committees, review boards, etc. are all excellent forums to ensure that light is consistently shed on work in the organization. If executed properly, our hard work will have an audience and the schemer will be faced with a choice as they continue to report less-than-excellent results: either take even greater risks or stop scheming altogether. Even the most ambitious person has a nose for self-preservation, but in some circumstances they will throw a "Hail-Mary," which will be their undoing. At times like these, we must remain calm. Schemers are never so clever as to fool all the people all the time and the "Hail-Mary" reaffirms what most everyone already knows about this kind of individual. The successful executive will remain calm, defend themselves fairly, and provide an opportunity for schemers to reveal themselves. The successful executive will never engage in schemes.

Schemes and machinations are distracting and can be damaging to the organization and individuals involved. When faced with a pointedly adversarial political scheme, the successful executive will pursue the only legitimate strategy: a string of decisive tactical wins in pursuit of the broader goal. These wins may take the form of winning or growing customer accounts, implementing a new training program, publishing a study, etc. In so doing, we will demonstrate not only that we will not acquiesce to political schemes but that we must be acknowledged and accounted for in every situation.

The Junior Executive will not engage in political schemes nor will they tolerate or enable the schemes of others.

FIGHTS

Very often a direct assault on a particular scheme will degrade into a fight, as opposed to a merit-based contest. To know how to deal with fights, we must understand their root cause. In the vast majority of circumstances, fights arise in an environment with no clear authority and no clear goals. Uncertainty around who should be doing what in which way causes the individuals involved, particularly if they are high achievers, to determine their own course. If the organization has no clearinghouse for conflict or an authority figure (senior executive, CEO, etc.) who can arbitrate and make a final decision, fights will arise between individuals in the organization as they each push their agenda forward. There is a clear difference between conflict and fights in this analysis. There will always be conflict in any organization as policy is crafted through differing points of view. Conflict is healthy and a very effective way of ensuring that strategies are vetted for problems. Fights arise when there is no single point of resolution in a conflict. For example, in a matrix-based organization where different business units provide similar services for different constituencies, conflicts may arise over who should service which constituency. If there is no clearinghouse for resolution, then a fight can arise. Fights of this type are damaging to both the organization and the individuals involved. Work is not completed on time nor at the appropriate level of quality, resources are wasted on competing organizational functions, and people will leave to avoid being tainted by the fallout. The individuals responsible for the conflict will have tarnished reputations and engender a perception that they are difficult to work with.

In the organizational context there is no good reason for a fight. As noted above, fights only arise in an environment lacking in decisive conflict resolution. The strategy for dealing with individuals who would proactively engage in a fight for political ends and those who find themselves beset by circumstances in a fight is essentially the same. A method for resolution must be established. For the executive, the absence of a standing resolution method is a golden-opportunity to demonstrate strong and thoughtful leadership. The methods for conflict resolution are well established—single points of leadership (e.g., managing director, CEO), third-party arbitration, board committees, executive steering committees, design boards, decision review boards, etc. They require that accountable decision makers in the organization meet in an open forum to discuss issues that are typically cross-functional in nature and agree on an appropriate course of action, typically proposed by the individuals directly involved in the conflict. In organizations of intellectual peers and relatively flat hierarchies, these types of conflict resolution methods are extremely effective. If the organization rejects any initiatives to establish a conflict resolution method, the smart executive will seek employment elsewhere. Organizational fights have no good outcomes, especially for those involved.

The Junior Executive will avoid organizational fights and push for clear methods of conflict resolution.

OVEREAGER

If we look at the spectrum of behavior in the context of willingness to do a task, we see at one end a complete lack of desire to complete a task and at the other excessive eagerness. We will exclude from consideration the lackadaisical end of the range and review the more active end. By examining over-eagerness, we will gain a better understanding of the optimum level of eagerness an individual should demonstrate with regard to work. By extension, this understanding will hold true for many situations: meetings, Q&As, etc.

As work enters an organization, it must be contextualized and decomposed into component tasks. The assignment of these tasks and responsibility for delivery of the final output are where we see over-eagerness expressed. At this stage of work, colleagues compete for responsibility for output, resources, etc. The motivation in these circumstances is to secure opportunities to demonstrate competence and position oneself for advancement. The instinctual behavior in a competitive situation is to control the communication thread associated with the decision. We see this often in meetings when an individual will endeavor to speak first and control the conversation—answering a question before it is fully asked in an attempt to be the first to speak. This is the classic example, and still pervasive for all its notoriety. This over-eagerness is a brute-force approach to controlling the communication thread. In high-achieving individuals, it can be a strong impulse—one that must not be entertained.

For the successful executive, over-eagerness prompts several considerations. For the most part, given a mature understanding of how decisions are made in an organization, any over-eagerness expressed by competitors is a golden opportunity to not only demonstrate their weakness but also demonstrate our maturity and leadership competence. If we break down a typical scenario of a new project, we see that several moments can be exploited. First, the presenter of the opportunity or issue will begin addressing the group in a standard manner: problem, solution, and benefit. The overeager individual will attempt to offer a solution without a full understanding of the issue, prior to the presenter having finished their briefing, placing themselves at a competitive disadvantage. To the spectators, it will be obvious that the overeager party has spoken prematurely. If at this point, they withdraw, a small advantage is gained. But if they proceed (and they often will) in an attempt to recover, there is even greater opportunity for advantage.

When the overeager party presses the issue, they will be doing two things for us: soliciting more information from the presenter and giving us time to evaluate and generate a suitable solution that can be delivered coolly and confidently.

In an attempt to recover, the overeager person will ask more questions, backtrack, change answers, and generally exceed their allotment of airtime. It will be clear to all around that they are floundering, and all parties will typically give the overeager individual a way to exit the communication thread. This second step is a critical point of advantage: offering a face-saving exit to the overeager individual. This magnanimous gesture not only eases the tension in the room and aids a person in the face of mounting embarrassment; it also demonstrates that we are focused on the actual solution and not on scoring cheap points. However, this offer must be followed directly by a third step, which is to present our more well-thought-out solution. Here the greatest advantage is gained and we see the appropriate level of eagerness toward a new opportunity: fully engaged and interested but mature enough to think through the implications of possible solutions before asking others to spend time and effort considering them. The successful executive will employ this strategy to ensure that overeager individuals do not corrupt the organizational decision-making process and to ensure that they are well positioned to demonstrate their competence and maturity.

As a leader, we must never allow an overeager subordinate to control the communication thread in meetings. While it is important not to dampen the enthusiasm of individuals in sorting through problems or developing solutions, it is critical that all of our subordinates understand that only well-reasoned solutions should be presented and that everyone have the opportunity to speak and be heard. This type of environment can be easily established in a single meeting through an overt statement. Once stated, our subordinates will either welcome the cultural norm or self-select themselves out of it.

The Junior Executive will resist the temptation to be overeager in addressing opportunities and demand the same from their subordinates.

READING PEOPLE

A common theme in this book is the will to power. This is a Nietzschian concept describing the imperative that many feel to express individual control over their fate. It has appropriate and extreme levels of application. There are many negative connotations associated with an extreme application of the will to power—most of which we will not cover. However, it is appropriate to understand the limits of the will to power concept in relation to other people and our ability to read their intentions. We must acknowledge our limitations in understanding what truly motivates others. Despite much literature and thinking to the contrary, we can never really know what is going on in another person's mind at any time. All attempts to "read" another person typically involve boxing them into a situation that has a reactionary bias and then judging their response's deviance from our biased norm. But developing mental models of possible reactions does have value. How do we implement a strategy to do such in a manner that is beneficial to all parties?

We assume that it is important to be able to read the emotional states of other people. This sensitivity demonstrates and hones our capacity for empathy and projected thinking, and also provides an evaluative medium for judging the applicability and reasonableness of our ideas, mitigated by a large enough sample. Thus, we become better able to sense that the CEO's grimace at our idea for a new product may not be displeasure with the idea but rather stomach trouble. Further, if we agree that in a modern economy, goods and services are judged subjectively to a large degree, it is critical that we establish a grounded mental model of people's reactions to many situations in order to realistically judge their reactions to our products and services.

So, we are stuck with a quandary: Reading people is very important but not consistently possible. Of course, with maturity and experience, we all establish a fairly workable mental model of people's reactions under like conditions. But for the executive, this is not sufficient. There is no shortcut for understanding other people, which is one of the reasons we find older individuals at the higher levels of authority. For junior executives, this presents a trap—how to learn to read people effectively without the benefit of extensive experience. Rather than approach this problem directly, we can side-step the trap of reading people.

To work around this hurdle, we refer to a method explained previously: objectify the work and leave individuals to find a way to complete it. We cannot know how someone will react to a particular scenario. However, as an executive, we can control the environment in which the individual operates and bring to bear tools for the individual to complete the work. Furthermore, we can ensure that individuals have the freedom to express their opinions in both public and private forums—to tell us what they are thinking. This requires us to understand our level of experience and maturity in the organizational setting. For example, if we understand that we have a limited amount of experience, that must factor into our judgment of an employee's pleas in private, be it for more control over a project, for more money or for less work. If we acknowledge our capacity for deficiency in discerning the validity of their plea, we realize the true benefit of empowering the individual. What would they do if they faced the obstacle without our capacity for intervention? By opening the environment and objectifying work, we put responsibility for interpretation on the appropriate person. We allow them to adjust the parameters of the work to suit their circumstances, while maintaining focus on the outputs.

The best strategy to avoid mistakes in reading people is for the executive to control the environment within which work is done and to objectify the work involved. The new executive will acknowledge their inexperience in reading people and implement a strategy that allocates responsibility for interpretation on the individual in relation to objectified work. Events within this environment must be allowed to play out, and individuals be allowed to suffer any consequences and enjoy any rewards.

The Junior Executive will acknowledge an experiential deficiency in reading people and objectify work to allow individuals the freedom to self-adjust.

MANEUVER

Executive work is ceaselessly competitive, from initial ascension to ongoing operations. These competitive dynamics, as well as intra-team challenges, provide ample opportunity for maneuver. Our basis for a discussion of maneuver is the asymmetrical distribution of power, resources and legitimacy. It is highly recommended that we research asymmetrical conflict (in warfare, politics, social causes, and business) to truly understand the challenges presented to the junior executive. We will move forward on the premise that we are on the weak-side of an asymmetrical situation—that is, lacking the resources, power or legitimacy of our competitors. Given this situation, we contend that maneuver, as a strategic and tactical concept, is the best tool for achievement.

Although the theoretical difference between strategy and tactics is discussed in a different chapter, brief definitions are in order. With regard to maneuver, a tactic is a discrete movement that proves advantageous for a specific action (e.g., changing seats in a theater to gain a better view). A strategy is an integration of individual tactics into the overall effort (e.g., only attending theaters that accommodate our viewing requirements or implementing a policy whereby tactical maneuvers for viewing optimization are automatically undertaken in all theaters).

So, what is maneuver, then? Maneuver is the act of moving quickly and intelligently, so as to disrupt the decision-making ability of our competitors through surprise and dissonance. Given our basic assumptions on the asymmetrical position of the junior executive in relation to competitors, maneuver has some straightforward benefits. If we are weaker than our adversary in the boxing ring, it makes sense to avoid getting hit. In marketing a new product against an incumbent in the marketplace, it does not make sense to try to match their advertising budget. Rather, it is better to reposition the product to avoid a direct conflict, or to engage in channels of promotion that blunt the advantages of the incumbent: guerrilla marketing, viral campaigns, influencer seeding, word of mouth, etc.

There are myriad implementations of tactical maneuver in this sense in all competitive scenarios (ducking in boxing, a flash mob marketing event, etc.). However, what concerns us here is the integration of strategic maneuver (choosing only slow opponents, hiring a guerilla marketing expert) into our thinking to help differentiate us from competitors and to engender a mode of working that enjoys both the discrete and leveraged benefits of movement.

How is maneuver disruptive? Fundamentally, all calculated decisions follow the same general formula: define problem, generate solution, weigh benefits. Maneuver, in this sense, is a calculus of action and timing—both are required to achieve disruption. The action to be applied is to change the conditions of the decision so as to modify the parameters of the problem, remove fundamental assumptions in the solution, remove benefits, redefine benefits, etc. In warfare, the position of our army presents the conditions of the problem for our adversary. If we modify those conditions (i.e., move our army), then their decision must be fully recalculated. The timing of the action provides the application of surprise and is a multiplier of the disruption (please refer back to the section on “Timing”). The application of action to present dissonant conditions at the right time will yield benefits that can fully overcome the asymmetrical advantage of our adversary. It is not easy to integrate, but we can break it down.

There are three key points in employing strategic maneuver: intelligence, rapid synthesis of information and team synchronicity. In order to integrate maneuver into our strategic thinking, these three points must be in place. When we discuss intelligence, we are referring to a disciplined, holistic and reliable stream of information regarding our adversary. There are chapters later in the book that go into greater detail on the application of intelligence. For the purposes of this discussion, it is enough to understand that if we do not have clear information on the movements, intent and disposition of our adversary, then our movements will be at risk. The successful executive will ensure that they have a solid intelligence network in place. Have we established trusted relationships with other team members in our organization? Do we cultivate these relationships and keep open lines of communication? To have a solid intelligence network in place means to talk to a lot of other people in various levels of our organization's hierarchy and establish trust.

The second key point—rapid synthesis of information—is a combination of innate talent and hard work. If the information from our intelligence network is consistent and reliable, but we do not have the ability to quickly understand the meaning, importance, application and likely implications of that information, it will be wasted. The successful executive will ensure that they and their team are highly adept at rapidly synthesizing information and applying it to their planning. Do we triangulate facts to gain confidence in them? How do we evaluate the narrative of a particular piece of information in relation to our company's strategy? Are there inconsistencies? To synthesize information, we first must have a contextual fabric of our environment to evaluate variance and trends.

Finally, team synchronicity is an absolute requirement for a successful maneuver strategy. In an asymmetrical contest, the more powerful opponent is often hindered by its size and complexity. Put simply, a group of five individuals can arrive at a decision and implement an action faster than a group of fifty. This decision and action attenuation gap is a calculus input of the complexity of the competitor or organization (a peer's team, for example) and the degree to which our team is synchronized on goals, tasks, work streams, outcomes, philosophy, etc. Given that we cannot control the complexity of our competitor's team, we should focus on ensuring team synchronicity to yield the smallest decision and action attenuation gap possible. Do we have regular one-on-one meetings with our second line leaders? Do they have one-on-one meetings with their subordinates? Do we clearly articulate our intent and goal structure within these meetings? Do we verify understanding? Team synchronicity requires thoughtful attention to ensuring that everyone understands why and where we're going.

Effective maneuver provides a means by which smaller and weaker teams prevail against larger, more powerful teams.

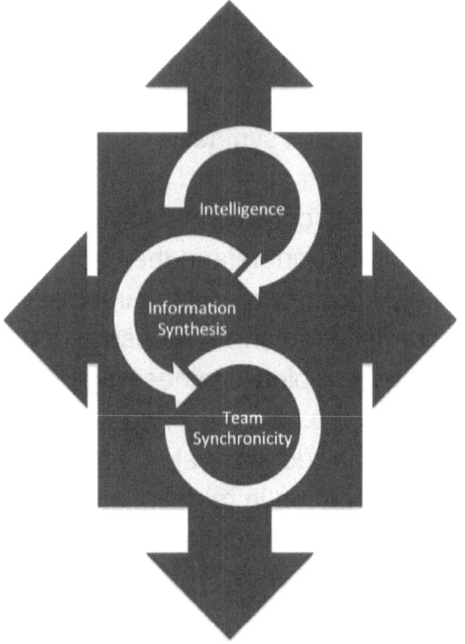

Figure 28 - Maneuver is only a viable option when three key elements are in place.

The Junior Executive will implement maneuver into their strategic planning and ensure that it is supported by an effective intelligence network, rapid information synthesis and team synchronicity.

RESPECT

The concept of respect is a source of significant uncertainty for junior executives—uncertainty that can often lead to mistaken perceptions, attitudes and actions. We will examine respect briefly within the scope of collegial interactions in an organization. In order to make sense of our analysis, we must frame the discussion. We are not concerned with establishing models of behavior for rare scenarios. Rather, we are concerned with the challenges in the other 98% of time spent in an organization. We will assume that everyone in the organization is of average intelligence and moderate temperament. Having said that, we must acknowledge that everyone is beset by a myriad of feelings and struggles with fear-based analyses, as discussed in previous chapters.

So, what is respect in the organizational context? In general, respect is deference given to another person or group, either positively or negatively biased. That is, we defer to others in domains where we view their presence as deserving equal or better treatment than ourselves. We are concerned here with the expression of respect in the organizational context. The period of time leading up to our executive promotion and directly thereafter is tumultuous in terms of respect. Within our domain, we must demonstrate an overwhelming competence that allows others to grant a face-saving level of deference. That is, we must exceed all expectations to the point that there is no risk of loss of respect among either our subordinates or peers within the wider group by their deferring prominence to us as a higher role in the hierarchy. The degree to which we succeed is the amount of positive respect we earn. For example, if we raise 100% more funds in a given year than any other individual in our charitable organization, others in the group lose no face by deferring to us in the fund-raising domain. This is a clear-cut example, but murkier scenarios are more common. For example, in a matrix-based organization where domains are not functionally delineated, performance-based respect will be more difficult (variability in the circumstances of one group's work make apple-apple comparisons difficult). In these scenarios, competition will be fiercer and behavior generally less congenial. Respect in these scenarios is based on several factors: relative value to the organization, personal integrity, and objectivity. As an aspiring executive, it is critical to demonstrate a model of behavior that engenders respect.

In the competitive arena, personal integrity rarely escapes scrutiny. In political contests, candidates are often judged on this criterion alone. It has been demonstrated over and over that in highly contested competitions, personal integrity will have a great impact on the respect granted by both competitors and spectators. The successful executive will demonstrate exemplary integrity in both their personal and professional life. This is far easier than we are led to believe in modern society. John McCain once gave the following advice to his son upon his arrival at college: “Don’t lie, cheat or steal—anything else is fair game” (CNN, 2009). At the heart of it, personal integrity is rooted in these three rules. We should follow them zealously. Despite our general disgust, ad hominem attacks are extremely effective. As a bulwark against personal attack, the successful executive will follow the simple rules that ensure high integrity. There will be challenges and temptations in this area and we must never underestimate the depths to which some competitors will sink. Our personal integrity—and its perception—must be defended rigorously.

Maintaining objectivity demonstrates maturity and the ability to fairly assess problems in view of current circumstances and reality. Our failure to remain objective will lead to an opportunity for our peers and subordinates to not respect us. Who would defer in decision-making or action to a person who perpetually internalizes external issues and frames issues in terms of their personal impact?

Respect for the executive is dependent upon our performance against factors that can be controlled. There will be hostile situations whereby nothing we do can affect the respect granted by other individuals in the organization. The important point is to remain steadfast in delivering value to the organization, maintaining personal integrity and remaining objective. Individuals who do not grant respect for exemplary performance in these areas will not grant respect to anyone.

The Junior Executive will foster opportunities to gain respect by creating value for their organization, possessing personal integrity and maintaining a strong sense of objectivity.

SLIGHTS

A scene from the movie "Hoffa": Jack Nicholson, playing the notorious Teamster boss, shares the screen with Danny DeVito, playing a confederate of Hoffa's. In the scene, the Teamsters air suspicions that one of their colleagues is potentially relaying their activities to enemies. DeVito's character asks Hoffa why the boss had shared some potentially sensitive information with this colleague in the first place. Hoffa's reply is something all leaders should integrate into their daily interactions with their subordinates. He explains that excluding the suspected colleague from sensitive information would have been taken as a slight: "If a guy's close to you, you can't slight 'im. You can't slight that guy. A real grievance can be resolved; differences can be resolved. But an imaginary hurt, a slight—that motherfucker gonna hate you 'til the day he dies" (DeVito, 1992).

The language is coarse, but the sentiment is dead on. When we slight someone, we treat him or her derisively and without respect. For the majority of people receiving perceived slights, their pride will never again allow them to deal with us fairly. This is particularly true with subordinates. It must be stated clearly: The successful executive must never slight a subordinate. In so doing, we will create an outright enemy with little to no hope of reconciliation—one who will seek us harm either directly or indirectly. Many will simply leave and work for someone else. Regardless of the specific consequences, this is a situation that must be avoided. As such, the advice and guidance is straightforward.

But how does the successful executive handle a situation like the one presented in "Hoffa"? What do we do with subordinates who may not be faithful to our team or the endeavor? There is only one way to deal with such scenarios. The successful executive will bring into confidence carefully chosen individuals. In entrusting sensitive information about our company or product or planning, we will also explain the consequences of breaking that trust directly and clearly. And once we have entrusted another individual, we must hold true to that trust. If they choose to break that trust, it is out of our control.

When a member of the inner circle or even the extended team breaks trust or betrays the team, the consequences can be disastrous. But only under extremely rare circumstances will the consequences prove fatal to a project. Rather, betrayals of trust are always more damaging to the individual betraying trust than to the betrayed group. Any short-term gain achieved by this sort of action is more than offset by the damage to reputation of the individual. Basically, no one who knows how they have acted will ever fully trust them again. They will never again experience the freedom of action and movement that comes with integrity. For the organization, the impact of betrayal can be overcome. If an organization is so fragile as to rely on a single individual's fidelity, then it will likely fall to other, more probable weaknesses.

In these scenarios, if we have managed our team well and have engendered a healthy environment, dealing with consequences is relatively straightforward. When presented with a betrayal, the successful executive will acknowledge it publicly and make clear the impacts. Further, they will explain the plan for mitigation and lay the moral consequences squarely on the betrayer. It should also be made clear that the level and degree of trust in the organization will not change.

The Junior Executive will place the moral imperative of loyalty on the trusted individual and never slight a subordinate.

COALITION BUILDING

Whether we are promoted from within or hired from outside, the root of our authority as an executive is the commonly held belief in our legitimacy. If the majority of colleagues do not believe that we belong in the executive role, we will essentially have no authority. There are myriad reasons for this, examined in part in other chapters. In his excellent book "Chimpanzee Politics: Power and

Sex among Apes," Frans De Waal presents a strong case for the biological roots of our predisposition for assigning authority based upon legitimacy (De Waal, 1984). We will not achieve the executive role nor be successful as an executive if we do not have a coalition of peers, colleagues and subordinates who support us. We will discuss high-minded and low-minded justifications for this, but the main reason is that all major decisions regarding our role in the company will be made without us. That is, the individuals with the power to grant or deny us authority will make that decision without our involvement.

This is the most critical reason to build a coalition within the organization: to become and remain successful we must have individuals within the organization who will defend and support us. This is also important for situations where we are in attendance, but it is mandatory for situations where we are not in attendance. Where we are not able to defend ourselves against doubters and competitors, we are at our most vulnerable. From the executive standpoint, such meetings will prove critical in relation to our advancement, our projects and our prospects.

So, what do we mean by coalition? In the context of the executive, the definition of "coalition" includes individuals who will support our efforts through word and deed for a period of time. This is not a formal arrangement, but rather an expression of affinity for another individual and a willingness to work with them in preference to others—and to take a stake in their advancement or success. This type of coalition is relatively straightforward. Would we rather support a jerk or a decent person in their career? Would we rather support someone with integrity or without? Would we rather support someone with teeth or a milquetoast? Would we rather support someone who will support us and deal fairly on our behalf when asked by others, or someone who will not?

The definition of a coalition may be simple, but building one is not easy. It requires sincerity, political savvy and an objective culture. There are two reasons that individuals build or join coalitions:

defense and offense, both of which are rooted in self-interest. Ultimately, there is no altruism in organizations—empathy and compassion certainly, but no altruism. Thus, especially at the executive rank, there will be a great deal of coalition building, coalitions that are malleable and circumstantial certainly, but coalitions nonetheless. Further, executives will endeavor to build coalitions for both offensive and defensive reasons. In the case of an aspiring executive, a coalition will be offensive. In the case of existing executives, coalitions will be established for both reasons.

Who should be in the offensive coalition of the aspiring executive? The answer is somewhat counterintuitive. Having a competitive peer in our coalition is not likely to help us to be promoted and could very well hurt our chances. Instead, aligning with a trusted subordinate of our competitive peer is highly advantageous. This is particularly true in situations where our competitive peers are prone to dark politics, in that they will be dissuaded from bad behavior for fear of losing legitimacy within their own team. It is also critical to obtain support from other executives who may benefit from our ascension. If we have a good relationship with the executive in charge of Marketing, they may be more eager to work with us in our new role than with our competitor.

Figure 29 - Coalitions are mandatory for pressing forward an agenda and our ascension as an executive.

The Junior Executive will develop the skill of coalition building in support of both offensive and defensive endeavors.

REPUTATION

The majority of the challenges that an executive faces are subtle, subject to interpretation and often tragic—that is, where both sides are arguably in the right. Much will be subject to providence or circumstances, but even more will be subject to active and detailed attention paid to critical matters in the organization and in our own lives. Among these personal matters, reputation ranks very high. It is a reflection of how we are perceived as a person or employee in the organization. It provides strangers an approximation of what to expect when meeting us and a basis for their decision to meet us at all. For those who don't know us, it is us. The same mistake made by someone held in high esteem has a substantially different impact when made by someone held in middling or low esteem. How people choose to interact with us on a day-to-day basis will depend in large part on our reputation.

Much of the material in this book is geared toward ensuring that our output and demeanor are consistent with a good reputation. This chapter is focused on protecting our reputation. In the competitive arena, some individuals will stoop to character assassination. While this behavior will inevitably expose itself, it can inflict considerable damage, particularly in organizations that experience significant turnover in personnel and structure. Character assassins, both clumsy and subtle, must be addressed. This typically involves two modes of behavior: how they attempt to treat us in our presence, and how they can affect our reputation by proxy.

Character assassins who attempt to malign our reputation in our presence are essentially bullies who hope to gain advantage by cowing us into submission. The remedy to this is simple, but requires courage and fortitude. No person can make us feel any particular way and people will most often treat us as we demand to be treated. The successful executive will refuse to be treated in a manner that we find inconsistent with our character or reputation. This is important enough to risk losing a job over. For if we are unsuccessful in protecting our reputation, we will lose that job in short order anyway.

Protecting our reputation in scenarios where we are not present is more difficult. In scenarios where others are discussing us and we are not present, we will be reliant upon the goodwill and respect that we have engendered in others. The talent of the character assassin is a factor in this setting. While they are typically clumsy and easy to spot, some are better at their craft than others. The best and only defense for this is to maintain a sterling reputation. For example, if a character assassin indicates to others that we are always late to meetings and that this means that we are arrogant or disrespectful, it will be easily refuted if we are not late to meetings. This is another reason why the successful executive will ensure that they cultivate a reputation for integrity and honorable behavior.

The Internet is rapidly extending our persona beyond our physical selves. It is an always-on record of who we are, what we do, and what we aspire to as individuals. Menacingly, it is also highly anonymous and subject to rampant abuse. It is relatively simple to anonymously malign a person's reputation on the Internet and the chances of being caught are minimal. As with the defense of our reputation in person, we must be vigilant and hit hard when our reputation is threatened unjustly. Of course, anything posted to the Internet is essentially there forever. That is a great and terrible truth of the medium. The successful executive will take an active interest in their online reputation and will work to control public representations of themselves to the extent possible. They will monitor these representations and ensure that related content is consistent with their reputation.

But what can be done when damaging content is connected with our online persona? It should be handled in much the same manner as our face-to-face interactions. If 99.9% of all online content associated with our persona is consistent with our good reputation, the 0.1% will be easily written-off by those with a non-cursory interest. On the face of it, this should be enough. But in the case of a character assassin, there may be an active campaign against our online reputation, in which case relying on established reputation will not be enough. This is particularly true if the assassin is successful in making these negative associations popular: search engine results, forum posts, etc. Under these circumstances we have two courses of action: short and long-term. In the short term we must contact the owners of the Internet properties where we have been maligned and inform them of the libel. We may remind them of their responsibility as publishers and ask them to remove the content. In parallel, we must counteract the negative content associations by creating positive content associations, which will require time and effort.

The Junior Executive will treat their reputation as a prized asset that must be maintained and vigorously defended.

LIEUTENANTS

Throughout this chapter we have discussed some of the challenges and contextual considerations of the intra-organizational competitive arena. In particular, we have covered concepts that are affected by competition for advancement to the executive role and, to a lesser extent, competition at the executive level. One final concept should be discussed: how to ensure optimal productivity. In an organization, virtually no competition is an end game. That is, most competitions are phases in an ongoing concern. So, it is critical that we consider the aftereffects of competitive engagements. Competition can be damaging to relations within the organization, particularly if extended over a period of time without resolution. Throughout the period of competition for an executive role or within the competitive executive environment, we must maintain positive relationships within the organization for two reasons: lieutenants and tribes.

Groups within an organization develop differentiated attributes that set them apart culturally from other groups within the organization—i.e. tribal characteristics. In a heated competition, groups may be inclined to become derisive toward their rivals along tribal lines. This is how slights on the individual level are projected as slights on the group level—individuals with a tribal mentality project their ego onto the group. Tribal conflict within an organization can be damaging to morale, operational efficiency, and growth. The successful executive will always ensure that intra-organizational competition is fair and objective. Further, all competitive endeavors will be undertaken with full exit planning so that work and operations continue smoothly after resolution. We cannot advance to the executive level by attacking another candidate's group attributes and then expect to work with them effectively afterward. It is often appropriate to highlight differences between groups, but this should not take precedence over ensuring organizational efficiency after the competition. This is especially true in circumstances where the leader of the other group has attacked our group's attributes. Maintaining tribal geniality is not only important for group morale, as future lieutenants may come from other groups.

Everyone wants to be on a winning team that is also fair and honest. By maintaining group integrity through objective and efficient competition, these traits will be conferred upon our group and us. The reward of this resolve comes after the competition, when the best and brightest in other groups will want to join us. In scenarios where reputations have been damaged through rough competition, the individual or group who has maintained steadfast resolve to ensure that the organization continues to operate efficiently will not only enjoy the immediate benefits of success, but will also be a magnet for the talent within the organization.

The Junior Executive will attract the best lieutenants through fair-minded competition and ensuring that group cultures are respected.

Chapter 7 Team

"Have very high expectations of your people and let them live up them."

-Warren Buffett

MICROMANAGEMENT

In general, the practices outlined in this book should help the Junior Executive avoid the expected behavioral pitfalls of management. However, many of the poor behaviors discussed are more nuanced than commonly acknowledged and worth further examination. One such poor behavior is micromanagement, whereby a person in position of authority directs and corrects work of their subordinates to a level of detail that essentially obviates that subordinate. The inefficiencies and resentments caused by this behavior are well documented, and all stem from the core fact that micromanagement removes the individual impact of the person being managed. But there are some instances where a measure of micromanagement is not only necessary but beneficial.

We are concerned with an appropriate use of micromanagement and how knee-jerk avoidance of it leads to confusion, disjointed teams and high-risk activities. Our deep involvement in a mundane set of tasks assigned to a subordinate will remove their personal impact and cause damage. However, this kind of deep involvement can be extremely useful and lead to great efficiencies when applied appropriately. There are two essential scenarios that call for a degree of micromanagement: initial setting of expectations and work of high uncertainty.

As a new executive, we must set expectations for the quality of our team's work. This can be a source of great consternation and confusion among our team as they seek to modify their outputs and style of working to our expectations. In times where new expectations are set, it is critical that the successful executive take a granular interest in their team's work. This is not to endorse a dictatorial style, but to highlight the importance of the alignment of responsibilities within the organization. This time of micromanagement should be collaborative to the point of ensuring an environment where feedback is rewarded. But we must employ force of will to ensure that our vision is expressed through the expectations we have as a leader. As an executive, we have responsibility for every aspect of the team outputs in all circumstances—not just the core product itself. E-mail formats, document formats, use of terms, use of colors, level of polish, etc. If we do not micromanage our team during a period of expectation setting, they will not fully understand those expectations. Until they do, our team's output will suffer. The successful executive appropriately micromanages their team during times when expectations for outputs must be set. It is important to note that this period of micromanagement must be openly acknowledged so that the team understands that it is necessary and temporary.

A second scenario where we see micromanagement as appropriate and required is times where the team is involved in work of great uncertainty and importance. These times are rare in most well-functioning organizations and should be noted as such by demonstrating unsustainable levels of focus and work time. During times like these, it is incumbent upon us to be deeply involved in as much detail as possible for a number of reasons. First, without an intimate understanding of important work, we will be unable to properly assess and communicate the impacts of crucial decisions that may be made. The second reason for micromanagement during work of great uncertainty and importance is that rapid decisions will need to be made based on a large number of unknown parameters and intuition. As the executive, we must ensure that our subordinates have as much guidance and direction as possible to ensure that they are not frozen by uncertainty. Without a degree of micromanagement, suboptimal decisions may be made and the overall team and organization will suffer.

In general, micromanagement of subordinates is damaging and

inefficient. However, these two scenarios demonstrate a benefit to this type of deep and overbearing involvement by a leader. The successful executive will avoid micromanagement during the course of regular work in the organization and enforce a policy of personal responsibility with the two notable exceptions of setting expectations and handling work of great importance and uncertainty.

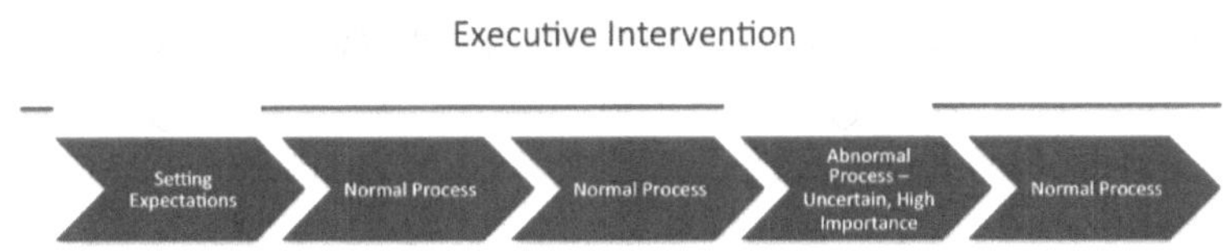

Figure 30 - Executive micromanagement is a benefit in specific circumstances.

The Junior Executive will avoid micromanagement except in cases of initial expectation setting and during work of great importance.

SET THE TONE

As an executive, our behaviors and expectations, both stated and unstated, will serve as the model by which group members conduct themselves. We must set the tone for acceptable behaviors within our team, given that the outputs of the team will be the measure of our value to the organization. We have discussed how a large measure of the value delivered by our team is derived from the environment that we create as the executive. As the executive in charge of this group, we have a personal relationship to them. This should be reflected in the goals and vision that we have laid out for the group, but it must also be reflected in the tone of the aligned work of our subordinates. This is not an easy task and requires fortitude. If it is not implemented successfully, we will not likely maintain the executive role or advance. Why should we personally succeed or advance if we personally cannot make our mark?

The executive role is a journey. Without other aspects of the fundamentals already understood, our advice to set the tone could be misinterpreted and implemented in a dictatorial manner. Successful senior leaders do set the tone, sometimes ruthlessly, but we must also embody the work. How we set the tone will be highly subject to circumstances and the makeup of our team. For example, if many of our subordinates have already reported to us previously, it should be relatively easy to signal any adjustment to tone. When working with new hires, we will rely on the groundwork that has been done with our existing team, as they can provide many necessary signals to the new team members. Some general notions on tone-setting follow.

> **Non Ad Hominem**: We must never make a critique of a subordinate's work a judgment of their personal worth. It is very common for tone to infer personal judgment. The successful executive will focus all attention on the quality of the work only. We should aspire to the advice of Colin Powell to "surround yourself with people who take their work seriously, but not themselves." Further, we must signal to our team that personal judgments are not tolerated by anyone. This is a substantial step in opening the collaborative spirit in the team.
>
> **Excellence**: We should not hesitate to insist that our subordinates rework an output. This is the only way that they will achieve excellence. There are several constraints: The successful executive will take time to ensure that the level of critique is consistent with the experience level of the given subordinate. There should be little tolerance for their making the same mistake more than once. Any output should be received with the implicit question, "Is this your best work?"

Empathy: There are few attitudes more damaging to an organization than demonization on the part of an individual or a team toward another individual or group. One of the most important traits an executive can demonstrate is the ability to empathize with others. It shows to our subordinates that will we grant them that benefit and that we have control of our environment. Individuals and teams who demonize others demonstrate a lack of control and imagination as well as unwarranted arrogance. As an executive, we will do well to set a tone of empathy among our team.

These are only two selected attributes. The organization is a complex entity that encompasses the full range of human emotion and interactive drama. We must serve as a rock within this chaos by setting the tone within our teams.

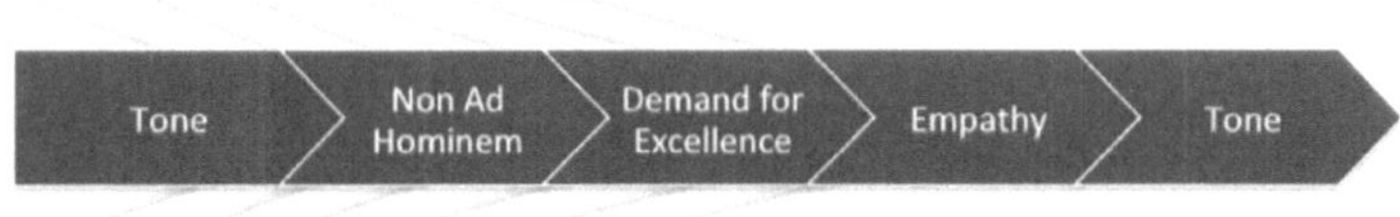

Figure 31 - Through disciplined interaction with our teams, we will set the tone by which work is completed and optimize team alignment.

The Junior Executive will work intelligently to set the tone within their team to ensure focus on outputs, excellence in quality and an empathetic view.

LINES OF INQUIRY

Many individuals and organizations rightly view change as an opportunity to further their cause. As a new executive, we will represent such an opportunity to both external and internal parties. This presents a challenge for us in the early days as the ripples of change fade, particularly in how we handle inbound information. As a new executive, we will encounter many untruths and half-truths. This is not a cynical view, but a practical one. We will discuss aspects of information management related to intelligence gathering and processing in a later chapter. How we process this information into action is our concern here. How do we avoid being manipulated by others seeking to further their cause? The successful executive will develop an evaluative style for lines of inquiry that leverages deductive reasoning (e.g., detective work). Organizational work is not a crime scene, but there is a great deal of value in employing a proven method of sorting incoming information. This is particularly true in cases where another person suggests a course of action or attempts to induce a course of action. Deductive reasoning is also extremely useful in evaluating the actions of our subordinates to avoid prima facie judgments.

So, what are these lines of inquiry? Essentially, they seek the same information that would be used in investigating a crime: motive, means, opportunity and most importantly, intent.

> **Motive**: Given what we know about the actor (individual or team), the circumstances, the environment, and reward flow, what is the motive of the action that we are evaluating? How good is our intelligence on these questions? Do we fully understand the circumstances or environment? Motive is particularly difficult in the organizational context because the reward flow may not be easily traceable—that is, what rewards could be gained from which actions, in which sequence. Is one of our subordinates telling us about the misdeeds of a colleague out of concern for the team or to further their own standing in our eyes? Is a colleague

offering to assist in a customer meeting to help win the business or to wedge into our relationship and move the customer to their portfolio? By evaluating what we know of the actor (are they passive-aggressive, forthright, proud, arrogant, sneaky, a coward, etc.?) in light of the circumstances of the action, and the environment, we can make a judgment as to their motive. This will be an imperfect analysis and should be weighted as such. But in lieu of perfect information, ours is a solid approach. The successful executive will always evaluate the actions of others in light of a likely motive.

Means: This is relatively straightforward and reflects the level of intelligence we have about the actor in question. Do they have the means to carry out the action suggested? If so, then we must take the proposed action somewhat seriously. If they lack the means to carry out the action, then why has the action been attributed to them or why are they suggesting the action?

Opportunity: Does the actor have the opportunity to execute the action? If a subordinate is asking for funding authority to initiate a piece of work in the next month, do they have the actual opportunity to complete it? Do they have a customer for that piece of work? Or are they empire building? If a potential rival is sending signals that they might have a new product to offer our customer, do they have the opportunity to offer it (e.g., a channel into the customer or a relationship with the decision maker there)? If so, then this potential action represents a threat that must be addressed. If not, addressing the issue could be a waste of time and resources. For the executive, evaluating opportunities in this manner will provide valuable insights as to where to allocate resources or attention.

Intent: The question of intent is critical when mistakes are made or risks are recommended. What was the intent of the individual when the mistake was made? How confident are we in our understanding of their intent? The same questions hold true for evaluations of recommendations that incur risk. What is the intent in recommending this? Intent is a close cousin to motive in that it deals with the underlying motivations of actions, but it is more nuanced in that it seeks a moral attribution. That is, was the intent good or bad? Consider a drug dealer tipping off police about the criminal activity of a rival. The informant's intent is to remove their rival from the market rather than assist the law, and thus stains what might otherwise be a commendable action. The new executive must accept that intent is frequently not good and often solipsistic. The challenge for the new executive is to understand when intent is good and to treat individuals and organizations as such when mistakes happen.

Much like newborn animals in the wild, the new executive is more vulnerable than their mature counterparts. Other individuals, groups or organizations will seek to take advantage of this situation. It is critical that we implement a solid and reliable line of inquiry when considering the actions and recommendations of others.

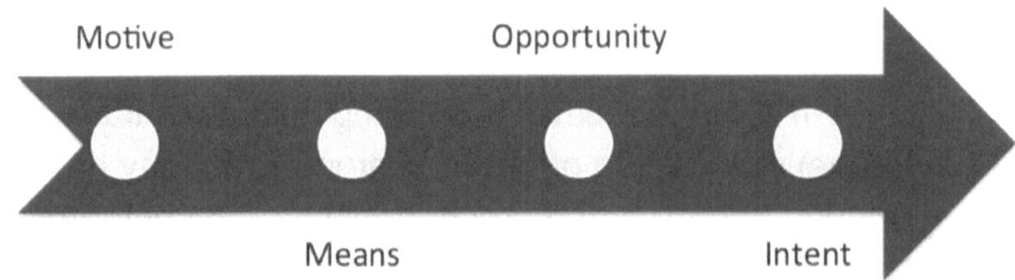

Figure 32 - The successful executive will make a strong habit of using lines of inquiry to evaluate inbound information.

The Junior Executive will establish a standard line of inquiry to evaluate the motive, means, opportunity and intent of others to seek greater confidence in their decisions.

VOICE AND DIGNITY

If we create an environment of mutual respect, our staff will possess voice and dignity. We will review these qualities in a situation that will be very common for most executives—multi-generational teams. As an executive, we will typically be older than many of our team members, but often we will be younger—in some cases, much younger. This can present a variety of challenges to us as the leader. The issue is rooted in a trait common to the majority of cultures—deference to those older than ourselves. This deference is so engrained that individuals who do not adhere to it are often ostracized. So how do we execute as a demanding, driven leader across a team that includes individuals to whom we have an instinctual deference? Outside of the level of confidence that we have in our position, there is one key point of consideration: the level of emotional maturity of the older staff member.

In many cases, an older staff member will have accepted that they are unlikely to advance in the organization and will focus on excellence in their current position. We see this with individuals in roles that are "senior" but not managerial. Organizationally, these individuals are crucial assets that provide continuity through organizational changes and serve as subject-matter experts for the core functions of the organization. In more unfortunate cases, an older staff member will resent their lack of advancement and generally carry a negative bias toward a new superior (it is worth noting that many individuals in organizations are negatively biased toward a new superior, regardless of age). In any case, the challenge for the executive is to accurately gauge the level of resentment and its likely expression. Subordinates who are outright mutinous must be fired. More difficult are those individuals who are maliciously compliant—that is, they will comply with the new order but will seek ways to subvert their new superiors. Of course, all individuals working with a new supervisor will fall across a spectrum, from the trusted senior employee to the borderline mutinous. Many new executives fall into the trap of attempting to tailor an approach to each unique individual. As we have noted in previous chapters, it is imperative for the executive to establish an environment whereby individuals can excel. Tailoring an individual approach or attempting to weed out subversives is a major distraction from the real work of the team and a sign of failure.

First and foremost, the successful executive will ensure that the accepted behaviors and environment of the team are based on a foundation of moral authority. We must behave in a manner that is exemplary of the morals and ethics that we expect from our team. If we expect senior employees to set aside their cultural encoding and accept us as a leader, we must acknowledge their worth irrespective of relative status. This means trusting them. Further, it means trusting them enough to explain our rationale and include them in the decision-making process. By including all employees in our plans and thinking, we demonstrate a culture of trust. We grant to our team and especially older employees a voice in decisions and influence on the team's work. By including them in this discussion, we grant them a level of dignity that any individual craves—belief that they have value to offer to the team.

As a new executive, we will likely inherit and build a multi-generational team. This will present significant challenges that must be addressed by the environment that we establish for acceptable behavior. Poor behaviors, such as a dictatorial style or insensitivity to the individual, may be tolerated by younger employees. But older employees will seek to punish this type of behavior. It is best practice to demonstrate the moral and ethical behaviors that are the bedrock of basic human dignity. By including our subordinates in our decision-making and rationale, we grant them a voice in the direction of their working life.

The Junior Executive will craft an environment where everyone has a voice and receives dignity through honest acknowledgement of the value they bring to the team.

DEFENSE

Very often, executives develop a callousness toward subordinates. In the majority of instances this is not some sort of overt, malicious disdain or cruel attitude. Rather, it is a lightly dismissive tint toward individuals who are of a lower rank and is typically expressed through demeaning humor. However, it can express to a larger degree whereby executives will be overtly harsh with other executives' team members. These behaviors are prevalent in many organizations to some varying degree. None are acceptable.

These particular behaviors present an opportunity to directly impact a negative event and demonstrate our commitment to our principles. Objecting to demeaning comments about subordinates requires courage, especially for the newly minted executive, given asymmetries of power. However, we suggest that it is actually easier for the new executive, given that there is typically no other precedent of behavior upon which to judge our commitment to values. That is, if we demand that our team members are treated with dignity when an opportunity presents itself, our demand will most likely be accepted. If our objection is executed well, it sets the tone for future interactions.

We should examine how another person's ill treatment of one of our subordinates relates to us as the executive. In the organizational context, the executive has a pastoral relationship to their subordinates. When we see a situation where a fellow executive is mistreating our team, we have a duty to respond. But why exactly?

For two reasons: an enforcement of morality associated with dignity and an aggressive defense as policy. Human dignity is an inalienable right—defense of such is required of all decent people. All individuals should be defended from abuse. That is well and good, but a bit lofty for practical purposes. The far more mundane reason for defending the dignity of our subordinates is that a derogatory attack on one of them is an indirect attack on us. If another executive is dismissive or demeaning to one of our subordinates, they are essentially conferring that damage upon us. If they respected us, they would not demean our staff. This is the practical reason for defending the dignity of our team members. There are few other situations that allow us to directly and forcefully act from the moral high ground, especially when on the weak side of an asymmetrical power situation. The successful executive will defend the dignity of their subordinates because it is the right thing to do and because it allows them to directly attack instances of disrespect by other executives.

There can be some consequences to this behavior. Namely, it risks alienating us from the individuals guilty of the demeaning actions. This could be a good or bad thing, depending on the circumstances of our organization. If the majority of the executive team favors a demeaning disposition, then we will eventually have to compromise our morals and join them to some degree or leave the organization. This is not a binary. There will be significant uncertainty and variability in the behaviors of the team. It will be our challenge to determine the appropriate responses. In some cases, declining to join in these kinds of behaviors is sufficient to quell their nastier aspects. In others, more direct action is required that may result in a confrontation. It is important to remember that dignity is worth fighting for in any circumstance, but we must weigh the underlying intent of demeaning behavior to understand if they are indeed an attack on an individual's dignity.

Dignity is incredibly important to an individual. There will be many openings for morally weak and cruel individuals to express their underlying failings by attacking the dignity of our subordinates and ourselves. These moments will be a test of our fortitude as a new executive. In any case, to not defend dignity is to open our team and ourselves to subsequent abuse and disrespect.

The Junior Executive will aggressively defend the dignity of their team members.

ATTITUDE VS. EXPERTISE

One of the more common mistakes that a new executive will make is spending an inordinate amount of time perfecting their organization chart. We will obsess over identifying roles with extremely specific attributes and seek perfect fits for these positions. Such mistakes often come from inexperience, but are also frequently a byproduct of the initial phase itself. The new executive has little time for training or taking hiring risks. In hiring our team, we will often be faced with the following choice: attitude and intelligence versus expertise. The reason for this is relatively simple: individuals with the specific expertise we require will be rare and much more likely to have some significant negative attributes—unavailable, too expensive, difficult to work with, etc. We will avoid discussion of the "rarity of specialty" aspect, given that it is outside our realm of control. Rather, we are concerned with the decision to hire an expert versus a novice. Some points of consideration:

Raw Intelligence: It is generally acknowledged that an individual of average intelligence requires approximately 10 years of experience to become an expert in a particular discipline. That is, there are few jobs (e.g., astrophysicist) that most people cannot master with dedication over a decade. Even in many specialized jobs, an average person can very likely at least obtain a competency through focused work. When considering a novice versus an expert, one key question is our assessment of their raw intelligence. If we are interviewing an expert in this job, the question of raw intelligence is still important, but not necessarily paramount. They need to be smart and intellectually curious. However, we also assume that in this case, the expert has some other negative qualities. Thus, the question the level of raw intelligence in the novice we are considering. How much time can they shave off the 10 years? The answer to this is important when we think about changes in the discipline in the next 10 years. An expert at this point in time has learned the discipline over the preceding decade-plus. Will they maintain that learning curve going forward? Could the novice overtake them in the next 2–5 years, as the discipline evolves? Very often, a novice with a high degree of raw intelligence is far more valuable from a mid-to-long-term standpoint than an expert.

Proximity of Need: An important consideration in the hiring question is the proximity of need. That is, how quickly do we need this role operating at full capacity? To clarify, the core question is not when we need the role filled—a hire with a solid educational background and a high degree of raw intelligence can perform adequately for a short period of time. Rather, the question is when we need the role operating at full capacity. If that need is immediate, then we must seriously consider overlooking any negative attributes of the expert in order to fulfill this proximity of need. Does the pinnacle of this role's output need to be delivered immediately or is there time to grow a person into the role? The successful executive will consider the practical need for expertise in a role versus the time needed to grow a novice into the position.

Attitude: The right attitude is absolutely critical for all team members. The best-case scenario is an expert with a great attitude; but expert candidates very often have some deficiencies in attitude. These shortcomings are a common decision point in hiring a novice. Experts very often carry baggage with them, gathered through their experience, which may make them difficult to integrate into the team. The charm of a novice lies in their lack of baggage. So how do we evaluate attitude—good or bad—in potential hires? Luckily, there are some telltale signs of a great attitude that can be determined through open-ended and Socratic questioning. How does the candidate deal with a problem? If their answer does not convey in some form "I will never bring you a problem without a suggested solution," then we know that we will have a problem training them quickly. Another excellent point of consideration is how they deal with uncertainty. If their answer does not convey in some form "there are no blocks, just hurdles to overcome," then we know that we will have a problem with them. Finally, they will need to provide good examples of their innate need to internalize responsibility. Without this, every failing will become a setback rather than a learning experience. In the end, when considering attitude in a novice versus an expert the key attributes are resiliency and energy. The successful executive will seek candidates who are resilient to challenges and energetic about achievement.

Maturity of Team and Organization: Some mature organizations are very ill-suited to novices, and some immature organizations are very ill-suited to experts—and vice versa on both scores. The successful executive will spend considerable thought and analysis on understanding how well a possible new hire can integrate with the team and broader organization in relation to their level of expertise. Would more experienced team members be offended or threatened by a novice? Or would they take on a mentoring attitude? The outcome is directly tied to the culture of the organization, but there is no easy answer. Much like an organ transplant in the body, even a potentially life-saving new hire may be rejected. The successful executive will ensure that their choice will be set up for success in the team and broader organization, based upon the prevalent culture and level of maturity.

Very often, taking on a position as an executive will require expanding, integrating and growing a team of subordinates. Hiring is obviously of importance in those processes. The effectiveness of our team will directly and significantly impact new employees' performance. Thus, we will take great care in hiring and integrating them effectively.

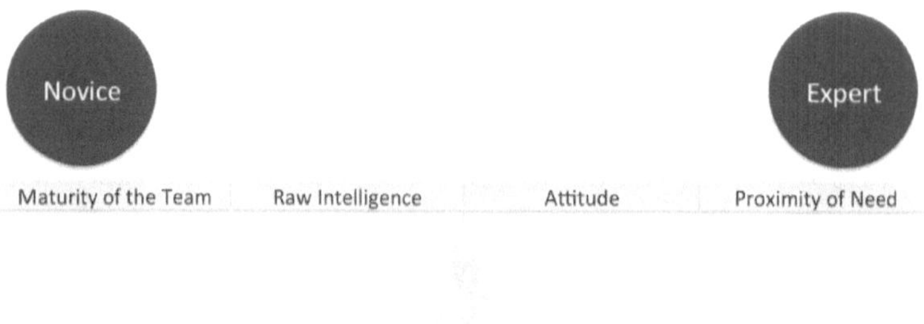

Figure 33 - Several key factors weigh our decision to hire a novice versus an expert.

The Junior Executive will consider raw intelligence, proximity of need, attitude and the maturity of the organization in determining the suitability of candidates.

COMPENSATION

Compensation is a sensitive and complex topic of discussion, and there is much debate as to the merits of one approach versus another, and even on the nature of compensation itself. In general, there are two bases for compensation: reward for showing up (loyalty) and reward for achievement (leveraged benefit). The common discussion of compensation is typically misguided in that it focuses on compensation as a top-level goal, which it is not—even for commissioned salespeople. Top-level goals of individuals are fundamentally ego-focused: respect, knowledge, power, security, etc. These goals are derived symptomatically from lower level goals, and compensation is a prime example. An individual is less concerned about the cash value of the compensation than about what that cash value implies with regard to their top-level goals—respect, security, etc.

A single person with no dependents will focus much more on knowledge or power than security. As such, their point of view toward compensation will markedly differ from that of a person with two small children at home. The compensation packages for these two individuals should also differ in recognition of their respective top-level goals. However, in the majority of organizations their package will be the same, due to the complex nature of compensation in society at large. So how does the successful executive approach this delicate and complicated question? As always, we favor practical approaches based upon a first principle. In this case, we must find an acceptable common denominator of compensation and adjust via a system that considers the varying circumstances of our employees.

During the initial phases of our tenure as an executive we should spend time with the relevant human resources representatives reviewing the compensation levels of our direct reports and their teams. Many new executives accept the existing policy or offload it entirely to human resources. This is a mistake and deflective in nature. An executive with the power to hire and fire individuals must be able to change policy and speak intelligently about the compensation policies of their organization. Once we have a clear understanding of how the organization manages compensation, we can adjust our strategy. If we think about compensation temporally, it encompasses two frames of time across two bases of purpose. Thus, there are four components of compensation that must be addressed:

> **Base**: Base pay is the familiar bedrock of any person's financial life. For an hourly employee, base pay is their hourly wage. For the salaried worker, it is their annual salary. The level of base pay is dictated by market forces that are essentially out of our control. We should rely heavily on our human resources representatives or other experts to determine the appropriate level of base pay allotted to an individual role. There is some flexibility in this component that is worth discussing. Many compensation experts recommend that employers pay at the top of the scale or even overpay for individuals. The reasoning is that this will secure the best talent as well as demonstrating an expected

level of performance that the individual must live up to. There may be some truth to this, but we think it relies too much on hope and not enough on practical application. Our recommendation is that the level of base pay for most employees, and particularly new employees, should be at or below average. Base pay simply provides a reason for the employee show up. There are other compensation components that will boost a mediocre base pay into an overall package that is above average.

The level of base pay should be tempered by a number of considerations specific to our organization and the individual. What is the expected level of growth for our organization? A general rule of thumb is that growth and base pay are inversely related. That is, a low growth rate would dictate a higher base level of pay. The risk-aversion disposition of the individual is also relevant here. A general rule of thumb is that risk aversion and base pay are correlated. That is, a high level of risk aversion calls for a higher level of base pay (there are several indicators of risk aversion, but it should be discussed openly with prospective employees). This is an important consideration, given that many individuals will plan their personal budgets based upon the base level of pay. The base level of pay is the basis for an individual to show up every day and do work. It is important, but only one component of the overall compensation package that should be considered.

Near-Term Incentive: Near-term incentive compensation refers to the ability of the executive to use cash to influence behavior. Bonuses are common in many organizations and with good reason. Bonuses typically are either structured or unstructured. Structured bonuses are sales commissions, annual bonuses tied to a percentage of base pay or some other systematic calculation (e.g., Management by Objectives). Unstructured bonuses are merit bonuses, holiday bonuses or any other unsystematic calculation. We do not recommend unstructured bonuses, as the associated benefits are virtually impossible to calculate or integrate into planning. Whereas base pay is used to secure the presence of an individual at work, bonuses are used to secure leveraged benefits of the individual—that is, outputs higher than the mean expected. If our planning has indicated a certain level of achievement for the year, exceeding that level through extra effort is incentivized by additional compensation. There is a further, often-unacknowledged purpose behind the structured bonus. It establishes targets for individual performance that, if crafted properly, will yield greater organizational performance (individually-controlled goal achievement yielding greater performance than company-wide goals). We must exercise discipline in setting targets; a lackadaisical performance-measurement process is a frequent pitfall. What if a team is operating at an optimal level of performance but the bonus targets were unrealistic or external events obstructed achievement? It is extraordinarily demoralizing for individuals working on a bonus compensation scheme to fail to achieve a bonus. This is a scenario where we can easily lose employees. So how does the successful executive leverage the real and substantial benefits of bonus-related compensation? Our answer is a more frequent assessment of targets and bonus packages. If we craft a compensation package comprised of low base pay and large bonuses, it is foolhardy to only evaluate targets and performance on an annual basis. It is far better to acknowledge the considerable unknowns in the organizational context and evaluate both targets and individual performance on a quarterly or even monthly basis, with weekly checkups. Not only does this more fully engage the employee in the process of target-based compensation, but it also allows us to adjust targets nearer to reality and our goals. The main reason many organizations do not do this is because of the administrative burden associated. It is up to the executive to leverage the tools available to overcome thls burden. The successful executive will ensure that performance-based compensation is a major part of the overall compensation package of their employees and is frequently measured and adjusted to maximize leveraged achievement.

Long-Term Security: A third component of the overall compensation package is long-term security. What are the policies and benefits available to employees for the long-term? It should be readily acknowledged that employees are no longer likely to work for the same organization for a significant portion of their career. However, our organization will be some part of their career and we must provide benefits that are long-term in nature. From our perspective, there are no special considerations with regard to long-term security. It is enough to say that it must be at the expected norm of the organization type and job role. 401(k) schemes, IRAs, etc. are all standard and portable. The successful executive will ensure that their employees' compensation packages include an appropriate long-term security component.

Long-Term Incentive: The final compensation package component is often referred to as "golden handcuffs." The intention of long-term incentive compensation is to tie an employee's future benefits to their involvement in the firm. In the majority of cases, this means a package where the employee will attain some level of ownership in the organization. This could be evergreen stock options or more direct employee ownership. In any case, compensation at this scale will likely not be under the control or influence of the junior executive. Rather, we must ensure that it is considered as part of the overall compensation package of our employees and is reflected as such in communication around compensation.

Compensation is a complex area and difficult to implement perfectly.

It is the culmination of not only labor market conditions, but the psychologies of the organization and the individual. The successful executive will thoughtfully consider the variables associated with the individuals on their teams and the labor market in general. We will ensure that the compensation packages of our employees favor enhanced rewards based upon performance to leverage achievement and attract those who are motivated by achievement. The successful executive will ensure that the long-term interests of their employees are served by their compensation package. In total, the compensation packages we offer and deliver to our employees must provide a reason for loyalty to the organization on a daily basis and a lever for achieving beyond expectations for reward. Finally, we will ensure that compensation packages are reviewed and adjusted frequently.

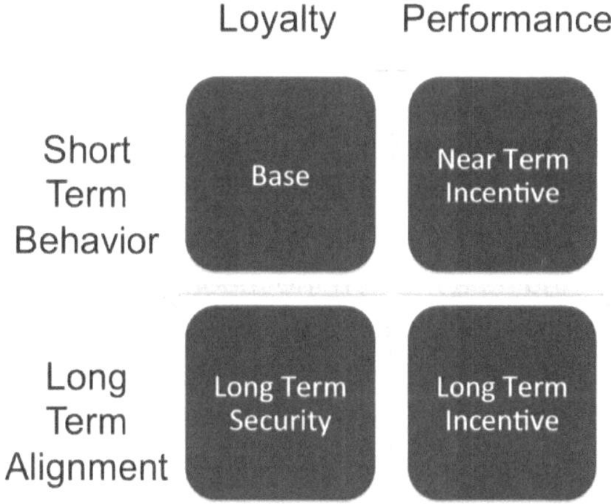

Figure 34 - Compensation is comprised of both time and purpose elements that must be considered in aggregate.

The Junior Executive will craft compensation packages that provide appropriate weighting to Base, Near-Term Incentive, Long-Term Security and Long-Term Incentive components.

GRAND CAPER

Inspiring people requires enormous energy and attention. The typical advice to new leaders (more energy!) to inspire their team is virtually impossible to implement reliably. Although some individuals have a talent, either innate or trained, for inspiring people, they are the exception. We need to better understand the root of inspiration and how it can be leveraged as simply as possible for the benefit of the team and ourselves.

So, what is inspiration? It is the excitement associated with the undiscovered country—a realization that the work we are doing as an individual will yield a transcendent reward. In essence, inspiration is a self-defining aspect of our work. The benefits of inspiration are significant: optimal motivation, imperviousness to privation, and persistent optimism. Inspiration allows individuals to break free of normal constraints and achieve outsized results. Inspiration that yields such outsized results should be a goal of the successful executive.

A project that is intrinsically inspiring is a rare event. For those lucky enough to find such a project, the burden of work is often much lighter. If we look at great historical feats, like the mapping of the human genome or landing a man on the moon, we see that these projects and their promised outputs produced inherent external inspiration to the individuals involved. Even more, the individuals involved were able to derive transcendental meaning from the work even though their specific roles may have been minor.

This is a rare scenario in the organizational context. Most individuals are involved in work that is frequently mundane and results in incremental and middling outputs. So how can the successful executive inspire? If we understand that inspiration is attributed to the ego through attachment to an external result that represents a transcendental achievement, we see that an external result must be created as the first order of business. Thus, inspiration is not a program or scheme to motivate individuals through willful determination. Most everyone can see through these schemes and they often backfire to the point of salting the earth. To inspire individuals in the organizational context, the successful executive must create an external transcendental achievement. This has been referred to as a BHAG (big, hairy, audacious, goal) that, if achieved, would confer great benefit (Collins & Porras, 1994). This is well and good, if implemented honestly. But we recommend a more practical approach to this concept—the grand caper. The grand caper supplies many of the requirements for inspiration: A transcendental goal is to be achieved through the caper, standard procedures are to be exploited for achievement and there are great spoils to be earned. The result itself is not what is important—it is the psychological benefit conferred upon the individual that matters. A person who achieves this transcendental goal is someone to be admired. By viewing established goals as a grand caper, we automatically confer upon the team the benefit of the association: that we chose to include them in this caper means that we believe they have the necessary qualities to achieve this outsized goal. Further, by contextualizing goals in this manner, we make them visceral. No one is inspired to achieve a widget target of 1,000 units produced this month. But, everyone is inspired to develop the new processes that delivered 1,050 widgets against all odds in time to save the plant. The successful executive will contextualize their transcendental goals for a team in the manner of a grand caper. We will ensure that all team members understand that they were chosen especially for this team.

This type of approach relies on all of the concepts reviewed up to this point. If we (or our team members) are lacking in trust or integrity, it is wasted effort. If we acknowledge that most work is often mundane, we will contextualize it in a manner that allows all team members to feel as though they are part of a special project.

The Junior Executive will develop external, transcendental goals that can be achieved through a grand caper.

POLITE, FIRM, FAIR

The level of rude and disrespectful behavior engaged in by many executives is staggering. The underlying causes are many, but typically center around two nodes: insecurity and arrogance. In this section, we will discuss the root causes of these negative nodes, the gravitational pressure that pulls many to them and the importance in resisting such corrupting behavior. Polite, firm and fair behavior is absolutely essential to a well-functioning team. This is particularly important as individuals gain more power in choosing with whom they work. These positive behaviors are essential to maintaining an environment that engenders trust, risk-taking and congeniality. In the near-term, rudeness and disrespect will decimate productivity as individuals become distracted by interpersonal drama. If someone is rude to us in the hallway, how much time and thought do we waste thinking about it? What if they needed something from us later? Even with the thickest of skin, we will lose time and productivity this way. Further, given the opportunity for revenge, the vast majority of individuals will take it. Now multiply these effects across our team and the entire organization. Rude and disrespectful behavior is hugely wasteful—and has longer-term impacts on an organization.

A culture of pervasive rude and disrespectful behavior will eventually turn into a self-selecting organism. That is, individuals who do not need to put up with bad behavior will move on. The organization will gain a reputation that causes many people, particularly high-performers who have no cause to put up with poor behavior, to avoid the organization. Of course, there are anecdotes about high-performers often being difficult themselves, but these are often sensationalized anomalies. The majority of high-performers in any organization are productive because they get the best from their colleagues and themselves through congenial behaviors. We should note the exception of putting a high performer into a team of underachievers—often this is a recipe for problems.

Rude behavior is a pervasive rot that does great damage to both individuals within an organization and to the organization as a whole. It also raises costs substantially—higher turnover and lower productivity are direct effects. As noted above, there are two common nodes of bad behavior in organizations and at the executive level in particular: insecurity and arrogance. We will discuss arrogance first as it is the simpler of the two. Some individuals, upon achieving a certain level of success, begin to internalize that success into their egocentric view of the world. Because they have achieved success in some contest, they see their core worth as individuals as greater than others around them. This node of behavior is less damaging than insecurity, mostly due to the general level of sophistication of modern workers. That is, an arrogant person is obvious and known to all. Their behavior can have many negative consequences. The most common is an overconfidence in the ability to deliver. Arrogant behavior often results in missed deadlines and finger-pointing. When arrogant individuals miss their delivery, they begin a heated campaign to assign blame for the failure on some other party. This is a waste of time, goodwill and the resources involved in remedying the missed delivery. Worst of all, it can lead to a lingering and pervasive problem within the organization. All of these serve to decrease productivity and increase costs. Further, arrogance will serve to significantly decrease cooperation and destroy morale associated with overachievement. If we look at this psychologically, we see that the inflated ego of an arrogant person seeking to dominate the egos of others will yield a fight-or-flight response—neither of which is productive in the organizational sense. The challenge with arrogance is that it is actually a mutated growth of a good trait—confidence. Very often well-behaved individuals will, with consistent achievement over time, actually begin to believe in their greater fundamental worth. As a successful executive, we must continually evaluate how our confidence appears to others. A clear indicator of a problem is rude or disrespectful treatment of anyone.

Insecurity of position is the second primary node of bad behavior. This is particularly associated with the executive level. Individuals who are insecure in their position will often act in a rude or dismissive manner. This is a defense mechanism that signals that the executive is a bit dangerous—much like a barking dog. The insecure ego seeks to defend itself against potential enemies by ensuring that everyone around fears their possible harshness or cruel words. This may seem trivial or silly but it is not. There is a large amount of incidental bullying of this type in most organizations. From the egocentric perspective of the perpetrator, it is extremely effective in many circumstances. To those who are aware of the underlying cause, such bullying is a demonstration of a weakness of character. The organizational impact is negative in both the near and long terms. For the rank-and-file individuals in the organization, this type of behavior will establish a threatening environment—risks will not be taken, questions will not be asked and individuals will throw up defensive walls. Bullying is a bit like being the first person to bring a gun into town. Eventually, everyone else needs to get one, and eventually one needs to be fired. Longer term, allowing such individuals to remain in the organization and behave in this manner will create the same sort of self-selection scheme as noted in our discussion of arrogance. High performers will see it a mile away and will avoid our team and organization. Costs will go up and productivity will go down.

Insecurity is a particularly problematic trait for newly minted executives. As a new executive, we will be insecure—probably greatly so. Executives who eventually fail often start down that road through insecurity. It is incredibly important to acknowledge our own insecurity and address it in a forthright manner. Further, we should monitor and measure our general level of insecurity over time to understand how we are maturing as an executive. Lingering insecurity is exhausting and we cannot maintain an executive level of performance with a high degree of insecurity.

So how does the successful executive manage and control for these two nodes of bad behavior? As with many strategies noted in this book, we rely on objectivity and maturity. The best approach to dealing with arrogance in others and ourselves is objective analysis of output. The concern is not how fast we or some other person can get a job done, but how fast it can be done at all. This is a subtle but crucial shift in outlook. As a successful executive, we must remove ego from consideration of performance. This separates the task from the individuals so that they may judge their own performance against the task rather than being judged by us or the group regarding their underlying worth. The successful executive will ensure that work and outputs are analyzed and evaluated in objective terms that neutralize the individual egos involved.

Insecurity of position is difficult to manage in others and ourselves. Addressing it directly amounts to peeling the onion of a person's psyche and is unlikely to yield real results. Rather, discipline in our behavior and the behaviors that we demand from others is the best approach to managing insecurity. By controlling the tone of communication, we remove the opportunity for insecurity of position to corrupt the process. The successful executive will ensure that all communication at all times is polite, firm and fair. By so doing, we send the message that we are secure in our position and that we will not denigrate ourselves through base behavior. There is a temptation to respond in kind to rude or disrespectful behavior, but it is bait. The successful executive will never resort to rude or disrespectful behavior in relation to others in the organization. It is unlikely that we see a change in the communication style of other executives immediately, if ever. But, by taking the bait and responding in kind to rude behaviors, the situation will most certainly get worse.

The Junior Executive will be polite, firm and fair in their dealings and communication and demand the same of their team.

PRODUCTIVITY

As a new executive, we will very often need to make decisions and execute work based upon abstract and nebulous plans that do not necessarily have a basis in tangible milestones or tasks. For some, this can be extremely disconcerting and prove beyond their capacity. This ambiguity results from the fact that we, as executives, are not directly responsible for lower-level work. Rather, we ensure that it gets done and is rolled into higher-level outputs to achieve abstract goals for which we are directly responsible. Much of this book is groundwork for dealing with this abstraction of work and output. For executives who have leapfrogged the management level, it will be difficult to understand the complexity of this issue. For those who moved up through the management ranks it will be less of a challenge but still require dedicated thought and effort. We will focus on three key aspects: productivity, follow-up and delegation.

> **Productivity**: We will not be able to manage our team or their subordinates by counting hours worked or individual widgets produced. This is an outmoded way of thinking no longer applicable to the majority of organizations—even those involved in producing widgets. Rather, the successful executive will view outputs as goals in and of themselves that must be assessed holistically in the context in which they are produced. Our measurement of productivity must also be modified. It is no longer sufficient to say that team members must punch the clock at a certain time of day. Rather, working hours must be dictated by the outputs produced. It is very likely that these requirements will align to normal business hours, but they should not be constrained by them. Productivity must be measured in higher-level goal achievement rather than incremental measurements of static indicators—hours worked are not strongly correlated to actual work completed. The successful executive will rely on project compartmentalization of work, as aligned to goals, to dictate the management and measurement of productivity. If our projects are too numerous or intensive, our team may be working more hours than is sustainable in order to keep up. If our projects are too few or fat, then we need to bring on more projects, move team members to other areas or reduce positions.
>
> **Delegation**: The task of the executive is to break out the work of the organization into interdependent projects that

align with the higher-level goals. These projects must be managed at the executive level to ensure overall productivity. Delegation of projects based on higher-level goals is the most efficient method of implementing this requirement. Once a project has been delegated, it must stay delegated and be managed as such. Delegation's greatest power is to ensure deep engagement of our team and to grant them a stake in the success or failure of the project. If they do not viscerally feel that responsibility, the power of delegation is squandered. The successful executive will manage productivity of the team and organization through disciplined delegation of project work.

Follow-up: In this productivity model, success can only be gained through assiduous and continuous feedback—hence the importance of reports and project communication. But we must also conduct detailed and consistent follow-up on delegated projects to ensure optimum productivity. There are additional aspects of follow-up that we have covered elsewhere regarding objectivity of communication and candor in reports. Detailed, line-by-line follow-up is critical for successfully managing productivity.

The successful executive will understand that the post-modern work environment cannot be managed with old methods of leadership. A highly educated and socially networked workforce must drive their own success. Productivity is neither managed nor measured through incremental tracking of hours or widgets. Rather, projects aligned with goals must be delegated to trusted lieutenants for delivery. The successful executive will establish metrics and policies of measurement based upon achievement of goals and delivery of projects.

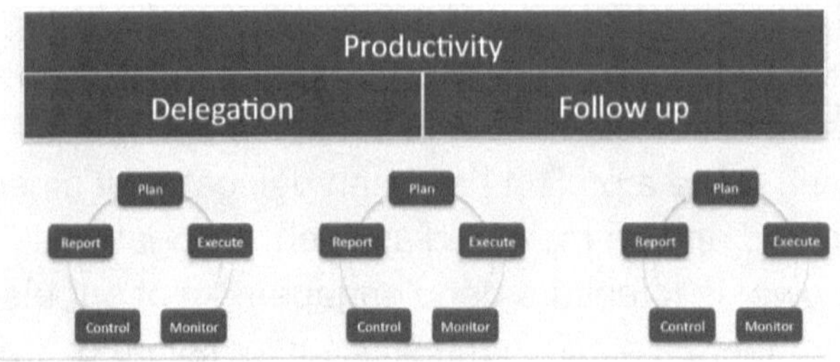

Figure 35 - Productivity is the top-level measure of delegated work.

The Junior Executive will drive optimum productivity through delegated project-level work and ensure a policy of disciplined, detailed and consistent follow-up.

TALENT

Talent is a gift, not a goal. There is much hand wringing regarding the question of talent. How to acquire those with it? Who has it? How did they get it? Are we born with it? How do we keep it from being wasted? All of these questions are valid, given that a trained and talented individual in a particular discipline can be ten or more times as productive as the average worker. But the rarity of trained talent and its fleeting nature should give us pause in consideration of our own teams.

What is talent? Talent is an innate aptitude for a particular action. Talent manifests itself in an inexperienced individual having the ability to complete an action in the same manner as a much more experienced person. It also manifests itself in an experienced person far outperforming their equally experienced contemporaries. Talent is a wonderful thing, but it must be understood, contextualized and properly managed within the team or group. Talent is sufficiently rare that when we actively seek it, we must expend resources to secure its benefits. In the case of individuals, this means recruiters, incentives and time. Of these three items, regardless of the resources of our organization, we most often lack time in acquiring talent—if for no other reason than the rarity of the trait. Unless we enjoy extreme good luck and have a complete team of talented individuals, our time will be fully employed helping our team do excellent work despite a lack of innate talent. Time spent chasing talent could be better spent raising the level of performance of individuals already on a team. If we have hired well by accounting for attitude and energy, working to improve our team should prove fruitful. The successful executive will see talent for what it is: a gift to be stumbled upon, but not a goal to attain.

As John D. Rockefeller said, “good leadership consists of showing average people how to do the work of superior people.” The vast majority of our time as an executive will be spent working with our team to raise their level of performance. The overall output of the team will be constrained by the minimum level of competency of the individuals on the team. If we are not driving average people to do superior work, we will not succeed—regardless of the number of talented individuals. As noted previously, new executives often fall into the trap of heroism. This is a pernicious side effect of a focus on talent, because a talented individual can often heroically overcome organizational problems to achieve a goal. The dazzling show screens the underlying problem. There should have been no need for heroics in the first place. If the executive had been focused on ensuring the maximum level of competency within the team, the talent would not need to save the day—they could be focused on raising the bar of overall performance. The successful executive will ignore heroics to work with their teams to raise their competencies. If a talented person joins the team, this is a gift.

The Junior Executive will avoid chasing talent and focus instead on developing existing team capacities above their perceived limits.

PRESENTATIONS

Every organization has a wide variety of presentation styles. Generally, entropy will degrade presentation quality to the minimally acceptable level. This is true for both oral and written presentations. Changes to this trend will come from two places: signaling of higher expectations from senior leadership and competition within teams. As a junior executive, this second source is important, but more consideration must be given to the first. We must be acutely aware of the effect of our presentation style in the organizational context. Imagine a scenario where we are slated to give an oral presentation to a group of colleagues, and so is one of our fellow executives. It is a certainty that there will be differences in style and quality between the presentations, and that the better of the two will set the standard for the next presentation. This holds true for written communication as well. A successful executive will prepare for competition within the organization with regard to presentation. Particularly, we must be prepared to continually improve both the quality and relevance of our presentation—always above expectations but never outclassing senior leadership. Once promoted, we should encourage similar competition among our teams—it leads to an indirect increase in quality and attention to detail among the group.

How is this accomplished successfully? Presentation and communication output are the manifestation of the culture and the attitudes of the individuals within the organization. The style of presentation and communication provides fertile ground for interpretation: intent, quality of thought, attention to detail, importance of message, respect for audience, mood, et al. Presentations represent an opportunity to create value, but also a challenge: understanding how presentation is perceived in the culture of the organization. A startup will likely be informal while the Federal Reserve will likely be formal.

In discussion of presentations, we will exclude one-to-one conversations and focus on one-to-many conversations and written communication. We must critically evaluate the quality and formality of these types of communication. Are written communications formatted in a commonly accepted style—salutation, body, and complimentary close? Or are they full of monosyllabic words and typos? The level of quality is not that important in an objective sense, but it establishes the baseline against which the successful executive's communication quality will be measured. For oral communications, is there a structure—greeting, introduction, agenda, action-biased discipline, record keeping, wrap-up and salutation? Or are they handled like informal round-table discussions? Are there artifacts—diagrams, PowerPoint slides? Are they dynamic with whiteboard interactivity, or a subdued roster of status updates? Once this analysis is complete, a communication strategy must be put together. How do we raise the bar?

As noted, communication conveys meaning beyond the actual content of the communication. It conveys intent, quality of thought, attention to detail, importance of message, respect for audience, mood, etc. Thus, subconsciously or not, both the presenter and the audience derive meaning from the message as it fits their worldview and particular psychological state. If they resent us or do not respect us, this will color their understanding of our communication. The first step in developing our communication strategy is to remove our ego from all aspects of our presentations. We may not be able to influence our audience's opinion of us, but we can objectify the subject and mood of our communication. Rather than, "Tim, you told me that you would have this done today, why are you late?" we say, "Tim, this task had to be done today to maintain the current schedule. Now that it is late, how can the time be recovered?" The protagonist in this scenario is never us; it is the deliverable schedule—our communication should reflect that objectively. Thus, Tim is free to answer how he can address the schedule, and does not have to deal emotionally with our admonishment.

This communication style is substantially bolstered by structure—not necessarily formality or embellishment, but fundamental structure. Informality or overfamiliarity with the audience denotes an introduction of ego into the presentation, which leads into a minefield. At the very least, we must introduce a minimal structure into our communication: salutation, body, and complimentary close. Although this sounds simple, it is a rarity in the modern workplace and will serve not only to raise the bar of our presentations but aid in removing aspects of our ego from them.

From this point, the question is one of gauging the improvement of our communication. There are generally two considerations:

What is the sensitivity threshold for our current culture? What is generally acceptable within our organization? How can we align the level of quality of our presentations such that they are above the norm, but not so far above as to be embarrassing for senior leadership? It is important to consider this as a ratcheting process—as we raise the level of quality, we must allow time for the organization to adjust before doing so again. From a competitive standpoint, timing of these ratcheting maneuvers is critical. We must be prepared to nudge the level of quality upward the instant before competitors reach our current level.

What is the gap between our current level of presentation quality and the level of the executive role? If we feel that we have a long way to go in order to raise the level of quality of our presentations, the point above must be tempered by time—we may need to implement a longer-term approach. If it will take too long to intelligently raise the quality of communication in the organization, it may make sense to either consider a more radical, step-change strategy or consider moving to a more professional organization.

The Junior Executive employs a strategy for presentation that both removes ego from consideration and inexorably improves quality over time.

DISINGENUOUS

A running theme in this book is the risk present in the initial period of appointment for the junior executive. There will be many individuals and groups who will attempt to take advantage of the change in the organization to their own benefit. One of the more common behaviors that will be noted is disingenuousness among colleagues and staff members. It is important to remember that the focus of the disingenuous behavior is not material. Rather, it is the behavior itself that must be addressed. Disingenuous behavior can immediately cause a loss of trust due to perceived and real betrayals. As such, we must recognize disingenuous behavior and address it immediately. We are concerned with two varieties of disingenuousness: known and perceived. Both should elicit the same response, but the two types have different knock-on effects. The consequences of disingenuous behavior should be based upon the intent and value of the individual involved.

Very often, disingenuous behavior results from an individual sensing an opportunity to advance some agenda item and then attempting to either manipulate or control information associated with that opportunity. If all stakeholders are aware of the parallel agenda and agree on the approach, there is not a problem. Disingenuous behavior thrives in an environment of confusion, which is a common scenario for newly minted executives. Their appointment causes a period of confusion within the organization that others may seek to take advantage of for their own purposes. This advantage seeking may be overt attempts to convince us of something or covert attempts to induce changes before we are aware of the implications. It will vary greatly depending upon the organization and the context of the appointment. In general, it will become clear when behaviors of subordinates or colleagues would cause some deviation or change in the understood purpose of the organization or our authority. We recall the advice in previous chapters that it is critical for a prospective or new executive to deeply understand their organization and group. This will establish a baseline for judging the nature of disingenuousness.

We generally see three types of individuals involved in disingenuous behavior: Peters, Empire Builders and Defenders.

Peters: The Peter Principle (namely, that individuals will rise to their level of incompetence in an organization) is a useful base to understand disingenuous behaviors. It is a theory, half in jest, posited by Dr. Laurence J. Peter and Raymond Hull (Peter & Hull, 1969). "Peters" are typically beyond their level of competence and thus seek to assert themselves in other ways. They are often the most disruptive simply because they lack other redeeming qualities. That is, their behavior is destructive because it serves no other purpose than to protect their undeserved position.

Empire Builders: Empire Builders are relatively straightforward in that they seek to use the period of uncertainty to expand their scope of responsibility to include some or much of ours. The underlying case for this may be justified if the organization was misaligned in the first place and this may be a useful opportunity to open discussion about that misalignment.

Defenders: Much like Empire Builders, Defenders are relatively straightforward in that they seek to ensure that no part of their existing scope of responsibility is reduced. Again, the underlying cause of this may be justified and warrant open discussion.

All of these types and the scenarios they present must be dealt with in the roughly the same fashion. The temptation is to directly confront the individual on the issue and seek to resolve through conflict. Although this makes for good television, it is not a productive approach. Rather, we must acknowledge that a person, when faced with accusations of embarrassing behavior, will seek to deflect negative attribution. That is, they will fall deeper into disingenuousness. As our goal is to resolve the behavior rather than prolong it, we must pursue a different course specific to the type of person. In general, Peters should be dealt with harshly as they have little value to be salvaged. Their behavior should be openly acknowledged and blocked. The Peter type should be ostracized from future work as much as possible, whereas the other two will likely remain with the organization. For example, if a colleague seeks to control the communication channel with a supplier who directly impacts our team by establishing a secondary line of communication, then an open communication from us to our colleagues should be sent asserting that ours is the only channel of communication that will exist and that all others will be closed, explaining the reasoning behind the decision. If our colleague persists, then it is worth a fight in any of the three circumstances. In general, though, disingenuous behaviors among colleagues—particularly among those colleagues with value to deliver to the organization—will not survive the glare of scrutiny. It is important in case of Empire Builders and Defenders to acknowledge their concerns, where legitimate.

The successful executive will scrutinize disingenuous behaviors in team members and colleagues to determine the nature of the individual involved and the appropriate response. The successful executive will sidestep the original act in favor of openly declaring the appropriate course of action, thus defeating the underlying purpose of the disingenuous behavior.

The Junior Executive will be watchful for disingenuous behavior and address it according to the underlying source in the offending individual.

TRAVEL

The amount of travel required of us and our team will vary depending upon our organization and type of work. In general, travel for work is a common requirement. Rather than debating the good and bad aspects of work travel, we will start with a practical assumption and then move into how to best manage travel. Despite what vendors of teleconference, telepresence and videoconference technology tell us, work-related travel will not go away any time soon. Travel is an essential part of the working world. Humans are local by nature and anything not local is automatically categorized as "other," subject to both good and bad connotations. As such, we will likely be required to travel to meet with colleagues, customers, suppliers and other peripheral players involved in our organization's work. Of course, communication technologies can reduce the amount of travel required and will serve to decrease the sense of "otherness" associated with the distance, but some travel will be required. Certain roles in certain organizations may require nearly constant travel while others require none. It is entirely subject to the needs of the organization.

In general, we should determine the absolute minimum amount of travel required for our team. Reasons for travel may include training, conferences, meetings, etc. The successful executive will plan for a 50% overage on this minimum throughout the year. This over-allowance will smooth out both our expense budgeting but also our resource time allocation. Emergencies will come up and so will opportunities. Travel should be one of the least difficult decisions we have to make throughout the course of the year. It is far more important to spend time and effort ensuring excellent work output than to deal with travel budgets and arrangements. By planning for at least a 50% overage on the minimum expectation, we free up thought and effort for more important tasks.

Work travel is both expensive and relatively unpleasant. However, depending upon the nature of the travel involved, some consider it a perk—at least on an infrequent basis. Both of these considerations need to be pulled into our calculus around travel. We again look to fall back on a minimum plus premium strategy. Given our planning and overage for the amount of travel required for the year, the next calculation is to understand the nature of that travel. Is our organization a bootstrap startup sending a low-level engineer to a conference 180 miles away? Or are we traveling to a meeting with a supplier 1,800 miles away? Or are we taking an emergency trip to a patient 500 miles away? All of these scenarios will dictate our travel spending and planning. In the first scenario, we may simply reimburse the engineer for mileage or buy a train ticket. The other scenarios will incur greater expense. A bootstrap startup using cash from friends and family to get a hold in the market would be ill-advised to pay for first-class tickets. But a multi-national corporation that frequently flies salespeople overseas would be ill-advised to fly them economy class. In both cases, misalignment between organizational culture and travel policy can lead to bad outcomes.

Depending on the person and the role, travel is viewed as either a burden or a reward. In both cases, the minimum standards apply. To ease potential burdens, travel should be made as painless as possible within reason. This calls for business-class flights for long hauls and a loose per diem budget in general. Easing the burden and providing a minor incentive to travel ensure that more actual work is done. The successful executive will develop a travel policy that provides the least amount of burden and greatest degree of comfort possible within cultural and budget constraints. Even the toughest road warrior appreciates perks.

The policies that we enact as an executive will have an environmental effect on the work outputs of our team and the rate of employee churn. Travel is often a main reason for losing important employees. The successful executive will create a travel policy that ensures travel is a medium for excellent work output rather than a distraction for both themselves and their staff.

The Junior Executive will acknowledge the function that travel fulfills in their organization and ensure that all applicable roles and work outputs are aligned to minimize impact.

DENG'S GENERALS

In 1989, when Deng Xiao Ping ordered troops into Tiananmen Square, he maneuvered his military leaders in such a way that all of his generals were compelled to volunteer troops from their regiments for the action. The environment of Deng's decision was extraordinarily complex, but the fundamental reason was simple: legitimacy. At the point in time when troops were committed, the pro-democracy demonstrators had made it clear that force would very likely be necessary to quiet them unless their demands were met. Given that their demands would not be met in any acceptable form, Deng, as China's premier, chose to halt the protests with force. Such a decision is politically dangerous from both an internal perspective as well as from external witnesses. Deng's position could be used as justification for his removal from leadership by a rival, or at the least as an opportunity for a political fissure within the established leadership. What if the action was a disaster? The blame would go to Deng, but how would it travel down the chain of command? These questions led Deng to a simple conclusion: all principals had to share in the result, whatever it was. Given the actual result of the action, Deng's decision seems prescient. If he had only sent troops from one regiment or excluded some regiments, the excluded group would have enjoyed distance from a negative outcome—thus enhancing their attributed legitimacy for subsequent decisions and actions. By sending troops from all generals, Deng ensured that the legitimacy impact resulting from an unknown outcome would be equally shared among all.

This example presents a strong lesson. When a difficult and potentially damaging decision must be made, it is absolutely critical to ensure that all principals are included in the actions resulting from the decision. Doing otherwise creates an opportunity for internal fissures that are unrelated to the action itself, but that call into question the legitimacy of the principals involved in the action. The successful executive will ensure that all key subordinates are involved in actions arising from difficult and risky decisions. The resulting cohesion is driven by the shared risk and lack of opportunity for maneuver by the principals. Of course, we deplore the violent actions of Deng, but the lesson regarding managing principals is noted.

Very often, we will be faced with extraordinarily complex decisions that could serve as opportunity for internal fissures. We have focused a large amount of our effort in this book on encouraging an open and trusting environment for the executive and their team. But, we must acknowledge human nature—imperfect judgments will be made that will have long-term, rail-switching consequences. As we have noted, team alignment and cohesion are absolutely critical to success.

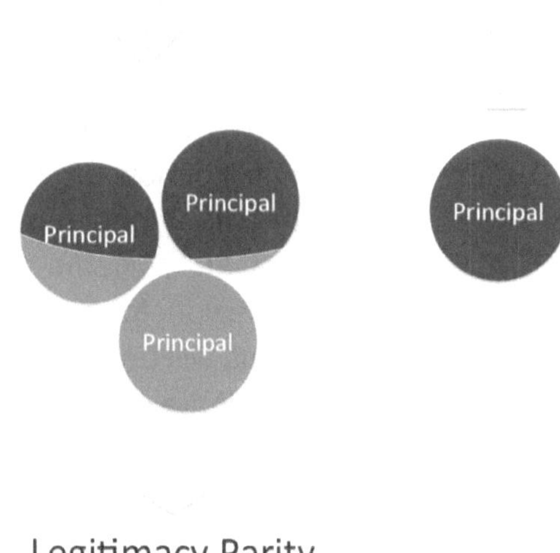

Legitimacy Parity

Figure 36 - To ensure legitimacy, all principals in our team must have a stake in key decisions.

The Junior Executive will ensure that all principals are suitably staked in any difficult decision.

Chapter 8 Delivery

STRATEGY, OPERATIONS, TACTICS

As a high-achieving individual, the executive candidate or new executive will have encountered the concepts of strategy, operations and tactics many times. These terms are often misused, abused and mired in misapplied dogma. We will not delve too deeply into the philosophical nature of the terms. Rather, we will acknowledge that in the majority of circumstances these concepts are the most efficient approach to organizing the themes, structure, and idiomatic architecture of an aligned group. That is, they represent the fundamental basis of how organizations should pursue their goals. It is important to understand the core purpose of these terms. As concepts, they are powerful tools for organizing thought and developing a framework for executing the goals of the organization. Often, these terms will be incorrectly presented in a hierarchical manner: tactics underlie operations, which underlie strategy. This is not conceptually correct in the organizational context, though. Further, strategy will often be misused to define the goals of the organization. That is not conceptually correct in any context. Much of this stems from a misapplication of these terms from their military roots to the civilian organization. Rather than delve into unending critical spirals, we will focus on how these terms can be applied at the most basic level to leverage the greatest benefit for the executive. There will be layers that can be added later, but only if the foundation is sound. To that end, we will examine each concept and the group.

> **Tactical**: We ignore tactics in reference to discrete actions of the individual. Instead, we view tactics in the organizational sense, which refers to discrete actions of the organization. From a corporate standpoint, changing a brand slogan is a tactic, buying a rival company is a tactic, and establishing a hiring policy is a tactic. Tactical actions are the base unit in organizing action within a group. The execution of these

tactical actions is likely broken into projects.

Strategy: From a hierarchical point of view, tactical actions are aggregated serially and in parallel to form a strategy. Consequently, a strategy is executed by completing one or more tactical actions. From an organizational sense, strategy is the highest-level planning required to achieve the organizational vision. Goals are milestones that are used to judge the effectiveness of a given strategy. Thus, we see that vision is achieved through strategy, which is delivered through tactical actions, which are delivered through projects.

Operations: Operations in the military sense are discrete events—a middling organizational format for bridging strategy and tactics. In our non-military context, operations refer to the standing policies and processes through which tactics and strategies are implemented. They are the organizational media. From a planning execution standpoint, operations represent constraints and opportunities that affect the organization's ability to achieve goals. As such, operations underlie both strategy and tactics and can be modified by both.

This chapter is relatively short and simple, much like our approach to these concepts. One of the traps that await the executive is the mess of misinterpretations, jargon, and double-speak that besets many organizations. We must understand the core purpose of these concepts so that they can be implemented as efficiently as possible. There is enormous power in simplicity and, as we have noted many times before, enormous opportunity for disingenuousness in complexity.

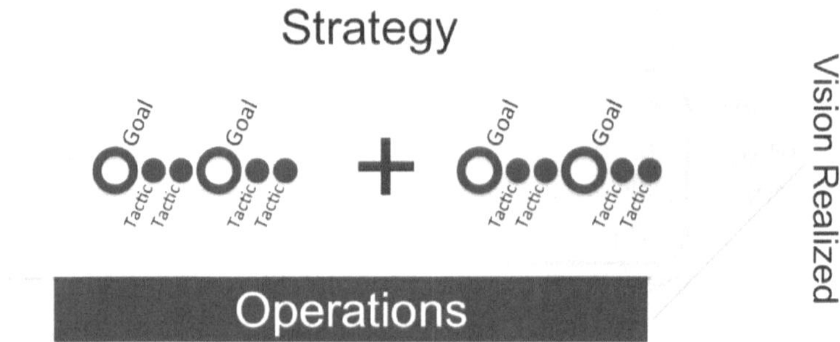

Figure 37 - Strategy, Operations and Tactics are somewhat hierarchical but mostly complementary in nature.

The Junior Executive will fundamentally understand the concepts of Strategy, Operations and Tactics as they apply to the organizational context.

CAMPAIGNS

At this point in the book, much of the groundwork has been laid for understanding our commitment to the executive role and our general place in time as it relates to the organization. We have reviewed a great deal of material that provides a ripe environment for success. But how do we make form from the void? How do we begin to set people in motion to achieve? We acknowledge that our particular circumstances may dictate one approach over another. Every organization and context of work is different. However, we argue that there is an optimally efficient approach to action that should be used as a baseline: the campaign. All other approaches are essentially elaborations upon it.

We have discussed how to organize discrete work elements and how these can roll up to provide general workflow intelligence. Further, we have discussed how these discrete work elements should be organized within the larger organization and monitored for performance. Yet there is still a piece missing: how we manage mid-term and temporally significant periods of work in a manner that carries meaning for both the executive and employees. There are many names and methods for this type of organizational division, but we prefer "campaign"—predominantly because it designates a degree of independence from the main work of the organization.

What is a campaign? For our purposes, a campaign is a temporally distinct work effort that is holistic in nature—holistic in that it requires representation and effort from most of the organization's resources. Or, in the case of more independent teams or business units, it requires representation of all of a team's resources. It is important at this point to clarify the basis of our use of the word "campaign." A strategy is not a campaign, but a campaign can be used in execution of a strategy. A tactic is not a campaign, but tactical maneuvers may be part of a campaign. A project or program is not a campaign, but campaigns may be executed using projects and programs. A campaign is a logical subdivision of organizational effort that delivers strategy in pursuit of the organizational vision.

The core purpose of a campaign is to render a temporal, real scope of effort with aligned goals that can be practically understood and executed by the organization's members. Planning and carrying out a campaign is a crucible for leadership and the executive who can successfully execute campaigns in support of organizational strategy is suitable for senior promotion. Campaigns have several key components.

> **Strategic Goal Alignment**: As noted above, the purpose of a campaign is to deliver strategic goals over a period of time. Campaigns must be directly and clearly aligned to one or more strategic goals with achievement criteria fully understood.
>
> **Time Frame**: A campaign must be temporally defined. Typically, campaigns will run in some frame of time under one year, e.g. "winter campaign" or "summer campaign." For a campaign to be successful, it must be delivered in a time

frame that is relatable and meaningful to the individuals involved. This is the only way to ensure fully leveraged participation. The successful executive will ensure that all campaigns are temporally aligned with the types of outputs delivered by the domains and individuals involved and adjust as necessary.

Clear Monitoring and Measurement: As with all work done in the organization, the campaign must be assiduously monitored and measured to understand effectiveness and to properly time any necessary changes. The successful executive will leverage existing monitoring, measurement and reporting systems to verify that all campaign metrics are fully understood within the overall context of goal achievement. The successful executive will ensure that changes are made at the most appropriate times within a campaign to account for inevitable surprises and changes in circumstances.

Executive Sponsorship: The successful executive will be the executive sponsor (accountable for the campaign, even if not organizationally responsible) of all relevant campaigns. As noted above, successful delivery of campaign outputs to the organization is a crucial test for advancement to senior leadership.

Domain Representation: All involved domains must have representation on the management council of a campaign. This can be a steering committee, decision board, or leadership team. But all domains must have a voice in decisions that are made and subsequently be held to account for domain performance.

Clear Lines of Communication: Campaigns must have a clear leader and there must be clear lines of communication to ensure timely decisions can be made. The leader of the campaign does not necessarily need to be the executive sponsor. It can be some other director or manager within the relevant domains. But this person must be empowered to make decisions and manage lower-level team members in pursuit of campaign success. This person must be subject and reportable to the campaign leadership and executive sponsor.

Campaigns are extremely powerful means by which organizational strategy is executed and vision achieved. They are a bridge between abstract goals and the actual work that is conducted within the organization. This is true not just for the discrete tasks and actions executed by individuals but also for the programs and projects that aggregate that work.

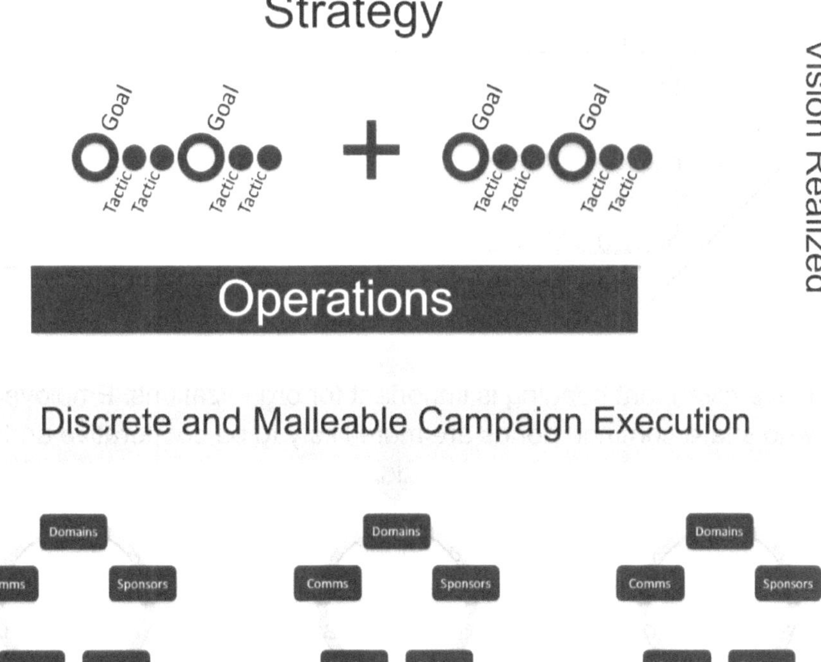

Figure 38 - Abstract strategic implementation is made real for the organization through campaigns.

The Junior Executive will understand the purpose of campaigns, know how to organize them in their particular organization, and serve as executive sponsor for campaigns involving their domain.

BONDING

Most organizational literature and thinking holds that bonding among members of the organization is very important for organizational effectiveness. In addition to reams of literature, a wide array of service providers exists to encourage bonding, such as corporate retreats and guided experiences that demonstrate shared value and interests. The literature and discipline around bonding and team-building is all well and good. But in many cases, it has been so abstracted from the core truth of bonding's importance as to become meaningless. We will very likely find those involved in these experiential settings asking why there is value in the activity. As a successful executive, understanding why bonding is important and what the fundamental lever is for encouraging it is paramount. This is not only important for the team-building that we will do in our own domain, but also important for the inter-domain team-building that we must do to increase our sphere of influence across the organization.

It is a given that bonding is important for organizations. Employees who share common bonds are more likely to be cooperative and empathetic in their daily work. Additionally, they tend to be happier and more contented with their position in the organization and in society in general. In this chapter we will examine why bonding is important to achieving organizational goals and how the successful executive can craft a program to increase bonding between both intra- and inter-domain team members.

Why does bonding truly matter? Bonding is not a core requirement of organizational operations. That is, good work can be done among teams that are not strongly bonded. What we are really talking about when we discuss bonding is incremental improvement in a standing operation. Bonding allows us to achieve near-optimum performance with non-automated resources—much like chemical bonding, bonding within teams decreases the amount of time and energy required to transfer information between the bonded partners.

Individuals can be trained to execute a minimum level of work, but if we want them to do their best consistently or exceed expectations, they must become emotionally vested in the outcome. There are myriad motivations and factors that drive this emotional attachment. All of them matter, but we are focused on the core emotions that affect bonding in the organizational context. To that end, we can look at studies on military effectiveness and training conducted since World War II on army combat troops. If we assume that the core goal of a combat operation is to kill the enemy, we see that one of the required tasks is to fire a weapon at the enemy with the intent to kill. This seems simple enough. But a study conducted by S.L.A. Marshall showed that during WWII, only 25% of combatants ordered to fire at the enemy actually fired their weapon (Marshall, 1961). Goal achievement in this context was dismal. What was the problem? The study found that the problem was not cowardice or fear of being killed, but rather a moral aversion to killing. Of course, a moral aversion to killing is a very good thing, but in the context of the goals required of a war, it is highly detrimental to success. Thus, the Army was presented with a difficult problem. Their ability to execute the core goal of combat was highly limited by the emotional investment of the combatants. This brings us to the core meaning of bonding. What the Army found through subsequent training evaluations and experiments was that combatants' moral aversion to killing was subordinated to their moral aversion to allowing a comrade to die by their inaction. Thus, intent was generated through emotional bonding with comrades. By refocusing their training effort on firing at the enemy with the intent of protecting their comrades, the participatory firing rate of combatants soared. Marshall's study went on to show that combatant firing participation rates increased to 55% in Korea and 90% in Vietnam. Subsequent studies have shown even greater improvement since Vietnam. This is admittedly a morally dubious example, but it cuts to the core truth of the importance of bonding. In comparison, applications of this concept to our organization should be relatively simple. So how does the successful executive use bonding as a tool to increase overall operational efficiency?

> **Moral Duty**: The most powerful lesson learned from the Army studies is that the majority of individuals feel an enormous moral duty to not cause comrades to suffer through their inaction. This moral duty is heightened by the emotional bonds we have with individuals who share our experiences. The successful executive will leverage this innate sense of duty by ensuring that team members understand clearly that their failure to excel will cause their comrades to suffer failure. If we look inside our own experiences, we will very likely find great pride and comfort in knowing that we have done everything possible to ensure the success of our colleagues. So, any exercises or events that allow individual team members to better know each other will leverage significant benefits.
>
> **Projected Self-Interest**: Less emotional, but just as important is the sense of reciprocation that underlies individual transactions among team members. The core of this is the understanding that our sustained success is reliant upon the sustained success of others. Thus, actions of operational excellence must be reciprocated. This serves the individual as much as the group. This basic understanding can be difficult for many to grasp. How do we teach someone that by enabling and supporting others to generate the outputs that we need, they enjoy leveraged benefit? The knee-jerk reaction in such instances is that this other party needs to step up their effort to provide us what we need to progress. However, if we look at the overall process with a discerning eye, we see that other parties are often not

capable of providing the outputs we need when we need them. In order for our goals to be achieved, we must assist them. The understanding that by helping a colleague, we are in fact helping ourselves is one of the most powerful benefits of bonding. This leads to a virtuous cycle of reciprocation that truly benefits the team and organization.

There is an entire industry devoted to promoting bonding among colleagues. However, the marketing associated with it often obscures why bonding matters. The successful executive understands that bonding is a means to greater performance efficiency among their domain members and within the broader organization. The successful executive understands that the benefits of bonding are leveraged by the innate moral duty that we all have to not allow others to suffer for our failings as well as the extended benefits of reciprocal actions.

The Junior Executive will create initiatives that leverage bonding to the incremental benefit of operational efficiency and excellence.

FRICTION

It is only through friction that true solutions are realized. No one can fully appreciate and internalize a solution without first enduring a great deal of frustration. In his treatise on war, Clausewitz hit upon a core truth of all endeavors and especially large ones. Large undertakings (wars, campaigns, standing organizational operations, etc.) are beset by friction. Friction is generated by the moving pieces of an organization as processes and plans are undertaken. Friction is the wasted energy thrown off by the infinite variability of circumstance that surrounds us. A large endeavor will inevitably have more friction than a small endeavor. While a large group may bring more resources to bear upon a certain point, a smaller group can maneuver faster, thus bringing an instantially more relevant amount of power to another point.[3] An army of 100,000 troops could overwhelm a smaller army of 20,000 troops in a pitched battle. But that smaller army can move faster to bring these 20,000 troops to a battle of their choosing. Napoleon demonstrated this masterfully in battles whereby he would bypass the enemy's larger force entirely and shoot for the politically sensitive capital with his smaller force. Despite objective asymmetries in power, Napoleon took advantage of the larger force's friction to achieve success. We see this same example in business where small companies are able to quickly bring new products and services to market. Many of the startups that have become successful since the dawn of the commercial Internet are perfect examples of this. This phenomenon is more prevalent in industries with lower barriers to entry, but also occurs in industries with high barriers to entry whereby new entrants introduce disruptive methods to business (e.g., 3D printing and manufacturing). All of this derives from the opportunity presented by friction—the attenuation and delay associated with aligning individuals and resources on a directed timeline.

It is important to note that friction is not a problem only in large organizations; rather, it exists even on the individual level. When we discuss discrete examples of small groups outmaneuvering large groups, it highlights the opportunity in asymmetries of power. But in truth, large groups are often competing against many small groups and the vast majority of these small groups fail. In many circumstances, the relative advantage of size and maneuverability is not leveraged as these small groups succumb to their own internal friction. This is particularly true when large groups are aware of and dealing with their internal friction in a methodical manner.

Here is the aspect of friction that concerns us—its potential use. While Clausewitz decried friction as an evil to be excised in the goal of optimal maneuverability, we see friction in a more nuanced manner. Counter to Clausewitz, J.C. Wylie makes a strong argument for harnessing the generative effects of friction to bring in

[3] "Instantially" is a term defined as an event occurring at a point in time, but which can be iterated in a parallel or serial manner.

the new (Wylie, 1967). Whereas Clausewitz sought to remove friction through efficient command and control, Wylie tells us to spend time analyzing the friction within our organizations to gain greater insight into the problems faced and to find innovative solutions.

Both of these perspectives can be integrated intelligently to gain the maximum leverage from friction. From Clausewitz, we see that organizations of all sizes must acknowledge the attenuation and delays associated with aligning varied individuals and resources to a single goal. Clausewitz would want to ensure that the energy input into a process yields the maximum output and that friction represents waste to be reduced—much like heat thrown off by a light bulb. From Wylie, we see that the heat from the light bulb can be leveraged to offset heating cost in the room or that a judiciously placed mirror can nullify the need for a light bulb entirely. In either circumstance, there is opportunity within the perceived waste. The successful executive must integrate both of these perspectives into the environmental culture.

How do we manage friction to our benefit? As with many of the topics presented, there is a mountain of literature on the subject. But it is often too systematic or full of jargon to be of much practical use. The successful executive sets their will and intelligence to overcoming friction in the most effective manner possible.

> **Acknowledge and Map**: The first sign that any organization will suffer a significant level of damage from friction is a culture that refuses to acknowledge that friction exists. If the status quo is acceptable to the organizational team members at any time, this is a strong sign of a lack of awareness of the dangers of friction. There is a common malaise that affects many organizations of all sizes based in a desire for equilibrium. We see in these organizations that the focus is on some future state at which the process will get better. This temporal thinking can never achieve optimal performance. There will never be a sustained point of

equilibrium—it is a target that is perpetually beyond our reach. If we believe that we have achieved it, then we are blind to the reality of what a new equilibrium should be. This is the point where many organizations find themselves when they are disrupted. They believe that they have achieved equilibrium, not realizing that it cannot be achieved. Their competitors, however, are chasing a new equilibrium set point.

Fatigue and a myopic view of the situation cause individuals and organizations to accept an existing level of friction as "the way it is." The successful executive must combat this attitude ruthlessly. The first step is to acknowledge the friction in the organization and to map it out. This is the lesson of Clausewitz—large organizations do not envision a scenario that does not include their current level of friction. As a successful executive in any size of organization, we must never accept the status quo and instead relentlessly expose and acknowledge friction. How do we do this?

Run Scenario Analyses: We have discussed various aspects of this in previous chapters and this idea should be engrained by this point. Once we have mapped out the friction in our organization, both intra- and inter-domain, we must evaluate how it can best be addressed.

Speed Up: If we fully understand the complexities of our organization, we see that the first logical set of scenarios involves speeding up processes by adding resources or removing steps, or pushing resources in the organization to move faster. This analysis may yield some easy wins as unnecessary constraints and bottlenecks are identified and remedied. The individual gains are likely to be marginal, but potentially significant in aggregate. This honing process is a discipline that the best organizations master as a core competency. The successful executive will continually work to speed up processes and outputs.

Go Around: In concert with speeding up processes, the successful executive will challenge both themselves and their team members to go around friction points. Often, the best approach to overcoming friction is to establish an insurmountable goal inhibited by the friction. As Machiavelli pointed out, in order to send our arrows to the furthest shore, we must aim at the moon. The successful executive will challenge themselves and their team to radically re-think their approach to points of friction. This is often the best way to earn significant gains in efficiency and avoid settling into a malaise.

Integrated Method: This work must be managed within an appropriate method. This may be Total Quality, Lean, Six Sigma, a mash-up or something else entirely. The particular method is not relevant to our discussion, just that it provides a framework for experimentation, controlled measurement and clear reporting. The successful executive will implement a method for managing friction under the umbrella of operational excellence that is relevant to their organization.

Simplify: The core message from Clausewitz and many other prescient thinkers is that friction represents a call to simplify. Only through simplification and elegance can we truly address friction as an ill. As noted, friction cannot be fully removed, so the only practical approach is to reduce its entropic effect. In so doing, we will minimize wasted potential while increasing efficiency.

All organizations have some level of friction. Only those organizations that seek to methodically address friction through both incremental process optimization and disruptive processes will succeed in minimizing friction and innovating in response to friction. As noted by Wylie, understanding friction as the source of asymmetric and innovative thought is tremendously valuable. Very often, the greatest innovations are caused by the greatest friction.

The successful executive will acknowledge sources of friction and compartmentalize them for evaluation and analysis. The successful executive will institute a method for operational excellence that allows them to identify, experiment, monitor and report clearly how friction is being addressed and what aspects of it can be leveraged for innovation.

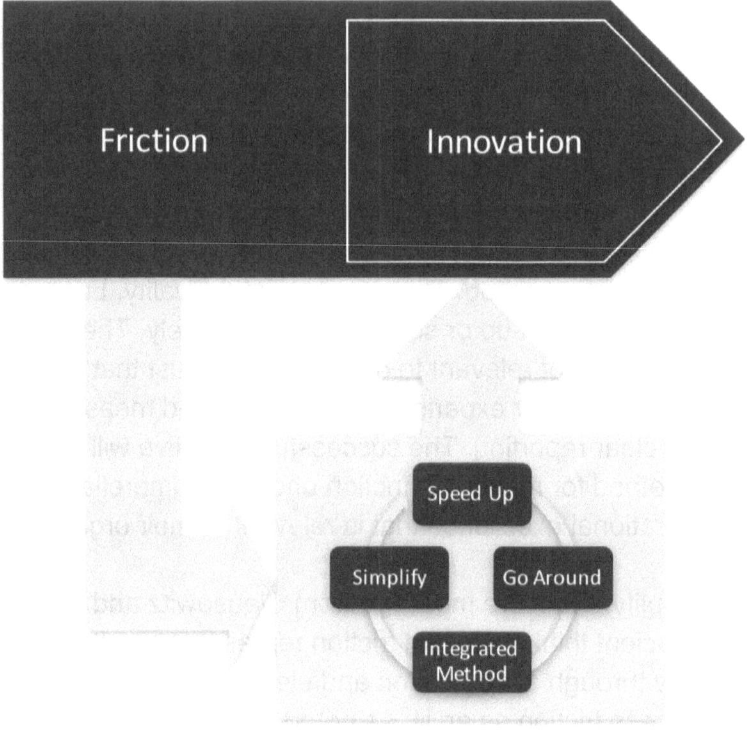

Figure 39 - Friction is an ongoing problem to be solved and an opportunity to generate innovation through managed scenario analyses.

The Junior Executive will make use of friction as a crucible for discovering and delivering innovation.

SITUATION AWARENESS

"If the mind is to emerge unscathed from the relentless struggle with the unforeseen, two qualities are indispensable: first, an intellect that, even in the darkest hour, retains some glimmerings of the inner light which leads to truth; and second, the courage to follow this faint light wherever it may lead. The first of these qualities is described by the French term, coup d'oeil; the second is determination."

- Carl von Clausewitz

The operating realm of the executive is relatively freeform, in that it lacks rigid structure with clear inputs and outputs. This is the challenge and the opportunity of the executive level. We should not throw ourselves into the wind, nor does it make sense to hide behind barricades and only control what can be touched. Rather, we must learn to operate clearly and confidently in a realm of uncertainty and confusion. It is not easy and this leads to much common advice about "listening to our gut," etc. We have dealt with this in other chapters and will do so in part later, but what concerns us now is the concept of situational awareness. This is "the perception of elements in the environment within a volume of time and space, the comprehension of their meaning, and the projection of their status in the near future" (Endsley, 1995). In contests, the individual with the greatest situational awareness coupled with a bias for action will typically prevail, all other factors being equal. Situational awareness is the basis upon which the executive makes quick decisions with incomplete or uncertain information.

Environment: As Endsley's definition of situational awareness states, it is a deep understanding of the environment as a contextual basis for deriving meaning from changes in that environment. Deep understanding is required to leverage changes in the environment to our advantage. This is true not only for external initiatives but also for ensuring continuity and harmony of existing work. The clarity of our understanding of the environment will determine the acuity of our sense of change to that environment and our ability to leverage our knowledge into an advantage. All of the investigative and evaluative work described in previous chapters now must be integrated in a higher-level process to ensure continual, deep understanding. The organizational members, inputs, processes, outputs and constraints must all be continually evaluated to ensure that our understanding of the environment enables situational awareness. Our mastery of the environment allows us to leverage that knowledge as we address chance and the value of anticipation.

Chance: Our clarity of environmental understanding allows us to address chance on more secure footing. The core purpose of situational awareness is to ensure the greatest likelihood of benefitting from chance and fortune; that is, to seize chance opportunities to create a new situation that leans in our favor. If we acknowledge that chance permeates everything we do, we see that it creates both opportunities and threats. The successful executive will follow the advice of Napoleon and have confidence in their ability to use chance to their favor. By having excellent situational awareness, we are able to acknowledge the variability presented by chance in a methodical way for longer-term planning and decisively for shorter-term planning. In terms of relative contests, chance represents a major success factor. We note this because chance affects all participants in the environment in some way or another. The successful executive will leverage the uncertainty and variability introduced by chance to gain advantage through anticipatory action.

Anticipation: Situational awareness enables greater success in anticipation of events through speed of action. In competition, greater situational awareness allows us to anticipate a rival's responses to changes in the environment

> and modify our actions to surprise them. There are two sources of advantage in this sense: Concealment of arrangements and greater understanding of the potential impacts of changes to the environment. If we have the greater understanding of the environment and an appreciation for the variability of chance, our ability to conceal our arrangements and plans is enhanced. This provides a source of advantage in anticipation. Our competitor's lack of understanding of our arrangements hinders their ability to anticipate how we might react to a change in the environment. This delays their ability to act and increases the likelihood that they will act inappropriately. Our greater understanding of the impacts of any changes to the environment will allow us to enjoy greater success in the decisions that we make and to better engage in feints and other distractions that can increase the likelihood that a competitor will make a poor decision. Both of these sources of advantage are rooted in the ability to increase friction in our competitors' operations—delayed action, poor planning, rework, etc. Over time, this added friction will erode any offensive advantage and our opponent will acquiesce without understanding why—other than that it began to cost too much. This is master's work and requires a great deal of thought, subtlety and understanding.

The successful executive will understand the importance of situational awareness. The executive role is overwhelmed with uncertainty and confusion—it is a realm of possibility. As such, we must implement a strategy and mindset that provides the greatest basis for successful decision-making and competitive advantage. A deep understanding of the environment, the role of chance in all events and the value and underlying influences of anticipation are critical to attaining strong situational awareness.

The Junior Executive will strive to hone their sense of situational awareness.

KEEPING SCORE

Unfortunately, it is often true that low-level conflict permeates the atmosphere at the executive level. Conflict is in the nature of the job and a symptom of the individuals involved—a group of intelligent and driven individuals competing over resources and opportunity. We have worked to demonstrate a path that will allow the successful executive to engage in this low-level conflict with as little collateral damage as possible. Low-level conflict is a trap that many fall into, as it triggers our basic instincts to combat threats. An atmosphere of low-level conflict and competition tends to raise the level of performance of the individuals involved and bring to light problems that might otherwise be hidden. But if low-level conflict remains unresolved, it can lead to more heated conflict and a culture of subterfuge. This book aims to help us avoid unnecessary conflict and expose bad behavior. Other executives and organizations will attack us and our team directly or indirectly, and it is imperative that we understand the implications of this.

Many newly minted executives do not understand the level of play in their new environment. The concepts covered up to this point are highly relevant to understanding the political atmosphere of the executive suite. They provide principles upon which we can rely to confidently make hard decisions. However, not all executives have these same principles or have eroded their reliance on them over time. This is common in many organizations and it is the root of much bad behavior. We find that many individuals feel trapped by their pride or fear of failure. Thus, they allow an erosion of their integrity or empathy or Randian self-interest, which then drives them to attack instinctively. The underlying intent is important for us to understand, because the successful executive must keep score.

An often-unstated truth at the executive level is that it is wise to neither forgive nor forget. As a new executive, we will be attacked directly and indirectly. While we have discussed how to respond to attack, it is also important to keep score—to understand who attacks us and why they are attacking. Perhaps a competing organization attacks the competency of our team within our organization in the hopes of taking work away from us. This is normal competition and not something to get overly emotional about. But we should keep score of the individuals involved and the nature of the attacks. This knowledge must then enter into our strategic and tactical planning as source material for changes we make to how our team operates. Perhaps they are attacking our team by intimating that we do not execute quality work or overcharge. All of these can be addressed in the messaging that our team sends to customers. The important point is to understand the intent of the attack. Was it based in fair play or FUDD (fear, uncertainty, doubt and distraction)? The same holds true for internal attacks but is more nuanced. Did another executive slight us? What was the cause of the slight: arrogance, fear? By keeping score, we understand, over time and with an ever-increasing degree of certainty, the atmosphere of the organization and executive team. This knowledge is critical to ensuring that we have the information needed to address subterfuge and defend ourselves and our teams.

The Junior Executive will keep score on both direct and indirect attacks against them and their team for use in crafting longer-term tactical approaches.

FLEXIBILITY AND ITERATION

We see that an individual with a relative advantage in a particular mental process will have a head start on others, all other things equal. What we are learning, however, is that what we call "genius" and "creativity" can often be attained through will and dedication. It has been shown that an individual of average intelligence, by spending 10,000 hours of dedicated and focused study, can become an expert in most any field (Howe, 2001).

But once they become an expert, how do they innovate? How do they learn? Many established creative individuals have provided the answer—flexibility and iteration. The successful individual must be flexible and continually iterate their work. Demonstration of excellence in leadership within our organization will require a level of genius and creativity that we were very likely not born with. Rather, we will have leveraged what mental acuity and prowess we do have into the position we currently hold. To be successful at the executive level and to grow beyond, we must show genius and creativity. Genius has often been defined by an analogy relating to an archery contest: the genius is the person who can hit the target that no one else can see (Howe, 2001). The core reason for this is that no one else knows to look for that target. The genius is the person who has worked against a problem so much that they have exhausted all possible known solutions and have moved beyond to find a solution that cannot be conceived using the tools available to the competition. Do they hit this target via a miraculous single shot or do they have a hunch that there is a hidden target and fire a thousand arrows at it?

When we look at the most creative people, do we see people of singular ability whose utterances are ostensibly perfect? Of course, the answer is no. Rather, the most creative people are the most productive—they iterate their work to an extreme degree, understanding that of a thousand hard-won ideas, one or two may be worth pursuing. Furthermore, those thousand hard-won ideas demand a level of flexibility in their thinking. The most creative people are often the best at integrating cross-disciplinary thinking into their outputs. To craft the most creative advertisement, the approach is not to create a thousand ads with slightly varied hues of blue. The approach is to create a thousand ads that demonstrate a wide spectrum of ideas and tease out of that variety something non-intuitive that will convey the perfect message. But perhaps the most effective advertisement need not innovate at all. After a thousand innovative ad reviews, the answer may be that the most creative advertisement is a tried-and-true simple message. Excellence in creativity is only attained through flexibility and iteration.

These concepts seem simple, yet it is difficult for many executives to truly demonstrate flexibility and iteration in their work. As we have noted elsewhere, there are significant mental and external forces that work against this approach. Pride and fear are the most directly responsible. We have discussed these previously, but they are worth examining briefly again in this context. As a highly successful person, we will have achieved our position through excellent work and a mature disposition. This provides a basis for pride and confidence in the methods by which we execute our work. By itself, this type of pride is great and serves as a bastion against indecision, but it can also ossify into dogma. It is prideful dogma that must be avoided. The successful executive will always have a greater respect for what they do not know than what they do. Thus, there will never be a point in time when flexibility and iteration are not the best approaches to executive work.

The executive arena is full of dangers, small and large. Fear of making a mistake can drive an individual to avoid flexibility and iteration. In fact, ad hominem criticism of honestly proposed new ideas is itself based in fear. The critic is fearful of losing the relative advantage of perceived superior knowledge. The successful executive will hold firm against this type of criticism and the fear it breeds. Ideas generated out of dedicated and willfully flexible iterative work should never be suppressed. Such disciplined work is the best method of ensuring that our team and organization remain competitive.

The Junior Executive will ensure that their teams execute work through flexibility and iteration in pursuit of creativity and genius.

OPTEMPO AND URGENCY

Executive success is a product of focused, intelligent and elegant orchestration of resources and processes. To make this happen, the executive must make real the abstract elements that guide our actions. Our focus here is on two of the more important elements of this process: operations tempo and urgency. Operations tempo—or simply optempo—provides a rough metric of how much work we are doing in relation to an average. It is typically measured in cycle time of actions and burn-down units for the resources and goals involved in an action. If there is a high optempo for a seasonal apple harvest, this means a higher-than-normal frequency of picking shifts will be conducted. A low optempo would call for a lower-than-normal frequency of picking shifts. Optempo can also tell us the failure risk of the components and resources involved. Increasing the frequency of apple picking shifts might illuminate inadequate trucking resources or the breakpoint of the apple-washing machine. The breakdown rate of the resources involved in operations increases geometrically as the optempo rate increases. This should be relatively clear, yet many new executives refuse to acknowledge this due to their pursuit of greater outputs.

The same holds true for urgency. A sense of urgency can vastly increase the rate and quality of output within a process. But it can be maintained for only a short period of time. The longer work is conducted in an urgent manner, the greater the risk of failure. Whereas in previous chapters we have covered how to efficiently and measurably control work, optempo and urgency are relatively unstructured. They reflect the attitude that we as the executive bring to the team every day. They reflect the intensity with which we impose our will on the work at hand. They are a direct reflection of the competitive drive within us. We will avoid the over-analysis and system-bias that typically beset these concepts. Rather, we advise the executive to think carefully about optempo and urgency as internal governors.

> **Optempo**: Optempo represents the spectrum of energy and enthusiasm that the individuals bring to the work at hand. As such, there are lower and upper control levels and a mean. As the executive, we must gain an intuitive understanding of the mean optempo of our organization. How energetic and enthusiastic are our team members on a daily-basis? How do they behave differently when optempo is high? What is

the norm in other domains within the organization? What about our competitors? What is the employee churn rate? These are very important questions that will help us evaluate our own mean optempo and how it should be adjusted.

Are there opportunities to increase the optempo? How is our team affected by the calendar? Are our expectations aligned to this? For example, expecting a high optempo in Scandinavia during the months of July and August is foolish, and the same holds of China in early February (national holiday periods). As a new executive, it will be important for us to understand how our typical optempo differs from that of the domain we are now leading. We must make clear what our expectations are for optempo mean levels. If our new domain has an extraordinarily low mean optempo and we arrive with a very high mean optempo, we must initially adjust our expectations down and adjust our team's expectations up a bit. Over time, we must seek opportunities to increase the optempo of the team to our expected level. Without tools, motives, goals or incentives, raising optempo will be virtually impossible. We may succeed temporarily but the components will break down. To raise the mean level of optempo within the team, it is incumbent upon us as the executive to modify the environment to support a higher optempo.

Urgency: One of the biggest failures of new executives is failing to realize the impact of their demand for urgency. It can be an exciting feeling to become a new executive, demand that something gets done, and actually have it get done. For many, this can be addictive. But the consequences of overuse can be severe. This should be clear from a quick consideration of the term “urgency.” This essentially means that other draws on capacity are ignored and all resources are thrown at the urgent project or task. By definition, urgency cannot be maintained and will eventually damage the entire system. With employees, this damage is typically characterized by burn-out and churn. This is not to say that urgency should never be applied. Rather, it should be applied with a careful understanding of its impact on other dependent processes and resources. For example, if a broken water main requires triple the usual technical resources to repair in short order, this means there is other work not being done at that time, or that the technical resources are being over-utilized. The challenge is to understand which tasks or projects are truly urgent. As a successful executive, we will have a deep and mature understanding of the organizational interdependencies that dictate urgency, in order to separate truly urgent matters from the noise of the standing organization.

There are many tools available to the executive for managing work. The energy and enthusiasm with which that work is conducted is managed best through intuition and understanding. Optempo is an excellent, intuitive guide to understanding how fast and frequent work should be done within a process, given awareness of constraints. Important to the internal morale and pace of work, optempo represents one of the best sources of competitive advantage. Our team's ability to out-hustle the competition can destroy their morale and ability to compete, particularly over the long term. In much the same manner, urgency is a powerful tool to energize team members and push through difficult challenges. But it can result in burn-out and failure in the long-term. The successful executive will develop a mature attitude toward the use of urgency and will deeply understand the knock-on effects of urgency to the domain and organization.

The Junior Executive will understand the mean and bounds of optempo in the organization and carefully manage the use of urgency as a motivator.

Reading List

“Good to Great” by Jim Collins
“Applied Anthropology” by Alexander M. Ervin
“The Goal” by Eliyahu M. Goldratt and Jeff Cox
“Genius Explained” by Michael J. A. Howe
“Twenty-Eight Articles” by David Kilcullen
“Sources of Power” by Gary A. Klein
“Seven Pillars of Wisdom” by T.E. Lawrence
“The Prince” by Niccolò Machiavelli
“The Design of Everyday Things” by Donald Norman
“The Person and the Situation” by Lee Ross and Richard E. Nisbett
“Chimpanzee Politics” by Frans de Waal

Say and Do

Chapter 9 Projection of Intent

SPHERE OF INFLUENCE

Throughout this book, we have referenced the ambient threat that surrounds the executive. There are much higher expectations for performance, greater risks of failure (and more opportunities to fail), and much higher competition. This reality can lead many to entrench themselves in their domain and seek safety in the areas that they can control. Others will become combative and engage in fruitless turf wars. Neither of these paths yield positive results; rather, they are career-limiters in the majority of instances. Of course, the executive level is harder; the stakes and rewards are higher. The danger can be managed effectively and serve as a platform for opportunity. Our ability to do so will determine our readiness and fitness for senior leadership.

How do we move forward from here? We rely on our understanding of the concepts presented to date and a basic truth—we were not promoted to the executive level to maintain the current level of operation; rather, we were promoted to make things better. By relying on this basic truth, we see that it is imperative that we not only seek optimal performance of the processes within our domain, but also seek optimal performance of the inputs into our domain and the downstream outputs from our domain. How can we demonstrate operational excellence if there is a bottleneck on the inputs into our domain? How can we demonstrate our increasing value to the organization if our outputs sit in a bottleneck waiting to be processed by the downstream domain? How can we leverage cross-functional resources in a matrix-oriented organization if training programs are not consistent across domains? All of these questions lead us to the point of this chapter. The successful executive will fully understand the intricacies of peripheral domains to ensure that inputs and outputs of their domain are optimally efficient. In short, the successful executive will seek to expand their sphere of influence. In doing so, we begin to significantly de-risk our situation as an executive. We will examine several aspects of this expansion along with their attendant benefits.

Empathy: Probably the most valuable attribute to peripheral analysis and process interoperability is empathy. Very often, domains will attain a level of tribalism that can be a great tool for team-building, but will often label groups outside the tribe as "others." This can destroy an organization. By working with other domains to understand the interfaces and the peculiarities of the inputs and outputs each generates, team members will gain an appreciation for the challenges faced by other domain team members. This is extremely important, not only for harmony of the greater team but for efficiency in problem solving. It is far easier to identify and fix an issue if the investigators understand how it relates to other teams and have empathy for those involved in the issue outside their own team. Finger-pointing is nothing but waste. The successful executive will guide their team to learn about and understand the processes and challenges faced by their counterparts in other domains. This understanding will serve as the basis for peripheral operations optimization and a growing sphere of influence for our team.

Asymmetrical Information: Very often, executives will rely on asymmetries in information to hide problems. These are a reflection of the challenges and dangers of the executive level, but also demonstrate an enormous source of inefficiency in many organizations. By pursuing peripheral understanding at the team-member level in the organization, we remove these asymmetries. Further, by having a common understanding of the specific needs of other domains in either providing our team with inputs or processing our outputs, we have the ability to begin a process of tailoring to accommodate these challenges of asymmetry. It is enlightening to find out that a downstream team must spend 10 minutes reformatting a report before their system can process it. The executive in that domain may not know about this and resent our team's delays or, even worse, know about it and use that knowledge against us. But unless we have done peripheral investigations and sought to expand our sphere of influence we will be subject to this asymmetry of information and suffer the consequences. The successful executive will work unrelentingly to break down asymmetries of information on how peripheral domains interoperate. Breaking down asymmetries of information in an honest and forthright manner yields enormous benefit to the organization and will confer credibility to our team.

Integrated Performance Metrics: In many organizations, performance metrics are domain-centric and only stitched together for an organization-wide view at the highest level. This provides only a cursory understanding of how the organization is actually performing. Very often, this is the result of defensive business units or executives who refuse to submit their team's performance to the greater organization for the fear-based reasons mentioned previously. This helps no one and will yield bad results for the organization. Once peripheral interfaces and their complexities are fully understood, the relevant constraints that relate to organizational outputs can be honestly understood. How can we effectively measure the performance of the organization if we do not understand the constraints associated with both intra- and inter-domain workflow? Is it more useful to know that it takes three days to get usability estimates from the data group for a proposal or that it takes three days because only one person in the data group knows how to run the report and they are overworked? Only one of these answers yields organizational benefit. The successful executive will ensure that senior leadership has not only a clear understanding of their domain's performance, but the performance of the interoperable interfaces with other domains. This clarity of reporting is critical to organizational success and will yield benefits to our sphere of influence.

Campaign-Level Benefits: Unless we have a clear and in-depth understanding of the peripheral interdependencies and process interoperability of our domain and those adjacent to us, we will not be able to manage a campaign successfully. As noted previously, campaign leadership is a critical test for senior leadership.

A discovery and analysis process to map and instrument peripheral interoperability for measurement should be initiated immediately under the direction of our trusted lieutenants. We may need to be involved, depending upon the disposition of other executives or competency of our lieutenants. It is best that peripheral interoperability be evaluated by the individuals who will be involved in it on a day-to-day basis. The aspects and benefits noted above can only be maximally achieved if the sphere of influence is projected from our entire team rather than us as an individual—this lends an inexorable quality to the effort.

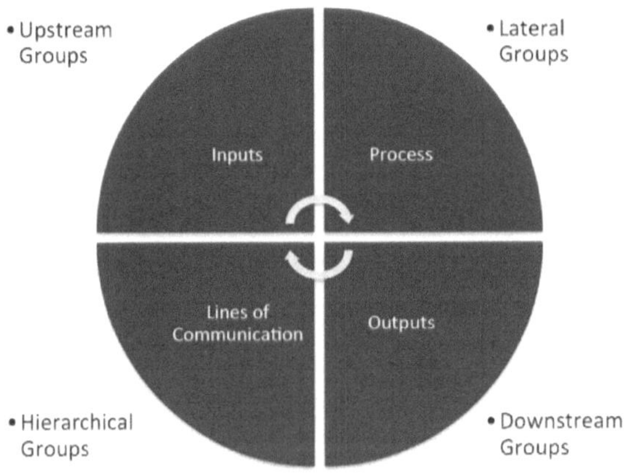

Figure 40 - Spheres of influence provide opportunity to optimize cross-domain efficiency.

The Junior Executive will establish spheres of influence to ensure the competency of peripheral domains.

EMPIRE

One of the greatest temptations for executives is the desire to build an empire. The executive is widely perceived as the leader of multitudes. But the responsibility and authority attributed to the executive role is necessity-based. That is, someone must have the authority and responsibility to make clear and impacting decisions. So executive power is not a mandate to implement our individual vision of the future irrespective of organizational goals. This truth holds with regard to building empire. Large and sustained organizations attain that size through necessity and the painful growth associated with continually seeking equilibrium between resource availability and resource need.

Very often, there is a significant resistance of will to reduce organizational size as need reduces. Sustainable empires are built over time through reflective analysis and experimentation—not through power of will. The clear truth for the executive is that building an empire in their early executive career will very likely result in failure to achieve their near-term goals and failure to advance to senior leadership. Before examining the framework for building a sustainable empire, we should spend some time acknowledging the source of the temptation to build an empire prematurely, which is typically rooted in fear. In turn, this fear is rooted in the psychology of the individual and the culture of the organization.

> **Rejection-Based Fear**: As we have discussed at length, the initial stages for new executives are full of risk. There are extraordinary pressures associated with the role that any new individual will struggle to overcome. The role is new and the scope of responsibility is significant. This will rightly yield a significant amount of rejection-based fear, i.e. fear of

failure. One way to cope with this fear is to build a team large enough to protect the fearful from failure. The thinking goes that if one has control of enough resources and a large enough team, then they will be insulated from rejection by senior leadership. This is calamitous logic. First and foremost, an executive who seeks to build a large organization signals a great deal of risk to senior leadership, irrespective of their job performance. This is particularly true for new executives. How can we be trusted with a large organization if we have not proven ourselves successful at leading a smaller organization? Further, how is a large team benefitting the organization as a whole, particularly if it is not built as a response to the pain associated with a lack of resources? The successful executive will understand and accept that their fear of rejection is really a fear of failure and that this fear is normal and unavoidable. However, the appropriate strategy is not to hide behind a bloated organization. Rather, we should address that fear head-on and demonstrate excellence in execution using only the absolutely necessary resources. This demonstrates to senior leadership that we able to succeed in our new role and that we are doing so in a manner that confers the greatest benefit back to the broader organization. This is the only honest strategy that will promote access to a senior leadership role.

Control-Based Fear: In much the same vein, many new executives have a strong sense of fear based upon a perceived lack of control. This is particularly true in highly functional organizations where there are clear lines between inputs and outputs, but can also be true in organizations where there is little structure. The root of this fear is that the executive's performance will suffer as the result of underperformance of some other domain or group. This is not an unreasonable fear, but its consequences can be damaging. As we noted previously, the appropriate strategy is to expand our sphere of influence into adjacent and interdependent groups to gain better insight on the processes that affect our domain. However, this process can be difficult and take some time. This can lead many hard-charging executives to seek to build redundancies into their organization to mitigate perceived or anticipated risk from other domains. This type of empire building is extraordinarily inefficient and speaks to several root problems that should be addressed directly and not through indirect means such as empire building (namely, the failure of other domain resources to deliver must be remedied directly). By building an empire of redundancy, the executive demonstrates a lack of maturity in interacting with other executives and domains as well as inefficiency in their use of resources. Neither of these outcomes is acceptable and both will limit our ability to be successful in our current role or advance.

Competitive Measurement/Status Anxiety: Finally, the organizational culture itself can be a strong motivator to build an empire. In many organizations with a competitive culture, there can be a temptation to build empires to demonstrate relative power within the organization. This is particularly true in organizations with unbalanced domains, where a great deal of relative power is held within one or two particular domains. We may see empire-building as a means of achieving parity. From the perspective of the executive, the challenge will be to hold firm in the understanding that willful empire building is inherently wasteful and damaging to both their career and the organization. The successful executive must have faith and believe that demonstrated excellence with the minimum resources will yield out the greatest benefit to both themselves and the organization. The truth is that as we demonstrate excellence with minimal resources, the larger domains will appear bloated and confer negative associations to their leaders. Parity seeking will continue, but to our benefit and the organization.

We must acknowledge the potential fallibility in our own thinking and our inherent lack of maturity as a new executive. Prematurely building an empire without direct and painful need is overshooting our target and brings with it all of the attendant disadvantages. Further, our desire to build an empire as a junior executive is very likely rooted in fear and anxiety. Until we have truly tested our domain's capacity in the existing scope of work and determined the optimal organizational model in terms of skillsets and roles, it is foolhardy to add resources. We must know which functions need direct and authoritative leadership and which can operate with independent resources. We must understand the true lines of communication in our domain and the broader organization as well as the attenuation associated with transmission of our intent to the furthest reaches of our sphere of influence.

We will create an appropriate equilibrium in which the organizational groups that we build ensure parity among the group leaders and preserve the shortest, most direct lines of communication. It must be stressed that this deep communication knowledge cannot be understood thoroughly before taking over a new group or even promoting into a position of leadership over an existing group. It must be evaluated closely, clearly and over time to find the optimal equilibrium. Further, it must be tempered by necessity. Creating three functional groups within our teams has no meaning unless the optimal flow of work necessitates it. Empires are not built by forcing circumstances into our preconceived notions of how work should be done by the organization; rather, they are built of necessity to ensure the greatest output with the least resources. As Clausewitz states in "On War," "Only the man who can achieve great results with limited means has really hit the mark" (Clausewitz, 1993)

The Junior Executive will acknowledge that their desire to empire-build is likely rooted in fear or anxiety, while working assiduously to only build their organization as by necessity.

INTELLIGENCE

The common understanding of intelligence in business literature is a misrepresentation of what intelligence really means as a competency in the organization. As such, we must examine the core meaning of intelligence before outlining an approach for its implementation. We should start by stating what intelligence is not, namely the disambiguation of just any stream of information. Thus, it is not "business intelligence," a marketing term that refers to the analytical understanding of the operations of our own business. There may be an external element to intelligence, but only as interpreted through the lens of our organization's outputs. Additionally, intelligence is not "competitive" or "market" intelligence. These are marketing terms for the subjective analyses of individuals with special access to major market players. There are only elements of real intelligence in these terms. The challenge for organizations is that real intelligence activity is administratively burdensome to implement effectively. But, intelligence must be implemented comprehensively and holistically to be of true use to the organization. We recommend a practical approach to that implementation based upon the core meaning of intelligence, allowing for an iterative, organic process. In truth, this is how all intelligence networks are established—organically.

So, what does intelligence mean for the executive and for the organization? Intelligence is the process by which we gain understanding of what our competitors do and intend to do. That is, intelligence is learning about near-term action and developing a framework for anticipation of the future actions of our competitors. The question for us as an executive is to determine the value of intelligence to our work. As with all initiatives, this determination should be strictly needs-based. An executive with product management responsibility in a consumer goods market has a tremendous need for comprehensive intelligence, whereas an administrator at a public hospital might have only a small need for intelligence, or none at all. Another definition of intelligence is the collection, analysis, processing and reporting of operational information on a particular target that represents a threat to our existing or future plans. In this definition, there are two types of intelligence: overt and covert. The goal of all intelligence activities is the clearest possible understanding of the actions and intents of our targets.

As an executive, a priority task is to identify the necessary targets of our intelligence activities. A target may be a competing organization or product line or an internal rival. We must weigh the relative value of the intelligence to be gained against the likely effort required to implement a program. Once a target has been identified, a plan of collection must be initiated. This can take many forms, each of which has both benefits and drawbacks. In general, the points of consideration in choosing a plan of collection are the level of effort and the relative value of the possible action derived from the information. There are some general parameters available to us, but it is the contextual triangulation of information that is the key confidence in the information. Multiple sources providing a consistent picture of the actions and intent of our target will improve the quality of intelligence and thus our ability to make operational decisions based upon it. There are multiple methods of collecting intelligence in a civilian setting:

> **Human-based Intelligence**: This is the most prevalent and cheapest manner of collecting information, but also the most unreliable and subject to machinations and subterfuge. In the organizational context, as we have noted in previous chapters, the use of human intelligence as a tactic is not recommended. It requires an individual to suppress their personal integrity and incurs all of the negative attributes of such behavior. However, we must note that human-based intelligence will likely very often be offered freely and should be considered when available. It can enhance other intelligence data and help round the picture, but it should rarely be used as the sole source of information for action.
>
> **Imagery-based Intelligence**: One of the most reliable methods of collecting intelligence is via image. In general, the level of effort required for deception is such that a picture

can provide a clear indication of activity by the target. In the organizational context, there is not much use for this. Yet there are examples. One of the most readily cited examples is in the use of due diligence for investment purposes. A very common strategy for firms conducting this type of intelligence is to take pictures from factory loading docks or parking lots of retail locations. Very often, this source of information is at odds with what is being reported overtly by the target firm. It is suggested that the executive carefully consider the costs and associated benefits of imagery-based intelligence and comply with any legal constraints.

Signals-based Intelligence: Arguably the most useful and reliable source of intelligence within the organizational context is signals intelligence, the discernment of information through the frequency and types of signals that are transmitted to and from a target. This is particularly useful in internal competitive efforts. "Signal" in this context means an event of communication. That is, an e-mail sent or received is a signal—the information is the envelope data, not the contents. Teleconferences, meetings, e-mails, packages, etc. all can provide valuable information on our target. In terms of a competitive bidding process, the signals sent from and received by both bidder and seller are very useful in anticipating both intent and actions. For example, if we hear from human sources that a competitor is going to be meeting with the prospective customer on a Tuesday and the customer either has already or subsequently delays an open-forum meeting to Wednesday, it will allow us to gain better understanding of the intent of the customer with regard to our competitor.

It must be understood that all intelligence targeting and collection must be overt—that is, legal. There is no benefit to covert intelligence in modern developed economies. We see periodic indictments, arrests, sackings and scandals associated with covert intelligence collection in the news. Any benefit associated with covert intelligence collection is vastly outweighed by the ethical and legal consequences.

In using overt intelligence, we need a framework for analysis, processing and reporting to develop a comprehensive picture from the intelligence data collected. This means standardizing reporting media and inputs, assigning commonly understood probability associations with various sources and developing the report format and associated algorithms for integrating multi-source data. Any one piece of data will likely be useless for near-term action. Rather, a multi-source aggregation of data must be established that provides a probability estimate for accuracy. This grants us confidence in the efficacy of our resulting decisions and allows for expectation setting amongst our constituents. How we implement this as an executive will be dependent upon our organization, its outputs and culture.

A final note on counter-intelligence: If the target of our intelligence collection is aware of the collection effort, then they may wish to remove that source or feed them bad information. As such, it is critical that our intelligence sources are vetted and kept anonymous.

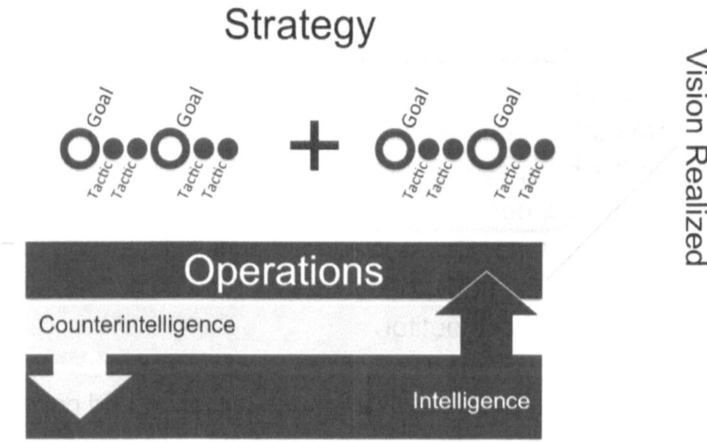

Figure 41 - Intelligence-related activities should feed our operations for tactical leverage, in support of strategy.

The Junior Executive will implement a comprehensive, lean and disciplined intelligence-processing competency within their domain.

TRENDS

The executive role is very often fluid and wide-open. That is, it is often unclear which direction the executive should go. An executive must understand the machinery of their domain and the organization in depth to ensure that it is running at an optimal level. But there is no machinery at the executive level. Rather, it is very often a new country rife with both opportunity and threat. At lower levels in the organization, we see an opportunity for laws of material application and control. As we move up the hierarchy and the targets of our actions become less fixed and more mobile and intelligent, our ability to apply such laws becomes far less useful and can even prove damaging. Luckily, there are tools available to us to gain control and understanding of our team and organization at higher levels. However, we must acknowledge that there are few if any tools or guidelines that assist us in determining a vision for our domain and the organization. In an uncertain environment that is ill-defined at best in terms of benefits and risks, how do we determine the best course of action? The truth is that this challenge will be different for everyone—there is no process that is universally applicable to every individual. But as Clausewitz noted, "This much is clear: [leadership], like any other [subject] that does not surpass man's intellectual capacity, can be elucidated by an inquiring mind, and its internal structure can to some degree be revealed. That alone is enough to turn the concept of theory into reality." With this in mind, how do we approach the question of determining the best course of action?

We have addressed discrete concepts that will assist us building a team and crafting organizational direction and vision. Institutional learning, situational awareness, and intelligence all contribute to a rich picture of our organization's competencies, capacities and deficiencies. Further, we have discussed the topics of cross-disciplinary study, innovation and genius, which give us insight into how to cast our eye ahead of what is currently in view. The task at hand then is to see the target that does not yet exist. This directive may seem cavalier, but this is precisely what it means to implement a vision, for our personal career and our work as an executive. What other options are there? Peg our movements and maneuvers to competitors? This certainly isn't interesting or inspiring; rather, it is a capitulation. The successful executive has little chance of advancement by following others. So how do we see the target that does not yet exist? As noted above, there is no universal prescription for this process, yet there is a reductive answer available. We understand the basic truth that no one knows what the future will hold—not even the most prescient analyst can tell us with any certainty what is going to happen in one year's time. If they guess it right this year, they'll be wrong the next. This is a certainty that we can use to anchor our analysis. If no one knows what the future will hold, then it follows that everyone is working through the same process of feeling their way forward. They are all operating within a system of analysis, experimentation and willful direction, all subject to infinite chance and advances in cross-disciplinarian studies and technologies.

We mostly understand the present and past. The task at hand is to project our understanding into the future. We can divide the future into two temporal ranges: near-term and long-term. Although the framework by which we gain our understanding is roughly the same in the near term and the long term, we must maintain greater flexibility the further into the future we cast. We need to analyze the data available to us now and push ourselves to think beyond analogs and mimics. By acknowledging our general inability to perfectly hit the unseen target, we can often ensure that we are in the best possible position to hit the target when it becomes visible. To do this, we must analyze trends. Trends in this context are past activities analyzed in a particular scope to extrapolate a line of progression of some factor against time. Thus, we might say that trends in home ownership in the United States are represented by new home purchases by year, new home builds by year or resale purchases by year in the market. All trends are some derivative of this process of statistical review. When we look at trends in other domains, we see that they can become standing rules or laws and take on an air of causality. For example, Moore's law of computing tells us that computational power doubles every eighteen months (Moore, 1965). These trends provide a foundation for assumptions in our own planning. If we are a computer software firm, we can use Moore's law as an underlying principle in our vision of a software program that will need greater computing power in the near-term future. Yet the trend identified by Moore's law is just one input factor. We also need to understand the customer need for this software (or whatever service or product we are providing) in the future. So, we must understand the trends in the consumer market. If we are a software maker, we must understand the market trends for hardware platforms and styles of user interaction over time. If we are a large university we must understand the trends associated with commuter students and their preferences for online coursework against in-class lecture. As we cast our eye further into the future, we should understand changes in teaching methodologies in primary school and the trends associated with computer-based training and consumer electronics used by primary-aged school children. All of these should influence our vision of the education experience at our university.

For example, we see that Nissan Motor Company's vision of electric vehicles, which allowed them to gain an eighteen-month advantage on competitors, combined analysis of the current market reliance on carbon-based fuels, anticipated cost rates of those fuels, market comfort with electric vehicles and green initiatives, previous tests and trials and a determination to make mass market electric vehicles viable. This vision was subject to highly variable fuel prices, which at many times did not trend in favor of Nissan's strategy, as well as adjacent cross-disciplinary technologies. Without advances in battery technology and the associated materials manufacturing as well as integrated wireless communication technologies, the vision of a mass-market electric vehicle would have been foolhardy. Yet Nissan's electric-vehicle vision is a case study in successful execution in a vastly uncertain terrain, and not a gamble. The successful executive will acknowledge the vastly uncertain terrain of their remit and implement a strategy to understand the complexities involved in crafting a vision of the future.

Our analysis of trends and market proclivities will assist us in crafting, experimenting with and adjusting our roadmap in the near and long term. On the path to our vision, what are the waypoints and what should be our positioning at those waypoints? Such questions are the framework within which we can artfully operate in the great uncertainty of the executive role. The successful executive will acknowledge that the future is unknowable. We will understand that our future success depends on being able to develop a vision that is in essence hitting an unseen target. The successful executive will analyze associative and cross-disciplinary trends and market proclivities to help craft this vision.

The Junior Executive will establish a flexible roadmap to guide analysis of trends in all peripheral aspects of their current and future work.

AGENCY

At the executive level, the temptation of callous behavior is always present and it is critical that we remain grounded in rock-solid integrity. We stress this point because it is fundamental to the concept of agency. Throughout our tenure as an executive, we must find agents in our team to work on our behalf. This is a critical step in the maturation process as an executive and in the process of establishing a bench of lieutenants who can be trusted. Further, this concept underlies our ability to establish a legacy of succession in our team and the organization as a whole.

There is a clear difference between agency and delegation.

Whereas delegation is the assignment of a scope of work to an individual, agency is the allocation of responsibility to another individual to act on our behalf. We grant an agent the legitimacy and creditability of our name. Traditionally, agency is relegated to discrete tasks or transactions (e.g., real estate, financial trusts, etc.). In the organization, agency is the means by which our personal authority is extended through other individuals in pursuit of our goals. It is a level above delegation, in that the individual agent is not simply executing a directed task within known constraints, but is acting independently on our behalf. The successful executive will spend time and effort grooming trusted individuals within their domain to take on the role of agent. These may be functional leaders or team leaders of matrix-assigned projects.

Agents are tremendously important in times of internal or external competition. Externally facing agents demonstrate a consistent message and approach to vendors, partners, and customers. This provides a great deal of comfort and ease of interface for these external parties. Further, it provides a consistent defense to machinations by those who seek to weaken our external relationships for whatever reason. Externally facing agents also expand our ability to manage externally facing work. Almost as important, particularly for the new executive in an asymmetric power position, agents provide extended opportunities to further our agenda within the organization. In particular, given that the actual work done in an organization is done at levels below the executive, internal agents have the ability to increase our sphere of influence through process enhancements and modifications, project ownership and resource allocations. In competitive endeavors within the organization, agents give the executive the ability to maneuver intelligently.

Agency is important to all executives, but particularly for the executive in asymmetric power contexts. A good analog of the utility of agents is the traditional use of dogs for hunting. We start with the assumption that a dog has minimal higher-level reasoning that provides motivations beyond their bond with their caregiver. That is, a dog is assured attention if it behaves as expected. If we hold this thought and then consider what we ask the animal to do when hunting on our behalf, we see an excellent example of agency. The dog is our agent on the hunt. We only make it aware of a target—its instinctual nature and predilection to hunt allow it to operate independently of us. Further, different dogs are better suited to different hunts, depending on the target (birds, boars, some other game, or even missing persons). By maintaining a variety of dogs, each suited to purpose, the dog handler has agents that can be engaged to achieve otherwise unattainable goals. Sending many agent dogs to field geometrically expands our reach. This is a simple example, but the same holds true for resources in our organization. Different individuals are better suited to different tasks. But only if we trust them enough to grant them agency are they able to expand our sphere of influence. It is appropriate to look at three tactical examples of the importance of agency in the competitive context:

> **Flanking**: In conflict, flanking means pivoting front-line forces into an oblique attack on the forces of an opponent. Beyond military terminology, flanking is the threat of action against a relatively unprotected area under management by competitors. Flanking in the organizational context is applying resources and will to an area controlled by a competitor that is not well protected. This strategy identifies areas that are under-resourced or ignored. For example, if we note that a large bank chain competitor has allowed their branch locations in a particular market fall into disrepair, this is worth investigation as a target for flanking. Rather than seek to slug it out in their strongest markets, we can attack this flank with a new business model and an energized workforce. A flanking maneuver of this sort requires a lieutenant to manage and drive the effort day-to-day in line with our broader strategy and goals. A flanking maneuver is a subordinated tactical move that is intended to progress a broader strategy. In order to execute an effective, integrated, and aligned flanking move, we must have an agent. To

follow our example, if the larger bank chain then pours resources and energy into competing with us in this flank area, we may have opened up an opportunity in their stronger market. As a single executive, we cannot manage both engagements fully; rather, it must be done through agents.

Skirmish: Skirmishes are often underutilized in the organizational context. The skirmish is an uncommitted contest between two opponents that will not result in a final decision. In other words, a skirmish is a small fight. Skirmishes are incredibly useful for several reasons: they relay intent to commit to a fight, they show commitment of will over the competition in question, they provide valuable feedback on the tactics and resources of opponents and they are excellent tools of distraction. Skirmishes require agents, for several reasons. An agent must lead and direct the skirmish and thus be the associated authority and responsibility holder of the skirmish. If our lieutenants enjoy true agency within our team, they will execute a skirmish of their own volition, typically to confer upon us its benefits or buffer us from its negative consequences in pursuit of a broader goal. We must mimic the dog handler and rely upon the known nature of the agent to deliver upon their exposure to the situation. Once released, we expect the dog to act as an agent and either confer upon us the success of the hunt or compartmentalize the failure. Our desired outcome should be reflected by which agent we choose.

Distraction: Distraction is arguably the most important tool in competitive engagements. It can draw our competitor's attention away from the focus of the contest and allow us to use our maintained focus to take advantage. There are myriad examples, but we are concerned here with the importance of agency in relation to distraction. As noted in the paragraphs above, distraction is often the desired

> outcome of a flanking maneuver or a skirmish. In fact, distraction is a causal effect of some other action and it is not itself an action. But creating distraction requires agents. To execute actions that distract our competitor, we must have an agent directing and controlling the action to ensure its success. Further, by entrusting an agent to conduct the distracting operation, if frees us as the executive to execute once our competitor's focus is lost.

Agency is a prerequisite for expanding our sphere of influence and maturing into senior leadership. Agency requires commitment to and thoughtful use of agents in the execution of strategy. Many components of strategic execution and campaign management require agency. Actions for flanking, skirmish or distraction require an individual of independent motivation to execute them whole-heartedly on our behalf.

The Junior Executive will seek to project their sphere of influence through the use of agents in competitive contests.

Chapter 10 Ascension

INTERNALIZATION

A very common reaction to criticism is a defensive posture, whereby we seek to deflect that criticism or otherwise blunt it by pointing out a deficiency in another. There are three troublesome aspects of such a posture. First, it redirects focus away from what may very well be an actual problem. Second, it corrupts the analysis of any issue by favoring subjective comparison over objective analysis (that is, how can another criticize our process when theirs is worse by comparison). Third, it initiates a cycle of defensive posturing that can permanently stall any actual attempts to remediate the problem. All three trace back to a critical point: the successful executive will ensure that their own yard is in order. Their domain and teams should be operating at expected levels of efficiency and quality such that there can be no real basis for criticism. The successful executive must both lead by example in this manner and demand the same from their team from the very start. We have provided a roadmap for establishing an environment where this is possible and have demonstrated the skillsets required to maintain that environment.

During our tenure as an executive, virtually any examination of problems within a workflow or output will lead to a discussion of the root cause of a fault. This will lead in turn to attributions of fault in which one domain points out a perceived or real failing in another domain. This in and of itself should be expected as part of how problems are examined. In general, fault can always be found, and we should never allow ourselves to hide problems or failures of foresight behind serendipity. Depending upon the culture of the organization and the personalities involved, the slightest attribution of fault can elicit a vehement defense. The resulting defensiveness can hinder any true analysis of the issue and follow-on remediation. Often, third parties must serve as arbiters. The coping mechanism of defensiveness and the original causal argument are both extremely wasteful. We seek to avoid this waste in two ways: avoiding defensive posturing and maintaining optimal processes in our own domain. Let us examine the first by looking at the three aspects of the defensive posture.

Deflection: Deflection indicates that the defending party perceives the criticism as an attack. This may or may not be true. In combative cultures with a history of conflict in this manner, a criticism very well likely may be an attack. However, deflecting criticism will only serve to avoid actual remediation of the issue. Rather, we must acknowledge the issue and the criticism openly. If there is an issue, the first point of action is to confirm its existence and examine the contributing factors of the issue. If they point to a process within our domain, we need to determine if there is indeed a problem with that process. If we have maintained our yard, this should be a quick and easy exercise. If we find that there is no issue with our process, the investigation can move on. Allowing ourselves or our team to deflect due to defensive instincts will only cause damage.

Subjective versus Objective Analysis: The quickest and most effective way to demonstrate our executive excellence is to achieve targets against objective milestones. Subjective analysis only serves to demonstrate relative worth against existing, running targets. The successful executive will demonstrate excellence against objective targets and thus confer the benefits of expanding the scope of operations of their domain and organization. Pointing out subjective comparisons between our processes and those of another domain really demonstrates less of a failure to grow the scope of the operation. If our domain and organization are operating perfectly, then we are chasing targets beyond the scope of current operations. Other domains must keep up with us—this should be the only cause of attributed fault with regard to our domain. The successful executive will ensure that they and their team are only concerned with objective targets and treat criticism of their processes in kind.

Defensive Cycles: By allowing ourselves and our team to indulge defensive instincts with regard to criticism, we open ourselves to a cycle of grudges and resentments. This is disadvantageous to the organization and the individuals involved. Poor practices and processes can ossify simply because the individuals involved refuse to cooperate on a solution that would benefit the broader organization. For the executive, this presents a very difficult scenario to manage. A policy of openly acknowledging discrete issues and addressing them in relation to objective targets will help in this effort.

The greatest defensive weapon available to the new executive is optimal process operation. It provides a clean yard from which any issues or deficiencies can be addressed. This is particularly true in asymmetries of power and cross-domain conflict. The successful executive will first ensure operational excellence. Furthermore, the successful executive will ensure a policy of engagement that avoids defensive posturing within their own team and doggedly exposes it in others. It is only by focusing on an issue, judging it objectively and avoiding recriminatory defensive positions that broader organizational issues can be resolved. If we have no skeletons in the closet, we have no worries of opening the door.

The Junior Executive will internalize process excellence to ensure that issues can be addressed openly and honestly.

ENERGY

We have discussed at length the level of trust granted to an executive, which is rooted in the purpose of the executive role to empower individuals to execute work on behalf of the organization.

We have also discussed the accountability and responsibility that this trust demands. As we move beyond the moment of promotion into the executive role we see that the love we feel for the organization at the point of ascension is very often short-lived. That is, the honeymoon will eventually end. After this short period of blind affection for the organization, we will be beset by frustration, disappointment and stress. This should come as no surprise. We should acknowledge the effect that this can have on our executive persona. One of the duties of the executive is to cheerlead for their team and organization. This is easy at the beginning of the executive tenure, as it draws from true emotion. The burden of duty steadily becomes more noticeable as we grow into the executive role and encounter some of the more unsavory aspects of the organization. We have laid a solid groundwork for protection against these challenges here. Yet the executive must go beyond mere protection. They must project a sense of energy and hope for the future that subordinates and others in the organization can use to anchor their own courage. The successful executive will demonstrate energy and hope in cheerleading for their organization and team. There is an element of duty underlying this mandate, but there are also morale-related benefits conferred back on the executive by fulfilling this responsibility.

Morale is commonly understood to be the projection of personal goals onto group goals and the capacity to pursue those goals in the face of adversity. The consistent maintenance of morale confers value upon the individuals involved, the leader and the broader organization. There are many Maslowian aspects to morale, but we consider them well understood. Rather, our focus is on the tenuous link that attributes personal goals to group goals. What is this link that goes well beyond our base needs as individuals? Essentially, it is deduced from a negative and a positive. If we look at the building blocks of morale and the link to the group, we see two key aspects:

<u>Things Cannot Get Worse Than They Are Now</u>: The best example of the negative deductive basis of morale is expressed by the Stockdale Paradox as defined by James C. Collins in a quote from

Vice Admiral James Stockdale, in the book "Good to Great." "You must never confuse faith that you will prevail in the end—which you can never afford to lose—with the discipline to confront the most brutal facts of your current reality, whatever they may be" (Collins, 2001). The paradox is essentially that we must always believe that circumstances cannot get worse than they currently are, and that our faith in triumphing over those circumstances must be maintained at all times. In so doing, no circumstances are beyond our endurance. We must keep our leadership persona in the present and demonstrate through word and deed that things cannot get worse than they are at that moment. Our example will serve as an anchor for our team. Without this, morale has no basis.

Greater Glory Can Be Achieved By The Group: If the basis of morale is a stoic stubbornness that circumstances will only improve, we must also ensure that our teams and the broader organization understand that greater glory is to be achieved by the group than by the individual. While it is an asset to have stars within an organization, they must have colleagues of like ability. There are few circumstances more corrosive to morale than star players who look upon their teammates with derision. The successful executive will not tolerate derisive treatment among their teams, and will also ruthlessly populate their teams with evenly matched individuals. This is the only way to truly ensure an environment where the individuals of a team can attribute their individual goals to the broader goals of the team and organization. The successful executive will not fool themselves that policies or programs designed to make individuals more sensitive to others will leverage the benefits of high morale. These may serve to keep the peace and put a floor under minimum performance, but they will never reap the truly impressive benefits of high morale. This is not to say that only star players are worth hiring; rather, it is to say that successful teams with common goals are made up of evenly matched individuals—both in terms of skillset and motivation.

The environment and basis for morale are relatively straightforward. Maintenance of both is a task of the executive, and in this work, we are a cheerleader for the team and organization. This directly delivers the true core value of morale—performance in the face of adversity. As we noted at the beginning of this chapter, after the honeymoon phase, workaday challenges will begin to take their toll. In terms of our focus on the objective measurement of performance, this can reduce efficiency, quality of outputs, etc. Our competitors are faced with the same friction. Morale is more often than not the decisive factor, even in asymmetrical contests. A faith that circumstances will improve and that there is greater glory attached to the team goals than our own individual goals underpins this advantage. Our team's morale must be dominant. It must be a juggernaut. This is the only defense against the corrosive effects of the stress and conflict that undermine many organizational endeavors. The successful executive will understand that in the face of both objective performance targets and relative competitors, morale is often the deciding factor and it is based on our energy.

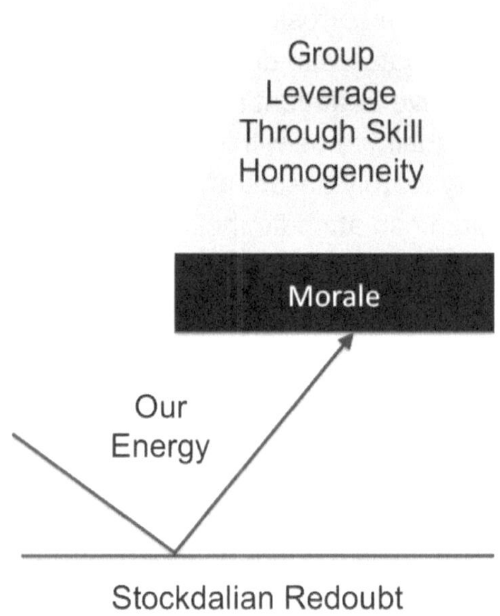

Figure 42 - Our energy serves as an engine for group achievement.

The Junior Executive will make a conscious effort to maintain high energy in the team and focus on optimizing the environment for high morale.

SUCCESSION

For the majority of individuals and organizations, succession is reactionary. That is, very few people think about succession until there is a vacancy that forces it. This is not necessarily a problem in the post-modern economy. Rigid hierarchies are no longer the norm, and it is becoming increasingly burdensome to manage individuals' career paths as a component of corporate policy. But there is still value in planning for and managing succession. First, we should address some of the reluctance associated with succession planning and then discuss what consideration should be given to it in our work as an executive. Succession planning is often resisted because it can represent a threat to the individual. The thinking goes that if a younger, cheaper version of us is trained into our job, then we can be let go with minimal consequences to the organization.

This is true, to a certain degree. If our organization sustains a culture whereby highly trained and valuable employees are replaced with cheaper versions, this says a great deal about the organization and the role. Namely, that the organization does not operate in a market or industry that requires value-added by employees. Thus, this is not an organization that will value us and should be avoided. This a worst-case scenario produced by a particular organizational failure and should not influence our approach to succession. Given the extraordinary difficulty of finding and training excellent employees, it is illogical to conclude that training a successor would result in our firing. Again, it is possible, but not probable. If we understand the direct value that we deliver to the organization in relation to our cost, it should provide comfort—assuming, of course, that we deliver more value than we cost. It is instinctual to believe that if we are required for the delivery of work in the organization then we are indispensable to the organization. Thus, training a successor reduces this indispensability. This line of reasoning is fallacious for a number of reasons and does not align with the ideas put forward in this book.

First and foremost, it directly contradicts a core assumption that we have made about ourselves: we are a successful executive who intends even greater positions of impact. Further, indispensability in our current role as a junior executive means that the organization cannot afford to move us into a higher position. This is common in highly defined staff positions in some organizations. How could a private hospital promote their best cardiac surgeon to head of surgery if there is no one available to replace them? By being indispensable we can enjoy a high degree of job security in that we will be unable to advance. Additionally, from an organizational perspective, indispensable employees represent a substantial risk. What if we were hit by a bus on the way to work? How would that affect the organization? Would the core outputs cease to be delivered? What indispensable really means to the organization is untenable. If we understand that indispensability is a false choice and actually represents a risk to both our career advancement and the organization as a whole, how do we obtain career security? For most of us, security is realized in always moving forward. To do this, we must put some effort into succession planning.

Succession planning is vital to our success as a junior executive for a variety of reasons. For ourselves, succession planning allows us to gain greater understanding of our role as an executive in the organization. There is no better learning tool for a particular subject than to teach it to another—we must reformulate what we know into a format that another person can understand. In this, succession planning allows us to grow in our position and make our work more relevant to the organization. Additionally, succession planning allows us to mold an individual to take our place in the organization when we are promoted to senior leadership. This not only ensures that our current domain will continue to operate at an optimal level but also provides a successor who we have personally trained and groomed and who will very likely be an ally in the future. For the organization, succession planning and training provides confidence that our concern is for the organization's success and that we are laying the groundwork to advance. It is far easier to promote an individual into senior leadership if we already know that their previous role will transition smoothly to a trusted person. For the organization, this resolves a substantial risk of indispensability. For our team members, succession planning and training provides comfort and confidence that a path to advancement exists for them. This assurance is one of the most important tools for morale-building and motivation, particularly if we have ambitious individuals on our staff. Without confidence in their ability to advance, ambitious individuals will soon depart. The successful executive will ensure that they have a plan for succession—no matter how simple—and will work to train appropriate individuals for the eventuality.

How does the successful executive address succession? We must bring the appropriate individuals into our confidence and allow them to see the inner workings of our role. We must create agents with portions of our authority in certain domains. Much of this we are already doing as a successful executive through agency and delegation. But succession planning goes to a deeper level in that we must allow a successor to see behind the veneer of executive leadership—negotiations, how work is allocated, how performance is measured, and how we lead our domain. In parallel, they must be given stand-alone responsibility to implement what we have shown them in a defined way. In many cases, this will mean putting a particular director or manager in charge of a single project and allowing them to run it as a stand-alone business. In time, they must be shown how this single project intersects with the rest of the portfolio, domain and the organization at large. Finally, they must be shown the roadmap and vision for the team and how these were derived. It is not the artifacts that matter; it is the thought process and evaluative discipline that must be taught to our successor. They must begin to think like an executive—they should read this book. Any particular implementation, as with all things, will be directly tied to the types of work that our organization does and the individuals involved. Additionally, the timescale will be dictated by our ability to advance within the organization. One common pitfall associated with succession planning is training too soon and losing a potential successor to another organization. It will be up to us as the executive to feel out the best method and timeline.

The Junior Executive will understand that indispensability is a trap, and plan for succession to excel in their role.

FORGIVENESS

As we have noted, the time during and after the promotion to executive is a psychological minefield. An imperative for navigating this phase is understanding the root cause of situations. An important aspect of this imperative is considering the ill intent of others. There will be individuals who truly wish ill upon us, those who will only seem so and those who will be guilty by association given circumstances. As with any high stress situation, the stakes seem higher and the emotions more intense. This is particularly true for the new executive who is very likely uncertain in their new position.

The focus of this chapter is acknowledging this uncertainty and the damage that can result if it is not addressed. The duration of this initial uncertainty is to a large degree defined by us as the executive. The faster we can demonstrate maturity in the new role and avoid overreaction, the faster we will feel secure and confident in our new role. Alain de Botton, in his book "The Consolations of Philosophy," addresses this trap in discussing the paranoid expressions of uncertain and unconfident leaders.

> "The governor of Syria had at once interpreted the applause of his soldiers as a wish to undermine his authority and to question his judgment. Cyrus had at once interpreted the river's manslaughter of his horse as murder. Seneca had an

> explanation for such errors of judgment; it lay with a 'certain abjectness of spirit' in men like Cyrus and Piso. Behind their readiness to anticipate insult is a fear of deserving ridicule. When we suspect that we are appropriate targets for hurt, it does not take much for us to believe that someone or something is out to hurt us: [thus,] 'so and so did not give me an audience today, though he gave it to others'" (Botton, 2001).

Instead of ignoring or suppressing an emotion, we must acknowledge its appropriateness. The successful executive will acknowledge their level of uncertainty in the executive role initially and understand how this uncertainty can taint their view of the actions of others. Furthermore, they must acknowledge how this uncertainty can taint their actions in relation to others. By knowing that our own uncertainty can skew our interpretation, we can overcome that uncertainty. Our aspiration is to internalize concepts, topics and values that will provide us with an anchor of confidence in times of uncertainty. One of the most important manifestations of that confidence is the ability to forgive. There are many circumstances that may require forgiveness, the nature of which depends on the intent of the act that required forgiving. Of course, it is easy to forgive a failing due to a lack of intent—for example, someone bumping into us in the hallway. Rather, we are concerned with two types of intentional failings that affect the executive: how they are affected by the level of uncertainty we feel in the role and how they should be handled.

As executives, those with the greatest ability to do us harm are those who have audiences with our stakeholders and those who we trust. There are really only two responses to harms, anchored in core truths of leadership based in integrity: ostracize or forgive. When we look at the two groups of individuals in a position to do us the greatest harm, it is clear that those whom we trust would be the only candidates for a "come-to-Jesus" approach, in which we benefit from our forgiving. Individuals who have audiences with our stakeholders must also be considered for this approach in that they are likely out of our sphere of influence and their involvement in our ongoing affairs may be out of our control if we stay in the organization. Rather, we should look at their actions and the likely intent with empathy. With this group, harms inflicted with direct intent must be addressed ruthlessly and directly. As a new executive, we cannot allow the precedent to be established that direct-intent harms will go unanswered. Our approach should always be consistent. We must openly acknowledge the harm and ostracize the offending party. It should be anticipated that this will cause conflict among the wider group and likely have consequences, but the alternative is untenable in any organization. The successful executive will ostracize external parties who inflict direct harm with intent. We must acknowledge that this scenario is rare, particularly at the executive level, where the players are more sophisticated.

When an external party harms us with intent, the likely source of harm is competition. The question is to understand the basis for the harm. Was it merely a harm we incurred because the external party beat us in some competition? That is, did our domain or organization suffer because the external party demonstrated a better case for their domain or organization? Or was there subterfuge involved? Our judgment of intent is critical to both our understanding of ourselves and the future possibility of working with the external party. Again, anchoring ourselves to the principles demonstrated so far will provide a good framework for analyzing these behaviors. The successful executive will understand that at times we will be indirectly harmed by other individuals and that the appropriate response is forgiveness.

When we consider harms incurred by those we trust, we use much the same thought-process. The only approach in response to trusted individuals directly harming us with intent is to ostracize them. Such incidents will often come in the form of intra-organizational rivalry. Much like above, these scenarios will be rare. Far more likely are the indirect harms received through intent by people we trust. Also, much like above these scenarios present us with a lot to consider. Our point on this concept is to acknowledge the role that our own uncertainty will play in our judgment. Understanding that we may be predisposed to a bit of paranoia in the early days of our promotion will go a long way in avoiding overreaction. Passivity is also a common occurrence in these situations, as most people are not predisposed to believe that others will actively work against them. But only by directly addressing the harm can we act in the best manner possible. Our options are to either forgive or ostracize. We leave it to the individual to determine their own outcome and own the moral responsibility of their actions. In the best outcomes for scenarios of this type, the trusted individual is forgiven and the stress of the situation resolved over time.

The Junior Executive will deal with all harms by evaluating the intent and either ostracizing the guilty party or forgiving them.

CEREMONY AND TRADITION

In many organizations, the mere thought of ceremonies and traditions is cringe-worthy (mandatory birthday parties, etc.). And in fact, organizational use of ceremony and tradition runs the spectrum from deeply meaningful to ironic. The particular alignment of an organization on this spectrum derives from many factors: age of the organization, type of work done, thoughtfulness of the leadership team, etc. It tends to rely heavily on two key components: intent and objectivity. What is the intent of the ceremony or tradition? How is it applied to the individuals within the organization? Both of these components determine the level of legitimacy of the ceremony or tradition and thus its value. If a ceremony or tradition is conducted superficially or non-inclusively, it will confer negative value on the organization. If the ceremony or tradition is conducted with deep meaning and includes all organization team members, it will confer a great deal of value upon the organization and leadership. The logic is simple, but practical implementation is very difficult. What does this mean for us?

First, ceremonies and traditions do confer real value upon the organization. Second, greater negative value can be conferred upon an organization if ceremonies and traditions are implemented superficially or non-inclusively. So, what are ceremonies and traditions? As discussed before, organizations exist as platforms for groups of individuals to achieve goals that otherwise could not be attained by individuals. Ceremonies and traditions are artifacts that serve to demonstrate a testament of this abstract concept of the organization. If ten people gather in a room to collaborate on a story, the output is the only tangible artifact of that collaboration. Once the story is complete, those ten people can go their separate ways. They were able to achieve something greater than an individual effort via the platform of an organization, but the organization existed only as an abstract concept and disbanded as quickly as it came together. Ceremonies and traditions serve as artifacts of a deposition process to give life to the organization. When we talk of great organizations with a rich history, that history is a product of such processes. As a junior executive, our control over these processes is relatively limited. However, we need to fully understand the implications of the phenomena. We must be able to clearly articulate the value of ceremonies and traditions to our subordinates. We must be able to provide feedback to senior leadership about the efficacy of existing ceremonies and traditions. And we must be able to create and hone ceremonies and traditions within our own domains.

> **Real Value**: Not only do ceremonies and traditions provide a real-life deposition of the abstract concepts of the organization, they provide a framework for achievement. Ceremonies and traditions provide a medium for acknowledging excellence that would otherwise go unnoticed. In practical terms, it means relatively little to be named "Salesman of the Year." But in the context of an organization, such an award enhances the reality of the organization. It is an entity that serves as a source of judgment and confers emotional value to the individual. While the broader culture may not value the achievements of

the "Salesman of the Year," that individual will likely have made a Herculean effort to achieve the results that warranted the award. Celebrating this achievement through ceremony and tradition demonstrates that the organization values the work of its members. This is real value and over the long term, will lend the organization life.

Negative Value: Misaligned or poorly executed deposition of organizational values through ceremony or tradition can result in significant negative consequences. If traditions are misaligned with the values of the broader culture or if the ceremonies are superficial and not supported wholeheartedly by senior leadership, they will erode the legitimacy of the organization. The typical symptoms of negative value attribution of ceremony and tradition are superficiality and subjective implementation.

Ceremony and tradition give life to the organization. They demonstrate that the organization is an environment where the emotional needs of the individuals involved are met and work is rewarded. But they must be inclusive of all members of the organization and supported whole-heartedly by the senior leadership. This demonstrates the deep meaning of the ceremony or tradition and thus its legitimacy. The successful executive will understand the importance of ceremony and tradition.

Abstract Organizational Concepts

Ceremony
Tradition

Figure 43 - Ceremony and tradition, if implemented correctly, serve to make organizations more real.

The Junior Executive will demand authenticity and inclusiveness in all ceremonies and traditions and support them wholeheartedly as a means of granting substance and legitimacy to the organization.

INSTITUTIONAL LEARNING

During many phases of our careers, we consider the groups that we move through to be transient. That is, they are what we navigate through on our career path. This is as it should be—these groups are the domains of others and are shaped by them. However, this mode of thought must be curtailed when we reach the executive level, for these groups become our domain. Even if the group or team is inherited from another individual, we will be responsible for the environment that exists under our leadership. Regardless of how our group became our group, we must establish a basis for understanding and growth. This is rooted directly in institutional learning. The successful executive will consider their group an institution and rigidly enforce a policy of learning.

Everything we do as an executive will be based to a large degree on what has been done before. So, it seems logical that a requirement for success would be a deep understanding of what has been done prior to our promotion or hiring. How does the organization deliver work? What do people in the organization need to know in order to do work? What meta-data are we collecting on that work or the inputs and outputs? How do organization members learn? As an executive, one of the most important steps we can take to ensure success is to answer these questions in a policy that governs how organization members learn. A quick review of any successful company demonstrates this—General Electric and Apple both have enjoyed monumental success and have created universities to manage learning within in their organizations. The US military manages several postgraduate universities that ensure a high level of learning among its higher-ranking officers. These are large organizations with enormous resources, yet what they are doing is relatively simple: setting aside some time for individuals to learn for the benefit of the organization. The key to their success and to understanding why many organizations fail at this is that they know what to teach. They understand how their organizations operate and what knowledge their workforce needs to enhance and optimize those operations, knowledge that is available to an organization of any size. The successful executive will methodically work to understand the fundamental operations of their organization and the meta-data associated with performance, as detailed in previous chapters. The successful executive will use this knowledge to craft a policy of institutional learning within their domain.

As we discussed in the chapter on performance management, there must be a framework within which individuals can be tested and measured. This discipline is required for institutional learning as well, based on the following key components:

> **Baseline**: The baseline of all institutional learning is deep understanding of how the organization operates. The successful executive will ensure that all team members have a deep and clear understanding of how the organization operates. This is a non-trivial task and requires significant work around documentation and process modeling.
>
> **Contextual Notes**: The key to establishing the basis for learning is to attach contextual meaning to events that take place during operations. Depending upon the granularity of reporting, these contextual notes may be highly normalized or more free form. At minimum, outputs, deliverables and events of note must be documented to elaborate the core result. What were the mitigating circumstances of the events under evaluation? How was the core result impacted by current circumstances? Can these circumstances be codified? If we are enforcing a project methodology, most of this contextualization will be done through the project

documentation. For more fluid organizations, throughput metrics serve as anchor points for contextual notes. In any case, they should be as normal as possible (codified in common terms) and as consistent as possible. The actual deliverables and events that we evaluate will not be that interesting or valuable in a vacuum—they must have contextual meaning for us to infer meaning. Regardless of our organizational resources, contextual notes can be captured with virtually no cost.

Repository: One of the major weaknesses of many organizational attempts at institutional learning is the lack of a usable repository of data. It is critical that all events and contextual notes are collated in a navigable repository that provides not only clear codification and summation procedures, but also actionable cues. A repository of notes and event data is useless unless it can be easily digested and processed into actions.

Review: If we consider the events and outputs of the organization's work as raw data, then the review we conduct for learning is based upon higher-level reports. The sophistication and automation associated with these reports will determine the efficiency with which reviews of learning materials can be conducted and translated into action. Reviews must be integrated with normal operations and not set aside as quarterly or semi-annual drills. In a fast-moving environment that requires all team members to learn and execute quickly, institutional learning must be continual and recursive. That is, once a pattern of learning is established it will provide a basis for higher-level learning within the organization that is self-sustaining—reviews beget deeper contextual understanding, and so on.

Depending upon our resources, these components may be highly elaborated or simple. But they all must be present in any organizational learning policy. Teams and organizations exist to provide a platform for output and performance that could otherwise not be possible. The key to maximizing the benefit of the organization is institutional learning.

The Junior Executive will make a priority of establishing a policy of institutional learning, and continually grow that policy.

INFORMATION FILTER MANAGEMENT (UP/DOWN)

There will be an enormous learning curve involved in taking on the executive role, even if we have been groomed for it for some time. It is critical that we be involved deeply in the work of our team and domain, but our role as the executive is to lead, and this requires some distance. Distance necessarily results in the establishment of conscious and unconscious information filters. They are put in place for a variety of reasons, but most often to maintain harmony and peace among the group. This is not without benefit. Harmony and peace among the group is important and sustains long-term satisfaction and performance excellence. However, these concerns should always be subordinated to the optimal performance of the organization and the individuals involved. Information filters are necessary but can pose a threat to optimal organizational efficiency.

To a large degree, information filters within the organization are defined by the personalities of the audience. It is clear that anyone who abuses the messenger will not get many messages. We understand that we must foster an environment open to honest communication and punishing of subterfuge. Our concern with information filters is not focused on blockages or machinations. Rather, we are concerned about information filters that ossify over time and lead to a general skewing of information received.

For the new executive who is deep in the details of their domain and organization, there exists a challenge. How do we ensure that we are getting clear and unfiltered information from our subordinates, and how do we ensure that we are not unduly filtering information that goes to senior leadership? Unfortunately, there is no universal prescription. Rather, the solution will be highly subject to the nature of the work conducted and the culture of the organization. As we will be struggling to get up to speed on the detailed work at hand, we will be highly reliant on reports from our subordinates and other stakeholders. Given the typical speed of work involved, there is often little time for skeptical evaluation of the information.

Subtle coloring of incoming information can skew our understanding of what is true. Over time, without correction, subtle filters on information can ossify into a cultural artifact. The effects can range from harmless to catastrophic, depending upon the circumstances. The information we receive from subordinates and other stakeholders will be skewed to some extent. It is human nature. As an executive, the truth of this will be clearly felt at the first point at which we deliver bad news to senior leadership. The impulse to color the information and filter the meaning will be enormous. From an organizational standpoint, we know that the aggregate effect of this across many domains will be damaging to overall performance. We must also acknowledge that individuals interpret the same information in highly divergent ways. Given these complexities, how does the successful executive address information filtering in their domain and in the overall organization?

The first step is to openly acknowledge the issue of filtering with the relevant stakeholders. By acknowledging that it is human nature to filter information, we shed light on the issue in a manner that allows the audience to be accepting of this and thus avoid the psychological games that often get built around secrets. How we handle this with senior leadership will be subject to the culture of the organization and the personalities of the senior leaders. It is naive to think that we will be able to have the same discussion with senior leadership that we have with our subordinates and stakeholders. However, we can make our approach clear and demonstrate how we as an executive ensure clarity of information reporting. Once we have openly acknowledged our concern around information filtering, we must establish the environmental basis for value-added information reporting. In any context, there are three core aspects to reporting information and to ensuring that our filters are not skewing the truth. How these are combined or presented is up to the circumstances, but the successful executive will ensure that the information they are presented and in turn present contains the following elements.

> **Core Message**: All good leaders want to hear the truth and they want to hear it as soon as possible. In all endeavors, a core message must be delivered clearly and correctly. One of the central duties we have as an executive is to ensure that senior leadership has a clear and honest understanding of the facts that relate to our domain and the work involved. The successful executive will hold firm in their actions to ensure that they demand clear and honest information from their subordinates and present clear and honest information to senior leadership. Anything less is manipulation and political gamesmanship.
>
> **Context**: The impulse to skew or otherwise filter information is often rooted in the context of the core message. The circumstances that surround the core message often are as important as the core message itself. If we report that the factory only shipped 25% of expected orders last month, this is clearly disastrous. But the contextual information that this was due to a labor dispute radically changes our understanding. How we present the context of the message and how we expect the context of the message to be presented to us will depend upon the organization and the culture. However, it should always be tied to root causes as directly and clearly as possible. This provides both the information provider and the audience opportunity to plan and prepare for action.

> **Suggested Interpretation**: Most presented information is subject to open interpretation. Core messages mean different things to different people. If they are presented raw, this is the expected case. But if we have delivered the core message within the most appropriate context, the scope of interpretation narrows. Yet, given the complexity and speed of most post-modern organizations, this is not enough. Not only must the core message be delivered with the most appropriate contextual information, but we must also provide a suggested interpretation. This is a transparent acknowledgement of information filtering, done openly and as a suggestion, which allows the audience to accept the logical framework presented or use the information in some other way. This approach ensures that the beneficial and useful aspects of information are conferred but that there is little opportunity for subterfuge or waste.

It is critical that we ensure that information filters are appropriately used and that their benefits are conferred to the team and organization. Rather than reduce focus on the work at hand to investigate and skeptically analyze internal reports for information filters, the executive must openly acknowledge the phenomena among their team. Further, the successful executive will establish a reporting environment wherein information is filtered with open intents by providing the core message, any appropriate context, and a suggested interpretation.

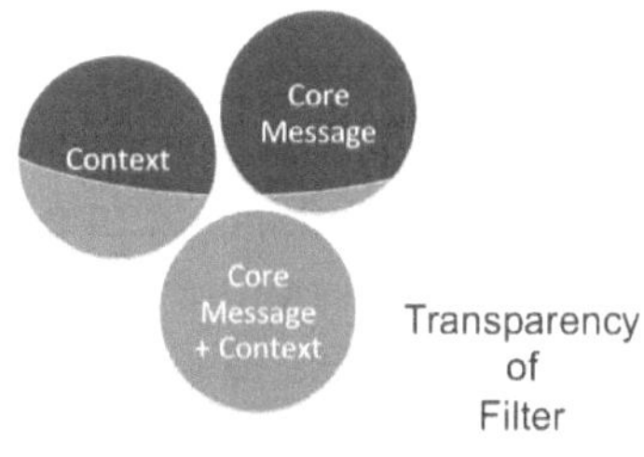

Figure 44 - Information filters are necessary for organizational efficiency, but must be managed.

The Junior Executive will use information filters transparently and so optimize their use by avoiding unnecessary investigation.

ALIMENTATION AND FOCUS

As we end this book and look to great achievement in the executive role and advancement to senior leadership, there is one final topic of great importance. At an open forum with a very successful CEO of a telecommunication startup, a question was asked regarding the challenges of maintaining a deep understanding of the business while also keeping a clear view of the vision and broader strategy of the company. Rather than provide some overly clever answer, the CEO simply said that the successful executive learns the ability to determine what is important. That is, which issues require their attention at a deep level and which do not—the ability to know when to dive into the weeds and when to rely on top-level reports. There is no formula for this and it is a skill that must be honed over time. This ability is a point of discernment between successful and unsuccessful executives, and thus an important topic for us to discuss. We deal with the question via two key aspects: alimentation and focus. For the successful executive, these can represent competing impulses of equal importance. The challenge, then, is to determine the balance between them.

Focus: "Focus" is the ability to allocate our attention to a discrete question for a non-trivial period of time. Thus, the question can be addressed with all of our mental and physical capacity. The cost is that all other questions will go without our attention. For the executive with limited time and energy, the ability to focus is both a challenge to execute and a detriment if that focus is allowed to remain on one question for too long. So how do we make the most effective use of focus? In general, we should bind this question with the constraint that our individual focus is limited by physical space and time. That is, our focus can only be applied to one place at a time and for a fixed period of time within a day. Instead of determining what we should expend our limited focus on, we might instead hone the need for our focus. How is our focus most efficient? Much like a knockout punch, our focus is most effective when we have pushed to a culminating point the following three factors:

<u>Concentration of the Question</u>: A complete distillation of the question to the salient impacts that underlie an executive decision.

<u>Concentration of Force</u>: Alignment of resources to execute against the question with overwhelming force (money, people, etc.) at the time of focus.

<u>Speed of Execution</u>: The speed with which the resolving action of the question and the output of our focus is executed and brought to full resolution, thus releasing our focus.

By limiting the application of our focus to the culminating points of the three factors noted above, we optimize our attention within the noise of workaday life. The successful executive will ensure that their team understands the value of focus and the economy with which it must be employed. The successful executive will limit their focus to culminating points as much as possible.

Alimentation: If focus defines discrete moments of exclusive attention, then alimentation defines the remainder of our attentive output. We must acknowledge that an executive's effectiveness is rarely defined by points of focus (although this is true enough to be considered). Rather, the majority of executives demonstrate their excellence and value to the organization through efficient and measurable alimentation of the processes of the organization. There are many examples of executives who fail to maintain or grow in their positions due to over-attention to points of focus while allowing their standing processes to atrophy. Thus, we see that alimentation is a core task of the executive. In fact, the majority of content in this book serves to promote operational excellence in alimentation. The successful executive will understand that organizations grow and thrive when their core processes and teams are sustained and supported consistently.

The Junior Executive will craft a working style that makes optimal use of focus while continually improving the standing operation.

Reading List

"The Meditations" by Marcus Aurelius
"The Consolations of Philosophy" by Alain de Botton
"On War" by Carl von Clausewitz
"Shogun" by James Clavell
"Man's Search for Meaning" by Viktor Frankl
"The Castle" by Franz Kafka
"Ogilvy on Advertising" by David Ogilvy
"Poor People's Movements" by Frances Fox Piven and Richard Cloward
"Military Strategy" by Rear Admiral J.C. Wylie

Final Comments

The executive role provides the ability for a group of individuals with a common interest in a particular domain of life to create an organization capable of delivering outputs otherwise unachievable. The executive role creates channels of growth for the organization through thoughtfully aligned goal achievement in pursuit of a common vision. As such, the executive role has an enormous impact on the life of the organization. In our pursuit of greater glory in the working world, many individuals will seek the executive role. The goal of this book is to present a foundation for attaining the executive role based upon core truths of what it means to carry the responsibility and accountability associated with it. The successful person will thoughtfully evaluate their desire and fitness for such a challenge. The role is not for everyone and the competition can be fierce. Honest evaluation of the concepts presented as they apply to us will help determine if the executive role is truly what we want. In the end, the pursuit of happiness is far more important than a job title.

Bibliography

Adams, S. (1995, September 15). Strips. Retrieved August 30, 2012, from Dilbert: www.dilbert.com/strips/comic/1995-09-15

Allen, P. (2011). Idea Man: A Memoir by the Cofounder of Microsoft. New York: Portfolio/Penguin.

Botton, A. d. (2001). The Consolations of Philosophy. London: Penguin.

Campbell, J. (1991). The Power of Myth. New York: Anchor.

Clausewitz, C. v. (1993). On War. New York: Alfred A. Knopf.

CNN. (2009, May 22). CNN Politics. Retrieved August 30, 2012, from CNN: http://articles.cnn.com/2009-05-22/politics/obama.mccain_1_naval-academy-graduation-naval-aviators?_s=PM:POLITICS

Collins, J. (2001). Good to Great: Why Some Companies Make the Leap ... and Others Don't. New York: Random House Business.

Collins, J., & Porras, J. (1994). Built to Last: Successful Habits of Visionary Companies. New York: Random House Business.

Coppola, F. F. (Director). (1972). The Godfather [Motion Picture].

De Waal, F. (1984). Chimpanzee Politics: Power & Sex Among Apes. New York: Harper.

DeVito, D. (Director). (1992). Hoffa [Motion Picture].

Disovery Channel. (2010). "Jaws of Death." I Shouldn't Be Alive. Television: Discovery Channel.

Dorfman, M. S. (2007). Introduction to Risk Management and Insurance (9 ed.). Englewood Cliffs, NJ: Prentice Hall.

Eckhardt, R. (1987). "Stan Ulam, John von Neumann, and the Monte Carlo Method." Los Alamos Science Special Issue (15), 131–137.

Endsley, M. (1995). "Toward a theory of situational awareness in dynamic systems." Human Factors 37(1), 32–64.

Gabriel, K. (1996). Gambler Way: Indian Gaming in Mythology, HIstory and Archeology in North America. Boulder: Johnson Books.

Hawkins, J., & Blakeslee, S. (2010). On Intelligence: How a New Understanding of the Brain Will Lead to the Creation of Truly Intelligent Machines. New York: Times Books.

Heidegger, M. (1962). Being and Time. London: SCM Press.
Howe, M. J. (2001). Genius Explained. Cambridge: Cambridge University Press.
Hume, D. (2003). A Treatise of Human Nature. New York: Dover.
Kano, J. (2005). Mind Over Muscle: Writings from the Founder of Judo. Tokyo: Kodansha International.
Kelling, G. L., & Wilson, J. Q. (1982, March). Broken Windows. The Altantic.
Marshall, S. (1961). Men Against Fire: The Problem of Battle Command in Future War. New York: William Morrow and Company.
Maslow, A. (1943). A Theory of Human Motivation. Psychological Review 50(4), 370–96.
Masters, B. (2009, March 30). Rise of a Headhunter. Retrieved August 30, 2012, from Financial Times: www.ft.com
Mayo, E. (1945). The Social Problems of an Industrial Civilization. Harvard University: Harvard University Press.
Moore, G. E. (1965). Cramming more components onto integrated circuits. Electronics Magazine, p. 4.
Nisbett, R. E., & Ross, L. (1991). The Person and the Situation: Perspectives of Social Psychology. New York: McGraw Hill.
Patton, G. S. (1947). War As I Knew It. Boston: Houghton Mifflin Co.
Peter, L. J., & Hull, R. (1969). The Peter Principle. London: Souvenir Press.
Wylie, J. C. (1967). Military Strategy: A General Theory of Power Control. New Brunswick, NJ: Rutgers University Press.
Yoshikawa, E. (1981). Musashi. Tokyo: Kodansha International, Ltd.

Made in United States
Troutdale, OR
02/15/2026

46969341R00176